# the COURAGE to DIVORCE

SUSAN GETTLEMAN
and
JANET MARKOWITZ

SIMON AND SCHUSTER • NEW YORK

*1979*

SBN 671-21748-8
Library of Congress Catalog Card Number: 74-945
Manufactured in the United States of America

1  2  3  4  5  6  7  8  9  10

# FOR THE FAMILIES OF DIVORCE

# Contents

## PART FIVE 175

)

*Learning to live with a person you do not love and respect, learning to live with a person who neither loves nor respects you, is merely learning how to die, how to walk around as a shell, how to deny what you feel, how to hate without showing it, how to weep without tears, how to declare that the sham you live is the true reality and that it is good.*

—JULES HENRY

# Preface

In the pages that follow we have taken a positive view of divorce, unlike most writers who argue that divorce is at best an unfortunate necessity which has catastrophic side effects for families. Our experience as participants in American society, and as psychotherapists, is that divorce can be and often is a wholly liberating and positive experience. After an exhaustive survey of the literature, we concluded that most of the "authorities" on the subject are unnecessarily judgmental and pessimistic in their speculations on divorce. By exposing and refuting those prejudices that masquerade as scholarship we hope we can help families in conflict achieve healthier and happier divorces. We have used as much contemporary case material as possible to illustrate the dilemmas inherent in modern-day divorce and to help people derive the strength to separate when they can no longer live happily together.

We do not advocate divorce as a universal panacea, nor do we disqualify marriage as a happy, healthy life-style for many people. Our concern is to minimize the suffering of those for whom divorce is a logical and healthy decision. We write for those families already divorced, for those families that contemplate divorce and even for those families that do not consciously envision divorce in their future. We believe that this book can also be useful to clinicians, ministers, judges and lawyers, many of whom have frequent contact with divorcing families.

We wrote this book in the form of essays on various aspects of divorce and post-divorce life in order to shed light on the joys and the hassles common to families of divorce. The data come from our own clinical experience, from popular literature on divorce,

11

from the experiences of our colleagues, and from a careful analysis of existing literature in the fields of history, psychiatry, psychology, social work, sociology, law, and pastoral and martial counseling. Much of the material on divorce that we have examined and criticized in this book is of a dogmatic nature, specifying a narrowly permissible set of behaviors and dictating "legitimate" feelings for a large class of people. We are not happy with what we have found in our reading and we are dismayed by the hostile and unenlightened advice available to people who are seeking help in freeing themselves from unhappy marriages. We know there are many people who subscribe to the ideas presented in this book; popular literature on divorce is becoming increasingly optimistic. Up to now conceptions and formulations about divorce have been confined to expression in short articles and essays. This is the first full-length book on the subject of how and why couples find the courage to overcome the powerful anti-divorce tradition in America.

Out of our own personal experiences we have come to recognize a need to demonstrate that divorced people are not deviants, that divorce does not need to be devastating to families and that the idea that the intact nuclear family is the only healthy familial arrangement is erroneous. We realize that as we write this book our society is in a transitional stage of social change. We have not attempted to chart the fluctuating statistics on divorce, as these data quickly become obsolete. Nor have we written a treatise summarizing the divorce laws of various states. We have tried instead to emphasize those practices from the past that have had a pernicious effect on families because they are based on unwholesome and punitive attitudes.

Not every divorce situation is discussed in this book; not only are there great individual variations, but there are class and ethnic ones as well. We are well aware that the examples we have chosen deal mainly with middle-class life. We make no attempt to deal with the much different pattern of working-class and ghetto matrimony and divorce. That is a topic that other researchers might well turn to.

As we studied and pondered the "divorce problem" we became aware of the fact that prevailing attitudes have deep historic roots. We have tried to explore and expose the genealogy of the anti-divorce tradition in order to help people free themselves from the oppressive weight of stagnant institutions and customs.

While the institution of marriage remains attractive for most Americans, others have begun to question the limits and dimensions of marriage and the common stereotypes about divorce. We hope that this book will challenge some traditional beliefs, undermine destructive customs, and help to generate further positive change. We also hope that our ideas will be relevant and helpful to the movement for women's equality and to other progressive forces in contemporary America.

We have included footnotes in this book for two reasons, first to distinguish this work from those books on divorce (and there are far too many) which rely almost entirely on hearsay and gossip; and second, to facilitate further research. The footnotes are placed at the end of the book, where they will not be cumbersome to the reader, and an annotated, selected bibliography is appended.

We wish to acknowledge our gratitude to the numerous friends, relatives, patients and colleagues who have openly shared their insights and experiences with us. Understandably, some of them would prefer to remain anonymous. We are also indebted to the following individuals for their generous assistance in our early research: Catherine East, Director of the Citizen's Advisory Council on the Status of Women, Sidney Ditzion of the City College of New York, Joan Gadol of Sarah Lawrence College, Paul Glick of the Department of Health, Education and Welfare, Eleanor Leacock of the City College of New York, Alexander Plateris of the Department of Health, Education and Welfare, Rosemary Ruether of Howard University, and Reb Leon Sales. We appreciate the very helpful copy editing of Patricia Miller, and our thanks go also to Diane Soroka for her rapid and accurate typing of our manuscript.

We are especially grateful to those friends and colleagues who studied and criticized our manuscript closely at various stages of completion. We would like to thank Dr. Louis Getoff, Mrs. Mary Getoff, Dr. Bernard Horowitz, Norman Rosen, Esq., Professor J. P. Sattin and Ms. Karen Smith. We are also very grateful to three special women for their confidence and vision: Cyrilly Abels, our literary agent, Alice Mayhew, of Simon and Schuster, and Diane Harris, who edited this volume with great care.

More than any other persons, our husbands, Arnold Markowitz and Marvin Gettleman, have shared our enthusiasm for this book. Their willingness over the past two years to lend themselves fully to our project at every stage has made the writing of this book an exciting personal adventure. Marv used his skill as a historian to teach us the relevance of history to the problem of divorce in America; without his guidance in specific problems of research and writing we could not have completed this book.

Those who have helped us are in no way responsible for the omissions or inaccuracies in this book and our acknowledgment of their assistance does not necessarily mean that they were in agreement with us on all matters.

S. G.

J. M.

# Introduction

The decision to divorce need not be a destructive one, but it often is. The reason can be largely ascribed to cultural taboos and erroneous beliefs and customs fostered and reinforced by the major institutions of American society—the schools, the media, the mental health professions and the courts. In varying degrees these forces all support the notion that divorce destroys family relationships, inhibits individual growth and encourages social chaos.

Despite these beliefs about the shattering effects of divorce, more and more people are abandoning bad and even mediocre marriages. More than a quarter of a million divorces take place each year in the United States and the numbers are rising. Mass media, legislators and social scientists have focused much attention on the "alarming" divorce statistics and have attributed the growing popularity of divorce to the lax morals of contemporary society. We are skeptical of the point of view that relates moral turpitude to rising divorce rates. The data seem to us to express a growing determination to achieve happiness and satisfaction, and to reflect a healthy distrust of social customs that hinder such achievement.

But while the divorce rate increases, the American anti-divorce tradition remains strong. Couples who divorce do so in a cloud of prejudice and misunderstanding, for it is very hard to escape the social scorn fostered by negative attitudes, especially if children are involved. Divorced people are often judged by society as either adulterous, criminal, atheistic, neurotic, immature, or at best frivolous and unfortunate.

15

Like any other change in life-style, divorce calls for reorganization of specific habits. It may initially be accompanied by confusion and uncertainty. Divorced families, however, often suffer extreme feelings of failure, guilt, remorse, hostility and loneliness that go far beyond the normal problems of adjusting to a new situation. For many people the mere *thought* of divorce arouses intense anxiety and doubt.

Such excess anguish is in part historically conditioned. Centuries of religious and secular indoctrination have helped insure that most people will not easily make happy and responsible post-marital adjustments. In fact, the prevailing negative interpretation of divorce acts as a self-confirming prophecy,[1] often bringing about the evil effects of which it warns. The notion that divorce is the enemy of marriage and the family, rather than a means of maintaining these institutions, makes divorce inherently unacceptable to many individuals. The irrational belief persists that divorced people have deviated from some benign entity called "normal family life."

In spite of the fact that our society's expectations of marriage are difficult to meet, individuals continue to react with surprise and dismay when divorce occurs. The romantic American evaluation of marriage obscures the fact that countless people endure unsatisfactory marital lives; archaic notions about the sanctity of marriage and the evil nature of divorce do not recognize that unhappy marriages can and often do destroy the lives of adults and children.

While our educational institutions do not lobby directly for or against divorce legislation, their organized propaganda for marriage and against divorce exerts subtle pressure on students. In the literature on "marriage and family living" sociologists hypothesize that the intact nuclear family is a social and psychic necessity of life. And since traditional morality demands that couples stay in marriage, textbooks focus on the traumas of divorce, remarriage and stepfamilyhood.[2] These orthodoxies need critical re-examination.

A more elusive but by no means less insidious force in shaping attitudes toward divorce is the mental health establishment. Professionals in the fields of psychiatry, psychology, social work, and marital and pastoral counseling typically use a health-illness model for understanding behavior. Thus clinicians usually discuss divorce as case studies in pathology. They often ignore the strengths that are required to achieve separation and to endure the social and economic consequences of divorce. A reformulation of professional aims and commitments is long overdue.

The state, a silent partner to marriage, is another active force in opposing divorce. In fact, the judgment of divorce as an evil is perhaps best displayed in the chaotic divorce laws of America. Marriage is a "civil contract in the United States, but it differs from all other such contracts in that it cannot be dissolved at the pleasure of the parties." [3] Our legal system operates to insure that divorce will be as painful as possible, thereby confirming and reinforcing the characteristic American anti-divorce tradition, which permits divorce yet surrounds it with inhibiting negative associations. The obstacles placed before divorcing couples not only encourage sham and collusion in the courts of the United States but also have a staggering effect on alimony and child-custody decisions.

The legal barriers and moral values that surround divorce are based on religious principles that originated centuries ago. Religion, social custom and historical tradition have been intertwined with current divorce practices so that economic and psychic adaptation to divorce is quite complicated. The principle of female inferiority in marriage and divorce derived from ancient Hebrew and Roman traditions. Christian teaching then elevated "holy matrimony" to the level of a sacrament. But most important, the history of divorce depicts with few exceptions an overwhelming effort to protect marriage and to censure or limit divorce. Religious and social institutions, mental health ideologies and legal complications form a combined barrier to divorce. To dilute and ultimately alter the damaging effects of such a powerful tradition will require an equally potent alternative view that is sensitive to people's feelings, attitudes and needs.

We believe that divorce, stripped of its gratuitous negative connotations, stands as inherently a "neutral" institution, in itself neither good nor bad for individuals or for society. Divorce does not have to result in emotionally crippled, hostile men and women or in embarrassed, maladjusted children. It does not automatically signal the destruction of the institution of marriage itself or the decay of civilized life. Nor does divorce merely undo a marriage and result in a "broken home," which then implies a "bad environment." Rather, it restructures family relationships and often results in new kinship groupings whose positive dimensions have never seriously been gauged. It also creates the potential for redefining traditional, often oppressive, stereotyped sex roles. Divorce potentially opens doors to new kinds of emotional fulfillment, unavailable to people whose energies are sapped by continuous marital conflict in the hothouse of the nuclear family.

Obviously we are not suggesting that current attitudes be completely reversed and that all married couples be considered dependent, neurotic and too fearful to divorce. We are addressing ourselves to the vast numbers of married people whose lives are torn by marital strife and who nevertheless continue to have paralyzing reservations about divorce. It is not our intent to paint an unrealistically jolly portrait of divorce or to defend without qualification the mental health of divorced adults. However, it is the purpose of this book to emphasize the often overlooked healthy, life-affirming motives that impel people to end their marriages.

While divorce remains a controversial issue in contemporary America, traditional family structures are undergoing vast changes. Divorced families in increasing numbers are experimenting with alternative forms of family living in place of the traditional nuclear model. The gradual obsolescence of marriage may make divorce unnecessary some day. But in the long meanwhile, traditional marriage is not hastily being rejected, and the present issues in marriage and divorce remain with us. From our point of view, it is an uncritical acceptance of monogamous marriage and nuclear family living as the only "right" way to live that adds a negative and unnecessary dimension to the "trauma" of divorce. We can envision a new entity in America, the liberated or creative divorce, based not on a frivolous rejection of marriage, but on a positive and thoughtful reorientation that grows out of healthy openness and willingness to learn.

# part one

# 1
# The Divorce Problem

The first problem of maintaining social equilibrium is to make people want to do what is required and expected of them. That failing, the second problem is to adopt other means to keep them in line.

—C. Wright Mills

Society could not care less about what gratifications you derive within the framework of its conventions. It merely punishes you if you break them.

—Jules Henry

The achievement of upholding the structure of marriage and family life, preventing divorce and making postdivorce life difficult has been the work of many hands. Academic courses and social science textbooks have met this challenge in a "scholarly" way. Religious leaders and mental health professionals have used the more subjective and personalized approaches of theology, psychology and counseling. But far more potent and pervasive have been the positive image of marriage and the negative image of divorce created by the mass media. Even in the early twentieth century, public attitudes on divorce were deeply affected by newspapers, magazines and popular books.[1] Nowadays, the

23

impact of the media is even more powerful because of the addition of television. A complicated network of indoctrination has taken shape to reinforce the importance of traditional marriage as the core of family life in America. Though not deliberately coordinated, these forms of propaganda have the effect of a powerful conspiracy to limit divorce, create and heighten post-divorce trauma and cast suspicion on alternate life-styles. Unsuccessful in preventing divorce, these forces are still powerful enough to engender guilt and cause a poor adjustment in many people to the potentially liberating experience of ending a marriage.

The intensity of the propaganda for marriage ironically and tragically tends to undermine the possibility of matrimonial happiness. As Simone de Beauvoir observed in *The Second Sex*, the pressure on girls to marry and thus live "normal" lives does not completely obiliterate widespread yearning for freedom and secret resistance to marriage. This pressure sets up conflicts which may forever prevent the attainment of happiness.[2] Hugh Carter and Paul Glick, in their 1970 government-supported research study, similarly concluded that marriage is so well entrenched as the normal and approved status of adulthood that a considerable number of people will marry even if they are temperamentally unsuited to marriage and incompatible with their prospective partners.[3] Meanwhile, sociologists and anthropologists have observed how false expectations in marriage reduce the chances of lifelong satisfaction. Marriage is supposed to provide sexual fulfillment, intellectual stimulation, congeniality, shared recreation, mutual security, companionship and a host of material satisfactions.[4] The physically repugnant notion of "one flesh" has been used to express the ideal that marriage should symbolize the "fusion" of two lives and interests.[5]

These notions, however, involve certain internal contradictions. Romantic love is the only acceptable rationale for marriage in our secular society, and middle-class youngsters are expected to defer the gratification of sex, love and parenthood until they are financially independent. Thus, on the one hand, marriage is supposed to be blissful; on the other hand, it signals the end of youthful and carefree fun. It means settling down to the awesome responsibilities of family. Men are advised to have their last fling before making a permanent commitment, while women tacitly agree to become annihilated as individuals in exchange for the status of wife and the right to bear legitimate children. As C. Wright Mills observed, "In so far as the family as an institution turns women into darling little slaves and men into their chief providers . . . the problem of a satisfactory marriage remains incapable of purely private solution." [6] Or, as Friedrich Engels wrote in 1884, "The modern individual family is founded on the open or concealed domestic slavery of the wife." [7]

Bronislaw Malinowski, the prominent early-twentieth-century anthropologist, was one of the first modern scholars to write about the dilemma of Western marriage, which promises bountiful happiness while demanding great sacrifices. He noted how our society teaches its members two matrimonial commandments: (1) if a man is to possess the woman of his choice and have children by her, then he will have to shoulder specific duties and burdens, and (2) if a woman wants to become a mother, she will have to stick to the lover of her choice and do her duty to him and his children.[8] Malinowski then concluded soberly that such rigid expectations meant that marriage could never simply be a matter of "living happily ever after." [9] In *Future Shock*, Alvin Toffler comes to essentially the same conclusion:

> It is safe to say that large numbers of people will refuse to jettison the conventional idea of marriage or the familiar family forms. They will . . . continue searching for happiness within the orthodox format. Yet even they will be forced to innovate in the end, for the odds against success may prove overwhelming.[10]

As the odds against permanent marriage prove more and more overwhelming, couples by the thousands divorce, only to face a new set of pressures, prejudices and expectations. Women, especially, are confronted with the consequences of their previous financial dependency on a husband. Their traditional role renders them financially and emotionally vulnerable, so that after divorce they often feel and function like helpless children. Their functional difficulties may be compounded by the failure of lenders (primarily banks) to regard women as creditworthy. Since a married woman who wants a loan has to depend on her husband's credit rating, after divorce she can be refused a loan on the grounds that she has no prior record of independent credit transactions. There is ample evidence of similar discrimination against women in the area of employment. At the 1972 hearings of the National Commission on Consumer Finance, witness after witness testified to the severity of this problem.[11] Some employers still consider the divorced women who might marry and quit work as a notoriously "bad risk." These are ways in which divorce drives home for many women the fact of their vulnerability and dependency in marriage and their consequent inequality in divorce; such discrimination demonstrates that much of the "trauma" is not inherent in divorce but in its socially conditioned aftermath. Economic discrimination against women is also demonstrated by means of occupational and other statistics showing that women have actually lost status in recent years in comparison with men.[12] For divorced women the situation is magnified.

Both spouses discover that an arrangement in which one party contributes most of the financial support while the other performs most of the domestic duties makes a mutually acceptable monetary (or custodial) arrangement unlikely after divorce.[13] Even in families of means, conflict often rages over money, as broad socio-economic problems are reduced to ugly personal vendettas in which each party feels cheated and self-righteous. Many contemporary books for the divorced male teach him that if he doesn't learn how "to take" he will "be taken." In *Uncoupling: The Art of Coming Apart*, authors Norman Sheresky and Marya Mannes present a variety of legal vignettes which show the folly of this approach.[14]

Ultimately, the feminist argument that discriminatory marriage practices enslave women for life may engender enough outrage to save future generations of women from such a fate. But in the meantime, a whole generation of divorced women, because of the way they have been conditioned, retain custody of their children, remain financially dependent on their ex-husbands, and then feel martyred, mortified, or trapped by their station in life.

After divorce, all family members usually become victims of the discriminatory marriage-oriented American society. For example, the tax burden for married people is alleviated through the privilege of the joint return. Divorced women sometimes find their friends abandoning them or jealously guarding their husbands against imagined sexual advances. Men are often responsible for this anxiety by assuming the "chivalrous" posture of offering to rescue divorced women from sexual frustration. The classic image of the sexually available "gay divorcee" lurks in their minds, somehow legitimizing their behavior.[15] The discrimination against divorced women readily becomes internalized so that often a woman continues to define herself as divorced, or as a divorcee, even years after the legal ritual. Women are indoctrinated from childhood to believe that their personal identities arc synonymous with their married status, present or former. (This is conspicuously not true of men in our society.) In America, one never goes back to single status after divorce; one is forever an "ex-spouse."[16]

Nor is the discrimination felt only by women; divorced men are often discriminated against as employees and parents. Data from a study sponsored by the University of Michigan School of Social Work shows that being married almost *triples* a man's chances for success on the job. If he gets divorced, he is less apt to move ahead; if he remarries, his prospects improve again. This study of six thousand men, ages forty-five to fifty-four, found that the pattern was valid for men in all kinds and levels of jobs. The report concludes that "the men who control job advancement in the system . . . view the man who has been married once and remains married as the most desirable person for promotion." The vice-president of personnel at General Motors said in an interview that those who moved ahead at work were "winners at relationships," and therefore also tended to be winners in marriage.[17] And in a management training program at the University of Michigan for executives slated for promotion by the companies, only one man in twenty was not married. The director of the program explained why: "Companies select and mold adjustable people. They look for those who set their goals and achieve them." Married men are more apt to have these qualities.[18]

Even men who are rich, famous and politically ambitious are vulnerable to the anti-divorce tradition in America. In 1964 Governor Nelson Rockefeller of New York announced his intention to run for the Presidency. However, his prospects were considerably dimmed by the fact that his wife had divorced him in 1962 and in 1963 he had married another divorced person, one who had lost custody of her children (casting some ominous shadow over her public reputation?). Before his divorce, the Gallup poll showed that 43 per cent of all Republicans wanted Rockefeller to be their candidate in 1964; after his divorce, only 30 per cent favored Rockefeller. His chance of being nominated at that time was ruined and Senator Goldwater was nominated instead.[19]

Marriage and family life "experts" frequently argue that people who are capable of building good marriages are contributing a positive good to the world around them and will be more effective in all life's relationships. "They are not the problem individuals who trouble society" write two such experts.[20] The implication, of course, is that those members of society who prefer not to marry, or who decide to unmarry, are not likely to contribute to the good of society. This cult of marriage and domesticity in America, combined with the Calvinistic reverence for people who "work at" and "build" solid marriages, dates back at least a hundred years and supports the ideological basis for active prejudice against single and divorced people.

It is not surprising that most people succumb to this indoctrination, for the consequences of deviation are severe. Youths are hurried into adult behavior by a host of social pressures but are discouraged from expressing "adult" desires as long as they remain adolescents, that is, single.[21] When single status does persist into chronological adulthood, it is looked upon as anomalous, unfortunate and peculiar.[22] The unmarried will be suspect, and eventually labeled as odd, possibly homosexual, neurotic, or immature,[23] not only by misguided laymen but also by members of the mental health professions, who have adopted, defended and largely reinforced old stereotypes. Family life experts gratuitously argue that people who fail to marry are by and large rationalizing their fear of responsibility, commitment and intimacy.[24]

Ironically marriage and divorce specialists show special alarm over the evidence that young marriages are more likely to result in divorce. In fact, the divorce rate is said to be six times greater for teen-agers than for adults.[25] Teen-agers are particularly vulnerable to the mass media's glorification of marriage. They marry to legitimize sex and pregnancy, to keep up with their peers, or simply to attain adult status. Some rush in by default because they are anxious to leave parental homes and have no place else to go. Evidently marriages which stem primarily from external pressures contain inherent flaws; since so many young couples never have a chance to evaluate whether they really want to be married (regardless of whether they want sexual relationships or children), they "take stock" by deciding soon after marriage whether or not to divorce. It is obvious that some people should not marry at all; but we are concerned about the destructive, biased assumption of many thoughtful writers that the *reason* some people ought not to marry is that *they are not healthy enough to adapt to "normal" life.* In other words, they are "too immature," "can't bear the financial burden," or are taken in by "sexual passion." [26] The obvious corollary of this view is that people who re-enter single status represent part of the unhealthy segment of the population and set a poor example to the youth of future generations. As long as marriage is considered life's most noble undertaking, then divorce must be one of life's most ignoble shames.

The myth of the happy nuclear family persists untarnished despite high divorce rates and evidence that many men and women are not satisfied with the conjugal roles they originally chose. Women are "processed" for motherhood from the moment they are born. They start learning what to want and what to be while still in their cribs, taught first by their parents, later encouraged by their friends, and urged on by relatives and teachers. The inevitability and normality of marriage and parenthood are assumed and then inflated out of proportion by those who guide the young. Ideals are first inculcated in the child through examples of parental interaction and teaching.[27] "When you grow up and get married . . ." prefaces so much of the advice given to children that by the time they are ready for school they have already learned that being grown up and being married are practically synonymous. Acculturation is then reinforced by the romantic rituals of marriage: courtships, engagements, showers, prayers, bridal gowns, tears, rice and honeymoons. While more and more people debunk marriage, 95 per cent of all American girls still marry and 90 per cent of these have children.[28] Even Dr. Benjamin Spock tells his *Redbook* audience that little girls will eventually replace their daddies with husbands. "A girl," he writes, "needs a fatherly man to admire and love from the age of three until she gets married." [29] The heat is on, from nursery school through college, to convince our youth that they can and should fulfill the American ideal of marriage. Even toddlers, urges one author, in their play, songs and stories, should act out potential forms of family conflict and be shown what makes and destroys a harmonious home.[30]

For those women who genuinely want a career of motherhood, raising children can be lots of fun and deeply rewarding. But "to assume that such an exacting, consuming, and important task is something almost all women are equipped to do is far more dangerous and ridiculous than assuming that everyone with vocal chords should seek a career in the opera." [31] If marrying and having children were not emotionally compulsory in our culture, then men and women who decided to become parents (in and out of marriage) could do so because they *both* wanted to raise children. If children were loved for their own sake, as opposed to their value as status and fertility symbols, then both parents could be equally "loving mothers," and in the event of separation or divorce, a fair and rational decision could be made as to which parent felt more able and willing at the time to assume "custody."

Even children from divorced homes have to face the anti-divorce tradition in America (which is *not* to say that divorce is bad for or destroys children). Depending on where they live, they may face a variety of pressures and prejudices. According to Morton Hunt, they are not as welcome in neighbors' homes as "normal" children from intact homes would be. They feel this discrimination even as minority group children do and know that "they are subtly and mysteriously held at arm's length." [32] According to Ralph Ober, some people feel their children will become "tainted" by association with children of divorce.[33] Prejudice also exists in our colleges, universities and hundreds of private institutions where young applicants are sometimes asked about the marital status of their parents; many administrators feel that such students are less reliable and less able to learn.[34] The children of divorced Catholic parents may have the additional problem of being excluded from active participation in the sacramental and social life of their Church.[35] The practice of excluding families of divorce from Church activities varies from parish to parish and ultimately depends on the convictions of the individual priest and his immediate superiors.

Given the intense and relentless pressures to marry, it comes as no surprise that more than 90 per cent of the people who divorce eventually remarry,[36] and that of the 90 per cent, 56 per cent do so within two years.[37] Remarriage is so prevalent after divorce that it is virtually "institutionalized" in America.[38] These figures are not necessarily a tribute to the glories of married life; one comparative statistical study concluded that second and successive marriages are not even as enduring as first marriages.[39] Remarriage rates simply suggest that divorced status still has too many disadvantages in our society to be anticipated as a positive and permanent alternative to unhappy marriage. It simply represents a transitory stage between marriage and remarriage.

The widespread view of divorce as a necessary evil, as a mere prelude to a new matrimonial tie, helps insure the unhappiness of divorced families. It is flaunted, advertised, repeated and spelled out *ad nauseam* that divorce is "regrettable but necessary," [40] that it is a traumatic loss for children, that the hardships may be insurmountable, and that the loneliness and misery are both excruciating and inevitable. Instead of helping newly single men and women develop a sense of mutual and communal concern to alleviate the hardships of earning a living while raising children, magazines, newspapers, books and other media all frighten them more. This relentless negativism acts as a self-fulfilling prophecy, helping bring about the evil effects of which it warns. In a famous essay, sociologist Robert Merton suggested how this process operates.[41] As applied to divorce, it would mean that people *expect* to suffer, *anticipate* pain, and then interpret whatever unhappiness they feel as proof of the equation that divorce equals suffering. What may not have been such a traumatic change is transformed into one by social forces which constantly reinforce that equation.

An anti-divorce orthodoxy reigns supreme in all media. The treatment of divorce in magazines and newspapers repeatedly reveals the horror, distaste and shame that surround divorce, compared with the sloppy sentimentality that surrounds marriage. In the most popular women's magazines of our day, divorce emerges as an ugly and feared last resort. For example, an article in *Good Housekeeping*, entitled "Stop Divorces Before They Start," [42] opens with the following sentence: "Divorce in America is a cruel and costly blight." The thrust of the article is that every American must realize that the high divorce rate, with the "agonies" it invites, is a drain not only on human resources but also on everyone's pocketbook.[43]

*Ladies' Home Journal*, "The Magazine Women Believe In," runs a regular feature article called "Can This Marriage Be Saved?" This exasperating title and the tone of the articles that follow carry the implication that divorce is the equivalent of suicide. The self-esteem of the woman reader who may be having serious doubts about remaining married is insidiously undermined when she reads that there is nothing more wonderful than "working" to achieve a good marriage. The point of this series is that professional counseling puts this goal within everyone's reach. The format of the *Journal* articles is "wife tells her story," "husband tells his story" and "counselor wraps up." The stories usually assume the position that when horrendous marriages are transformed into mediocre ones, the partners have achieved something eminently worthwhile.

The extent to which the present generation of adults strives to stay married is revealed in a *Redbook* article on divorced mothers: "They had struggled to avert divorce," says the author, "yielding to it only after being deserted or because marriage had become unbearably destructive and unrewarding." [44] Most of the time, couples just go on living with their resentments. Divorce is *not* the most common solution to unhappy marriage. Before writing *The Mirages of Marriage*, William Lederer and Don Jackson interviewed hundreds of "average marital pairs." They learned that approximately 80 per cent of the couples had seriously considered divorce at one time or another, and that many of them still think about it frequently. [45]

Every time a feature article appears on divorce, it turns out to be a hard-luck story about deprivation and trauma. *Mademoiselle*, for example, ran an autobiographical story by a young girl who grew up in a divorced home. She dramatized the pain of being uprooted from suburban Connecticut to urban New York, where she lived with her mother and sister (despite the fact that she had closer and warmer ties with her father). She described in detail how wretched and mean everyone was to everyone else, and how she felt "branded" and hurt by the ordeal. [46] Another article on divorce, recently appearing in *Newsweek* magazine, opened with a typically tragic view: "The pain is still blinding, the rupture still brutal. The desolation of the broken family has become no less stark." [47]

At least from the title, the *Redbook* article mentioned above, called "How Young Divorced Mothers Learn to Stand Alone," [48] promised to be a departure from the common pessimism and morbidity of divorce stories. But it opened with the usual list of practical hardships, followed by an impressive array of "subtler" problems that are "inevitable," including feelings of guilt and failure, loneliness, sexual frustration, an overpowering sense of isolation, dread of children's questions, conflict with ex-spouses, hovering families and the "worrisome" issue of getting close to a new man. In this article, one mother reported how she couldn't stay for the entire Parents' Day at her seven-year-old's school because she had to go back to work. Her daughter, "used to being shortchanged in this way," melodramatically asked her mother one day: "When I grow up and get married, will you stay for the whole wedding?" Whereupon the shamed mother "nearly" broke down and cried in front of her child. The author of this sentimental morality tale certainly loaded the dice against divorce. The type of experience invoked does involve disappointment, but it should be remembered that many working parents, not divorced,[49] are unable to spare a whole day for a school event. The need to care for other siblings might also have the same effect. A loving parent in whatever circumstance can usually make sure the children understand the reasons for adult behavior. But articles such as these project the idea that divorce makes it intrinsically impossible to be an adequate parent.

More chic and sensational magazines, such as *New York*, also feature divorce articles from time to time. One recent cover story portrayed the romance, marriage and divorce of a New York couple. This alleged "case history" described the pathetic, vengeful behavior of a man and a woman who move inexorably toward their dismal fate. Their breakup was preceded by almost nineteen years of misunderstanding, immaturity and selfishness. As usual, divorce is the ultimate evil, necessary only because these people have harmed each other beyond repair.[50]

It is no accident that healthy, strong people who can cope with stress and handle their children and divorce without guilt are never interviewed. Such people do exist, but their stories do not make good copy, and such people rarely come to the attention of "specialists." In America, where good news is no news, voyeuristic peeks at the misery and failings of others sell popular books and magazines and newspapers.[51] But they do not go a very long way in giving courage and support to troubled and divorced families. Before men and women can establish a sense of identification with other normal people who share their status, they must be convinced that they are not "sicker" than everyone else, and that their problems are neither unique nor entirely of their own making. If they could develop a consciousness of the ways in which they have been brainwashed to believe that divorce means failure for themselves and destruction for their children, they would be able to see the whole process in a new and more hopeful light. As Bertrand Russell warned years ago in *Marriage and Morals*:

> Emphatic and reiterated assertion, especially during childhood, produces in most people a belief so firm as to have a hold even over the unconscious and many of us who imagine that our attitude toward orthodoxy is quite emancipated are still, in fact . . . controlled by its teachings.[52]

In America, where almost six million families are headed by women, comprising a total of approximately twenty million people,[53] and where there are nearly two million young divorced mothers, there is *not one* popular magazine that *positively* caters to the needs and interests of these families. To our knowledge, there is not one series of articles, comparable, say, to the *Ladies' Home Journal* series, that shows how divorced families can and do live happily and raise healthy, loving children. There is no popular medium, with the possible exception of Parents Without Partners, through which divorced families can share constructive suggestions, pleasurable experiences, or new insights.[54] But there is ample room in the media for recipe swapping, housecleaning tips and new ideas for babyproofing the house.

As for contemporary newspapers, they enthusiastically exploit the misadventures and sorrows of divorced people in much the same way popular magazines do. Newspaper journalists, who are partial to divorced people who are rich, notorious, eccentric, or insane, recognize that along with the fear of divorce goes great public curiosity. They simultaneously sensationalize divorce as a bizarre and flippant Hollywood ritual, while asserting that for ordinary people it is at least a hazardous, if not tragic, fate. The treatment of divorce as a spectacular, newsworthy and curious phenomenon creates a public attitude that militates against serious understanding and acceptance of this widespread social process.

The countless tales told in the columns of Dear Abby and Rose Franzblau (both nationally syndicated) further attest to the ignorance that surrounds divorce. People who think that their problems can be solved in these columns also often believe the implicit bias found in them that married people, however miserable, can "work things out."

While the media relentlessly spin a web around the unhappily married, urging them to avoid "failure" at almost all cost, society reluctantly grants people the right to divorce. It then stigmatizes them for life because the socially conditioned pain of divorce acts as a punishment and makes the protagonists feel like criminals. The idealization of marriage and the praise bestowed on those who "stick it out" demonstrate that Americans are being conditioned, day after day, to believe that divorced people are inferior to married people, socially, psychologically and morally.

In the realm of divorce, people can hardly turn to religion for solace. If it were up to the Catholic Church, divorce would be even harder to get and more painful to live with than it now is. Determined religious foes of divorce are still on hand to reinforce secular propaganda. In an uninformed essay entitled "Divorce Court: Scene of Decay," Catholic writer Elizabeth Mulligan tries to scare people out of the mere thought of divorce. She claims that divorce *always* involves a bitter and hateful battle in a courtroom filled with "shrill voices and flushed faces . . . If either of the partners in a marriage is inclined to feel the 'I've had it' symptoms, it might be a good idea to visit a court of domestic relations." [55]

Even more disturbing than her article, however, is the recent news that the intercession by a powerful cardinal of the American Catholic Church has temporarily brought to a halt a movement to reform the Church's traditional stand on divorce and remarriage.[56] Catholic second marriages still have to be conducted outside regular Church channels and may not be reentered in official Church registers.

In the secular realm, big business, through its influence on television advertising and broadcasting, presents a constant source of anti-divorce propaganda. The public is bombarded by television images of marriage and family life at the urging of Madison Avenue, whose clients pay heavily for commercial time. The nuclear family is a great boon to industry. Until people marry, they usually do not own furniture or houses, but "every wedding sets in motion another spree," so much so that the pages of *The Wall Street Journal* gloat over predictions of the flood of new marriages in the coming years.[57] The family unit serves as the basic consumer of the goods on the market; a West Coast judge lamented that "merchants lose billions in uncollectable accounts through insolvency due to family breakup."[58] Since the happy family is a consuming family, it is understandable why businessmen simultaneously stress the desirability of marriage and family life while supporting liberal divorce legislation; the prevalence of *remarriage* means that divorce is not a major threat to the United States economic system. It is families that *stay divorced* that are not desirable for in such families there is often less money available for superfluous and luxury spending.

The image of the happily married, ever-buying family is supported by the media, which usually project a vision of life in which every "nuclear" household is filled with joy and good feeling. To our knowledge there are only two popular television shows that deal at all with divorce, *The Odd Couple* and *Maude*. The first, a comedy, centers around two divorced men who set up a bachelor pad together. One is rather bumbling and sloppy, the other fastidious and even effeminate. The message of the program is that you have to be weird or kooky if you are divorced.

The situation comedy *Maude* stars a woman who has been divorced twice and widowed once. While she is reminiscing about a past romance, her current husband asks her when she knew one particular boy friend. Maude can't remember whether he predated Albert or her other divorced husband, whose name she cannot recall. (This brings a big laugh from the audience.) In the same episode, Maude expresses concern about her twenty-seven-year-old daughter, Carol. She tells her husband that years before, Carol eloped with Pete and wound up in divorce court. Husband asks why she didn't put a stop to the elopement. Maude answers, "I was in Reno myself." (Another big laugh from the audience.)

In television land, divorce is for corrupt or childish people who are either wildly maladjusted or just unable to take life seriously. Television is not quite up to intelligent treatment of divorced and reorganized families. The place where divorce is most prevalent is in murder and courtroom dramas, where sordid intrigues require a network of hate-filled relations for their commercial and artistic success.

And yet despite the broad range of popular anti-divorce propaganda, the varieties of help now available to married couples suggest that there is more dissatisfaction with marriage than ever before and that people are becoming more impatient with unhappy marriage. The ailing institution of marriage is buoyed up by countless and diverse sources. The popularity of "how-to" books on making marriage work is evidence that marriage resuscitation is a vital part of American culture today. Acknowledging the strains in marriage, modern authors have found many clever ways to help people "revitalize" their relationships, short of divorce. Joyce Brothers, in her recent book, *The Brothers System for Liberated Love and Marriage* (how's that for a selling title?), outlines a detailed plan that every woman can use at home to become an equal partner with her husband.[59] In *Open Marriage*, George and Nena O'Neill outline their similar concept of a new egalitarian marriage based on mutual freedom and respect. Their positive approach to marriage is shored up by their negative attitude toward divorce. "The cost of divorce," the authors write, "both emotionally and financially, can be devastating." [60] This assertion is supported by a meaningless vignette about a man who could hardly keep up his alimony payments. That is their brief but effective reminder to the public that divorce is a negative experience and should be avoided. A more sophisticated volume, but in the same general tradition, is the William Lederer and Don Jackson book, *The Mirages of Marriage*,[61] which presents a very elaborate system for couples to use in diagnosing their marital ailments and finding ways to help themselves.

Since the pressure is as great as ever to preserve at least the outward structure of marriage, couples by the thousands resort to affairs, marriage encounters, crash courses in sex, group sex and swinging. They avidly study sex manuals which pour off the presses and which attempt to teach both technique and tenderness. A significant institutional development in the area of marital therapy is Marriage Encounter, Inc., of New York, a Roman Catholic organization presided over by Father Charles Gallagher, who expressed alarm over the increase of divorce in Catholic families. The annual budget of this organization is $1.5 million. "To date, some 150,000 couples in New York, New Jersey and Connecticut alone have had their marriages energized by Marriage Encounter, Inc." [62] Gallagher's stated aim is to get people to want to marry and stay married; he pursues this goal primarily through exhortation combined with weekend family retreats.

As long as couples believe the myth that any kind of marriage is better than divorce, all kinds and varieties of behavior are tolerated. There is much more curiosity, objectivity, and empathy, for example, in the literature on marriage than in the literature on divorce. The hypothesis has been advanced by historians that various forms of "deviance" are tolerated, perhaps even encouraged, because they act as "safety valves" which support highly valued social institutions. To divorce and then feel happier than you felt before is to flaunt a convention, not merely to experiment within it or use it as a means to some other end.

It is understandable, then, why people continue to dread divorce and why it remains surrounded by an aura of secrecy and circumspection. Divorce is not considered cheerful or polite "table talk," especially in front of children. It remains in the category of "adult gossip," with all the vulgar and voyeuristic sniping associated with such conversation. This problem is reinforced by the myth, now deeply ingrained in the American psyche, that divorce hurts children and undermines their self-love. We are reminded of a middle-aged woman who recently applied for help at a family counseling agency because of her sixteen-year-old daughter, who was becoming a "behavior problem." While taking the family history from the mother, the intake worker learned that the parents had been divorced for six years. When the social worker asked how the daughter had reacted to the divorce, the mother replied, "Oh, she doesn't even know we're divorced. I just told her that her father frequently stays in the city on business." Perhaps this woman's behavior is not as severely pathological as one would immediately assume; who can know how much she has been influenced by friends, family, religion and tradition to believe that divorce is a deeply shameful act.

# 2
# An Affirmative View of Divorce

Divorce is but a few weeks younger in the world than marriage.

—Voltaire

I don't believe in Morality. . . . Morality consists in being suspicious of other people's not being legally married.

—George Bernard Shaw

"Neurotic interaction in marriage" is not simply an abstract theoretical term or the subject matter of television specials and soap operas. It is a malignant pattern of life for thousands of Americans, eroding their happiness and driving them to endure years of bitter and hopeless emotional warfare with each other. In some cases it impels couples to drink, gamble, use drugs, be unfaithful, desert, divorce, act violent, apathetic, or suicidal. Among these alternatives, divorce and perhaps infidelity are the only healthy responses. Sometimes couples decide to seek professional counseling. In one way or another, and with varying degrees of success, unhappy people try to relieve their own misery.

41

It is more often women than men who are finally moved to do something "therapeutic" about their ailing marriages. This may be accounted for in a variety of ways: more exploited in marriage than men, women are more dependent on that institution to define their status; they are also somewhat more knowledgeable about therapy because it is the subject matter of popular books, women's magazines, television shows and neighborhood gossip.

Although there is an infinite variety of unhappy marriage patterns, some themes repeat themselves so often as to be almost characteristic of modern middle-class marriage.[1] For example, women frequently feel bored by the endless tedium of house and child care and the absence of intellectually stimulating daytime adult contact. They find that their husbands want them around only as sex objects and domestic servants, and expect them to be docile and subservient to their wishes. Men, on the other hand, frequently discover that their wives are dull to be with, that they want all the material rewards of affluence yet are indifferent to their husbands' work and resentful of his many hours away from home and family. Feeling mutually exploited and misunderstood, both partners complain that they are treated like jealously possessed objects instead of appreciated as growing, developing human beings. But no matter how stifled, enraged, or frustrated spouses feel, they are curiously unwilling and unable to extricate themselves from the most agonizing and destructive relationships.

When couples seek help, some improve their marriages, some end them, and others ventilate enough anger in therapy to return home and endure more years of familiar misery. Even after years of treatment, unhappily married couples may remain bound to each other because the task of *psychic* separation is so difficult. Partners cling to legal marriage, or at least to each other, sometimes out of love, but more often for a variety of neurotic reasons that even they do not understand. They can manipulate and depend on each other in a host of dramatic ways. We have seen many families, for example, in which all the people obviously detest each other and yet go on living together as cold warriors. Some of the common motives for staying together are guilt, inertia, fear of change, emotional insecurity, the hope (or fantasy) that things will improve, the fear that divorce will destroy children, the edicts of religion and the anticipation of poverty.

⌈One brilliant and talented father we know trapped himself in a desolate marriage because of his conviction that he was "superior" to the ordinary run of people in so many ways that divorce would be an admission to himself and the world that he was not only defeated but was also vulnerable just like everybody else. After he overcame his resistance to seeking therapy (which men more than women tend to look upon as a sign of weakness), he finally found the courage to divorce. Only in retrospect could he see that it took much more strength to leave his wife and build a new relationship with his children than it would have taken to adjust to his former misery. For years he had used his children and his stereotyped image of masculinity to ward off the anxiety of separation, although he was profoundly lonely, as well as sexually unfulfilled, in his marriage to a bitter, disturbed and unloving woman. While he recognized that he had married her for very unsound reasons, he was cemented into this relationship in part by his loyalty to the idea of marriage. Trapped by his self-image as a responsible father, he clung to a "reputation" as someone who was far above the sordid intrigues of "other people's grubby lives."

The fear of "losing status" and ending up "one down" in the marital struggle is a crucial factor in the perpetuation of many unstable and unhappy marriages. Sometimes a person wants to initiate divorce but is afraid that "as the deserter" he or she will be blamed for the rupture. (In fact, the *injured party* in court *is* the spouse who has been abandoned.) Rather than give the hated partner the satisfaction of *looking* innocent, husband or wife may tenaciously cling to the marriage in a spirit of pure vengeance. Obviously, in order to divorce, at least one partner has to be prepared to relinquish the neurotic struggle for status in the relationship. ⌋

Clinicians commonly observe how suffering, cruelty and unhappiness, instead of driving unhappy partners apart, often lock husband and wife into a pattern of mutually reinforcing, parasitic misery. Hate can sometimes be a more binding emotion than love. Even the most wretched, empty, or bizarre marriages seem to develop a life and momentum of their own, in defiance of common sense which would suggest that when couples are chronically unhappy together and cannot solve their problems, they should part ways. But the anxiety of abandonment, the anticipation of rejection, the fear of loneliness and the loss of one's children, coupled with the stigma that surrounds divorce, drive couples to torment each other psychologically rather than face separation or divorce. Some couples arrive at the unhappy compromise of repeatedly "deserting" or "throwing each other out," only to return, like moths to a flame, and continue their endless warfare. Thus, Pat Loud, whose marriage and family were recently exposed to ten million Americans in a serialized documentary on national television, remarked that her divorce from Bill came as no shock to anybody since she had previously thrown him out of the house on at least five different occasions. "They have been rehearsing for seven years," quipped their son Lance. "The divorce was really a relief," confided daughter Delilah.[2]

There are other typical behavior patterns which further convince us that divorce is not the *easy* but the *hard* way out of unhappiness, that a bad marriage is still more attractive to most people than the prospect of being divorced. For example, unhappily married partners often postpone separation until they are involved in affairs with other men and women on whom they can lean for reassurance and security. Others talk endlessly about divorce, as if it were something they *should* do, knowing full well that they have no intention of going through with it.

When both partners are clinging to marriage out of fright, they are likely to experience terrible panic at the mere thought or discussion of divorce. This feeling (sometimes called *anticipatory anxiety*), triggered off by the threat of separation, sets the stage for a dramatic display of sadism and masochism. For example, we have seen frightened people set psychological traps for their spouses by threatening to commit suicide if there is a divorce. Not only does the promise of suicide engender immense fear and guilt in the potential "deserter," but it gives an ambivalent spouse a convenient means of simultaneously flirting with and avoiding a tough decision. Each partner then has a powerful weapon of emotional blackmail to use against the other. We have known a number of men who have permitted themselves to be manipulated in this sad way by histrionic women who were not likely candidates for suicide. With little or no insight into their own needs, men who unconsciously prefer to stay married, but do not know it or cannot admit it, use their wives' threats as a smokescreen to mask their own dependency and lack of courage. When divorce does occur, in spite of such threats, those who are left behind often bear a burden of guilt and anger which erodes their self-confidence, their self-esteem and consequently their joy in living. Thus the "bad" marriage contributes to the "bad" divorce.

The tendency of many people to cling tenaciously to any kind of marriage is the logical outcome of our culture, which encourages young people to transfer intense emotional dependence on their parents to equally intense dependence on a spouse. The tragic flaw in these weak marriages may emerge only after there are thoughts and talks of divorce. The greater the panic, the harder a person has tried (and partially succeeded) to use marriage as a means of side stepping the struggle for personal autonomy and inner security. When people get married and move directly from one nuclear family to another, they are not necessarily making a psychic transition to adulthood. Often they are merely making a substitution. (The familiar complaint that one's mother-in-law rules the roost suggests that many couples do not even accomplish a satisfactory substitution in marriage.)

It is not at all surprising that so many people have reported to us that they began to thrive after divorce. It has been our experience with patients and friends that both spouses, after an initial period of confusion or depression, almost without exception look and feel better than ever before. They act warmer and more related to others emotionally, tap sources of strength they never knew they had, enjoy their careers and their children more, and begin to explore new vocations and hobbies. In one case a man who had agonized for years over getting a divorce reported that he "joined the human race" after dissolving a thirteen-year-old stagnant marriage. In dramatic contrast to the anger and desperation that consumed his energies and drove him from one casual affair to another, his post-divorce life has been filled with joy, creativity and relaxation. He earned his Ph.D. degree, became closer to his colleagues, developed a warmer and more loving relationship with his daughters, found what promises to be abiding happiness with another woman and enthusiastically started raising a new family.

He, like so many other people who marry and have children while they are still very young, feared that he could not survive or thrive alone, and that he would both destroy and lose his children if he got a divorce. Although divorce brings with it certain difficult adjustments, and sometimes even very painful ones (see Chapter 8), it usually turns out to be much less traumatic than the *anticipation* of it. We would infer that people's motives for divorcing are probably sounder and healthier than their initial motives were for marrying. One of the fortunate and healthy aftermaths of divorce is that the adults and children involved are much less likely to idealize marriage and to link the quest for intimacy with traditional, immutable, institutionalized roles.

The ability to live happily and intimately with another person should not be confused with the mere persistence of a legal marriage. As the late poet W. H. Auden once remarked, "There are so many happy marriages yet so many unhappy people!" It is our impression that many of the most neurotic, destructive unions never come to the attention of outsiders or specialists, and that the most profound unhappiness in marriage is often a very carefully guarded secret.

Assuming that it requires considerable ego-strength and openness to endure "exposure," to submit one's marriage to professional scrutiny, and to acknowledge that one is not "perfectly adjusted," it is probably the weakest and most troubled couples who keep their marriages hidden from view. For partners who are excessively dependent on the *form* and *status* of marriage, any kind of psychotherapy or counseling can be a threat. They may fear that both they and their marriages are too fragile to withstand therapy and that a close examination of their motives for remaining together would arouse disquieting thoughts of separation. In fact there is always the realistic possibility that if therapy proceeds for any length of time, especially if it involves only one partner, the spouses will grow apart. The "patient" may begin to see the other spouse in a new way, and if the picture is horrifying enough, one partner may want out of the whole marriage.[3]

Often the worst situations come to light only after a child becomes so severely battered or disturbed that outside agencies and authorities become involved in investigation of the home or in treatment of the family. Six years ago, one of the authors was working in a family agency in New York City and was assigned the case of a fourteen-year-old boy who was referred for help by his school guidance counselor; she had insisted to the mother that the child's depressed attitude was not normal and that he should be taken for consultation. The boy certainly was troubled, but compared with his parents he was in good shape. One joint session with the family revealed, in brief, the following situation: the parents, who had been married for nineteen years, had been discussing the possibility of separation for the last ten years. Father was a compulsive gambler who, although he made a decent living, chronically took his family's possessions and pawned them to pay off huge accumulated debts; most recently he had taken his son's bicycle which he promised to return. Mother worked part time to augment the family income, which was insufficient because of the father's habit, but she never told *anyone* about his gambling because she was so ashamed of the way they lived. Their son was under strict orders to do the same. Consequently neither friends nor relatives could visit them, because pieces of furniture kept mysteriously disappearing and the mother could not think of enough excuses to satisfy the curiosity of onlookers. She used her odd working hours and her fatigue as means of warding off visits. Rarely were the boy's friends (he had few) allowed to come to the house because they might overhear the stormy quarrels about gambling.

Determined to keep their marriage "intact," father and mother made certain concessions to each other. He dutifully attended Gamblers Anonymous, effusively and constantly apologized to his wife and brought her flowers every payday. He threw himself on her mercy, arguing that he did not deserve such a kind woman, that some day he would make himself worthy of her and repay her for all her deprivation. In exchange, she kept his gambling a secret, took care of the family on a marginal budget, and refereed fights between father and son. After a year of exasperating weekly therapy sessions (at which time the author left the agency), the family was still "intact," but the mother was ready to begin contemplating divorce and establishing a peaceful home for herself and her son. She actually had very little motivation to leave the marriage, and her son's obvious misery was the only thing that gave her the strength to continue treatment.

It is hard to say in a marriage such as this which partner is more emotionally deprived, which is more dependent on the marriage, and which has more potential for change. In their own bizarre way they had achieved an equilibrium that served them (but not their son) quite well. The parents truly feared that they could not survive without each other. Father was eternally grateful to the "good fairy" who in reality thought so little of herself that she considered it a miracle that *any man* could love her. She was intelligent and well educated (she had a bachelor's degree in psychology), was physically attractive and was a kind person. Father was a good-humored and attractive man. Although he was not dissatisfied with the marriage, she was torn apart with unconsciously ambivalent feelings. Their son benefited considerably from therapy, but for these adults, as for countless others, divorce remained terrifying although it was probably the most rational choice they could have ultimately made.

In his brilliant book *Pathways to Madness*, the late anthropologist Jules Henry shows how apparently intact marriages cannot only damage husband and wife, but often pose a lethal threat to children, physically and emotionally. Living with a series of intact nuclear families in which at least one child was severely disturbed, and implicitly designated as "the mental patient," Henry found some startling evidence of psychosis, neurosis and misery that had gone unnoticed for years. Of course, each unhappy family was unhappy in its own unique way.

If the existence of a legal marriage automatically meant that children were going to be cherished, warmly nurtured and well cared for, there would be ample and powerful justification for protecting and preserving the institution. But there is scant evidence that this is the case. *Marriage* does not protect children, *people* protect children. Every year countless numbers of children are neglected, deserted, beaten, abused and otherwise misguided by incompetent parents. Children can be resented, misunderstood and lonely in married homes as well as in "broken" or unmarried ones. A commitment and ability to love and to rear one's children adequately is not intrinsically related to the desire of parents either to get married or to stay married.

In light of the vast numbers of people in America who continue to enter matrimony, with all the traditional pomp and ceremony, it is perhaps premature to call marriage dead.[4] But there is much fruitful theoretical speculation about the nuclear family as a source of misery. The traditional image of home and hearth as a refuge from the troubles of life is being undermined as a more realistic and accurate model of the family emerges. Anthropologists, feminists, psychiatrists and social scientists have begun to demonstrate how and why the nuclear family is a major arena for social conflict and a major source of emotional breakdown as well.

Despite the prevalence of quiet marital desperation and hidden family pathology, a contrary stereotype prevails. The public still believes that children in intact homes, with full-time mothers, are the luckiest and best-cared-for children, and that married parents have reached the zenith of adjustment and fulfillment in life. Experience and research suggest that despite all the talk about new consciousness, and the inroads of the counterculture, many people, perhaps most, nurture traditional fantasies about marriage. Even if they are too sophisticated and urbane to admit it, Americans still think it is a shame when a child does not live with two parents, and still secretly wonder what is wrong with any man or woman who is not married by the age of thirty-five.

The never-married are even more suspect than the divorced. Single women constantly remark on the dearth of "adequate" men who are over thirty and available for a commitment to any intimate relationship. They are much more inclined to look for married lovers, or divorced ones, since it is considered a positive sign if a man at least got married once. Traditionally a lack of commitment to marriage has been considered synonymous with the inability to sustain intimacy and the unwillingness to assume responsibility.

History and culture have conditioned Americans to this rosy view of marriage. In the heyday of the Victorian nuclear family, men and women who desired abiding relationships, and children, had no alternative to traditional marriage. But as our generation begins to reject the "rotten compromises" and the exploitation attendant on keeping marriages together, it will become increasingly inaccurate to categorize unmarried and divorced people as a neurotic or alienated minority. The impetus for this change derives from the nature of American society; technological changes in the modern era have raised for the first time in history the possibility of lives free of grinding material deprivation, at least for the majority of people. In advanced industrial countries, where the family is peripheral to economic survival, men and women have become less tolerant of any form of personal misery.

There are many other factors as well that impel young people to create new life-styles.[5] Many of them have grown up in intact homes with married parents who were never happy together; youngsters are cynical, disillusioned and justifiably wary of marriage. They prefer to experiment with "mini-marriages," common-law relationships and communal life-styles. Many of the people who are now avoiding marriage are aware of its shortcomings, rather than frightened of intimacy or reluctant to assume responsibility for another person.

Other people who might like to marry are prohibited from doing so because their lovers are unable to get divorced. In certain contested cases, where there can be no amicable agreement, spouses simply drop the idea of divorce and start new lives and families without it. One close friend of ours recently faced such a dilemma. She and her lover wanted to have children together but he could not get his wife to agree to a reasonable divorce. Raised by very "straight" Episcopalian, middle-American parents, our friend could not envision herself as an "out of wedlock" mother. After contemplating the causes of her insecurity, carefully weighing her alternatives and warning her parents (who did *not* have heart attacks on the spot!), she decided to take the great leap into "illegitimate" motherhood. The proud parents adore each other and their "love child," and the mother reports that she has never felt more secure, independent and trusting in her life. For this family, necessity was in a way the mother of invention, but their child will not be bound by the conventional wisdom that marriage is more holy than love and that a legal contract is an automatic guarantee of security.

In spite of the myth that divorce is a psychological cop out (see Chapter 3), in reality it is considerably easier, legally and emotionally, to get married and stay married than it is to divorce. Marriage is therefore much more likely to be a cop out for young people who substitute artificial supports for genuine emotional maturity. It is easy to overlook all the "bad" reasons why people marry, because as a symbolic gesture, marriage is surrounded by a positive aura, enmeshed in a glow of sanctity and romance.

It is much easier, and far more common, for most people passively to acquiesce to custom than actively to defy basic cultural norms. Because divorce is still considered a form of deviant social behavior, it does not usually carry with it the blessings of family, friends and community. (Grandparents, for example, can typically be counted on to say something like "You're killing us" when they learn of the divorce plans. Their characteristic negativism, especially if they are *paternal* grandparents, can be understood in part as a reaction to the fear that divorce will mean the loss of contact with cherished grandchildren.) After many years of familiarity in marriage, especially when there are young children involved, it is hard to start a new life on one's own. It is the rare and fortunate family that has relatives and friends to count on for psychological support; therefore the desire to end an unhappy marriage often impels people to seek professional help, outside the family circle.

# 3
# Is Divorce Really a Death?

The American folk evaluation of divorce is constantly interfering with a scientific examination of it.

—Paul Bohannan

Most people believe that biological parenthood is the basis of the most intimate, enduring and important relationships. The exclusiveness of the nuclear family, predicated on the presumed inherent superiority of "blood ties," creates problems for both children and parents in divorce. What has happened in our culture, because of a peculiar American "loyalty fetish," is that the potential stepparent is perceived as an intruder who threatens the child's love for his "natural" parent and presumably competes for the child's affection. At the same time, the so-called "incomplete" or one-parent post-divorce family is a culturally unacceptable unit; social scientists and laymen alike believe that remarriage is both desirable and necessary.[1]

53

Divorced parents are thus put into a curious "double bind." On the one hand, they are told that remarriage reconstitutes a "whole" family, so necessary for children, and that it proves the parents' desire to live a normal moral life (historically, remarriage was condoned as the only alternative to a sinful life of fornication); [2] on the other hand, parents are warned that remarriage causes "stress and disturbance in children," [3] that stepparents and stepchildren are not likely to get along,[4] and that divorced parents should proceed very cautiously in introducing new adults into the family.[5] This latter set of attitudes is reinforced, in our opinion, by the unconscious belief of most people that love is a quantifiable and finite emotion; when new people are added to the roster of "loved ones," some love is taken away from the original set.

Because of these dilemmas and misconceptions, most people associate divorce primarily with the "destruction" of a family, the "loss" of love and the creation of "trauma." Dr. Benjamin Spock writes that "if a child has lost his father by death or divorce, he may have a strong sense of loyalty to him," and therefore mothers should move slowly and tactfully in dating.[6] Dr. Lee Salk cautions divorced mothers against sleep-over dates, which threaten the child with total renunciation of the biological parent to whom he may have great loyalty.[7] The projection of such possessive attitudes on to children creates a dilemma that divorced parents should not have to face. There is no inherent reason why a divorced parent should not live a new life in any way that he or she feels comfortable; it is the parents' privilege to remain single, to date, to live with someone, to remarry. The parents are the ones who have divorced and presumably fallen "out of love," *not* their children. It is *they* who want to *substitute* new relationships for old ones, *not* their children. The kind of conventional wisdom dispensed by Spock and Salk reinforces the worst aspects of post-divorce martyrdom by influencing divorced parents to deny their social and sexual needs on the basis of the unsupported assumption that they can damage their children.

In our opinion, the single most potent weapon in the anti-divorce arsenal that reinforces the pain associated with divorce has been the analogy between divorce and death. In countless books and articles, divorce joins death as a form of "social disorganization" (as if death were a form of impaired social functioning about which we could do something!). This analogy is brutal and crippling and cannot be justified as an aid to understanding divorce.

It is probably not out of malice that writers constantly reiterate the connection. At least some liberal authors make this comparison in order to help people recognize that they should be more sympathetic than critical when encountering divorced people, for they, too, have "suffered a loss." But the mechanistic application of psychological and sociological categories such as bereavement and mourning is careless of the meaning and impact of language. Although in their most important aspects divorce and death are not comparable, the analogy naturally frightens people and instills in them dread by association. The association persists because so many social analysts believe that both divorce and death contain certain destructive elements.

While divorce terminates a customary social relationship, death terminates *a life*. The alleged similarity between the two gratuitously assumes that anthropomorphic institutions can die. Such primitivism is characteristic of both popular and clinical literature on divorce: "Divorce is the death of the marriage: the husband and wife together with the children are the mourners, the lawyers are the undertakers, the court is the cemetery where the coffin is sealed and the dead marriage is buried." [8]

When the phenomena of death and divorce are distinguished from each other it is often only in the crudest way: death is a blameless and tragic quirk of fate, while divorce is a conscious and hostile repudiation of one person by another. The most diverse sources insist on this analogy, interpreting divorce as a form of death people inflict on each other, usually parents on their children.[9] Social anthropologist Paul Bohannan points out how it is sometimes suggested that a year should elapse between the divorce or death of a spouse and remarriage.[10]

Authors who are apparently convinced of the death-divorce analogy argue that both experiences are equally disorganizing. According to William Goode, America's foremost expert on the sociology of the family, there are six major common experiences shared by those who "suffer" divorce and death: cessation of sexual satisfaction; loss of friendship, love or security; loss of adult role model for children to follow; increase in domestic work load; increase in economic problems; and redistribution of household responsibilities.[11]

But the "deathlike" elements that Goode ascribed to divorce usually appear long before actual separation. In our observation of divorced families, sexual satisfaction and friendship go by the wayside long before the actual divorce. Adequate parenting is probably not being provided anyway, because mother and father are too busy fighting each other and feeling miserable. Furthermore, we have not seen any conclusive evidence that divorced mothers and fathers necessarily do more or less "domestic" work after divorce. In fact, it is probably closer to the truth that the opposite occurs! As one recently divorced patient reported, since her divorce she has felt no pressure to please her fastidious husband. She works full time now and therefore has less time than ever to clean and putter. And since family income, child support and alimony vary so much from case to case, divorce does not *necessarily* cause financial suffering; divorce often impels a nonworking wife into gainful employment, while child-support payments (and often even alimony) continue. This may mean augmented income for the wife and children.

But the "favorite" problem for the specialists is the alleged "loss of adult role model" for children when divorce occurs. Goode writes that "the missing parent [of death or divorce] cannot be an adequate role model for the children, or serve as an added source of authority in enforcing conformity to social rules." [12] It looks as though professional scholars of marriage and divorce are determined to commit homicide on divorced fathers.

Sociologist Willard Waller argued that no moral blame could be attached to death because it is an act of God; but when people deliberately divorce, they can expect to suffer a decrease in social status. But even Waller, in his deepest moments of pessimism and hostility, recognizes that the divorced father is still at least a live, warm body!

The image of an alive, involved divorced father was so alien to one Protestant spiritual leader that he recommended *voluntary exile* for these men. Divorce, argued Wayne Oates, ordinarily means that the child will sooner or later lose touch with one of the parents and therefore adjustment should be *eased* (our italics) by forcing a "clean break." [13] To assume that a divorced father is like a dead father is bad enough, but to urge that he deliberately act like one is bizarre! It suggests, despite the general recognition of the child's *fear* of rejection, that the best antidote to the *feeling* of rejection is *actual* rejection! [14]

The perpetuators of this fashionable psychological analogy go on to argue that post-divorce trauma is intensified because afflicted families are not sufficiently encouraged to go through an adequate mourning ritual. They assume that divorced people are always profoundly grieved. For example, Paul Bohannan writes that "emotional divorce results in the loss of a loved person just as fully . . . as does the death of a spouse." It involves an active rejection of another person, who "merely by living" is a daily symbol of rejection. The "natural" reaction to this is grief, since human beings mourn every loss of a meaningful relationship.[15] It is clear that when Goode and Bohannan refer to divorce, they mean the emotional process that takes place between people prior to the legal fact of divorce. If that is the case, then it is even more obvious that death and divorce do not belong in the same category.

Emotional divorce is most often characterized by a long-drawn-out process of alienation in which couples gradually sever their ties and cease to feel a deep, positive attachment to each other long before they legally separate. They give themselves at least some time to prepare mentally for the impending change, to muse over or even try out alternative arrangements. We recall, for example, the case of one of our patients, a married woman with two children, who came for psychotherapy because she was thinking about divorce but needed help in overcoming her guilt, in anticipating how everyone might react and in coping with her children. By the time she actually went through with a legal separation and asked her husband to leave, a full year later, she was prepared for the financial and emotional consequences of her decision. Because she was uneducated and unskilled, her financial worries were considerable, but she had given herself enough time to work up the courage to make it on her own and she and her children weathered the change very well. (In this case, the father, totally incapacitated emotionally and physically, was able to contribute very little to the support of the family.)

On the other hand, *deaths* among young married people are usually precipitous and shocking. It seems incredibly unfeeling to compare the stresses of these two very different situations. Furthermore, it has been our experience that divorced people, while they may experience some initial or even continued ambivalence, also characteristically enjoy the exhilaration of freedom and relief from tension. In most cases, the same cannot be said of death! (Under certain circumstances, even death, however, can bring welcome relief from prolonged mental or physical agony.)

When it is culturally expected that people should suffer and mourn, they are generally held suspect if their suffering is considered insufficient. Since people are supposed to mourn death in a certain way, they usually follow the socially accepted ritual. Relatives and friends are expected to act empathic and solicitous. But there is no institutionalized pattern of post-divorce reaction in America.[16] Bert Adams, a sociologist who argues that this is one of the three major reasons divorce is such a strain, writes: "What we may need is a divorce ritual similar to that surrounding death." [17] The problem with Adams' formulation is that the primary purpose of the rituals surrounding death is to give bereaved people an opportunity to accomplish what is called "grief work." That means the bereaved person struggles to accept fully the fact that the person who has "departed" is *physically* gone and can never come back, despite whatever heartache, anger and loneliness the death may have caused. If similar grief work were to take place after divorce, two things would happen: couples would be even less likely to become reconciled than they now are, and parents would be massively burdened in the task, which is hard enough as it is, of helping their children sustain healthy ties with the "other parent." Nobody can be expected to act as if another human being were both dead and alive at the same time. Unless a person is very comfortable with the idea of reincarnation, then telephone calls, checks, visits and letters from a "corpse" could prove very disconcerting.

The need for a set of mourning rituals is not as urgent as the experts would have us believe, although there is, even in welcome divorces, some sense of loss. Of course, a person who is divorced or abandoned against his or her will is likely to feel a profound sense of regret and anger; these feelings derive from the anxiety of separation, from the fear of being "out of control" of one's destiny and from confrontation with ambivalent attitudes toward the person who is gone. But for many couples who divorce by mutual consent (notwithstanding sham legal battles), divorce, unlike death, eventually provides welcome and sustained emotional relief.

Mourning rituals, at least for a time, enhance the feelings of despair and loneliness, and also symbolize love and respect for the deceased person. It is a positive sign of the vitality and enthusiasm that people have for life that they have *not* institutionalized a mourning ritual for a relationship which gave them more heartache and misery than anything else. Why should people *want* to mourn the "loss" of someone they prefer to be rid of or have outgrown?

Unlike most previous writers, we do not believe that divorce prevention can or should be accomplished by a campaign to resuscitate the traditional middle-class family. A more realistic aim would be to change the goals of family-life education and to recognize that marriage (i.e., nuclear family life) is only *one of many satisfying and normal options* available in life. Divorced homes, which are inevitable in our society, can be stable, healthy and happy. If education focused more on the process of change itself in a fluid and mobile society, it would be more effective in its task of wholesome socialization. A high incidence of "painful divorce" will be inevitable as long as people are indoctrinated to believe that happiness, adulthood and normality are synonymous only with marriage and biological parenthood. It is irresponsible and dangerous in our already overpopulated world to pressure people relentlessly into an institution whose primary historic function has been the production and rearing of children.

Since the "experts" have a very limited vision of the process of divorce, it is understandable why the larger community cannot decide whether to provide scorn, sympathy, or a champagne toast to the newly divorced. The assumption of liberal writers that divorced people (especially parents) always *want* to find new marriage partners, or "replacement parents" for their children, implies that mental health and remarriage are synonymous. High-pressure salesmanship for the institution of remarriage is perfectly consistent with the argument that "ultimately, most people in our society can bring their lives to a high point of satisfaction . . . only through marriage." [18] In *Open Marriage*, the O'Neills assume the same culture-bound position. In our world, they write, the *ultimate* step in the establishment of trust is the marriage contract.[19] Social scientists and popular writers have been hard at work convincing Americans that they cannot renounce by means of divorce the hallowed tradition of marriage and still expect to be happy *unless* they make a commitment to remarriage.

Since divorce, remarriage, stepparenthood and single-parent families are here to stay, they deserve more serious and positive consideration than they have received in the past. Having been indoctrinated to believe that a lifelong marriage is the healthiest and most worthwhile achievement in life, parents naturally have a hard time contemplating or facing divorce with pride, equanimity, and the self-confidence that accompanies a serious, mature decision.

It is particularly instructive to note that textbooks never suggest that couples who remain in hate-filled marriages should mourn *their* fate, although that would make a lot more sense. It is an infinitely greater personal "loss" to sacrifice one's emotional life for the sake of preserving a marriage that exists in form only. In *The Old Love and the New*, Willard Waller cites the case of a man who hated his wife so passionately for so many years that on his deathbed he kicked her every time she passed near. "His death was precipitated by one final attempt to express his hate in this fashion." [20] A much more serious concern than why "so many" couples divorce is why "so many" couples expect so much of marriage and accept so little from it.

# 4
# The Mystique of Mental Health

The characteristic tendency of modern society is to brand as sick that which is merely unconventional.

—Thomas Szasz

The helping or "care-giving" professions inherently support the status quo. The educator in teaching, the minister in counseling, and the therapist in healing traditionally want to bring their client to a state of greater harmony with his community. This is especially true for the theologian or the healer.

—Seymour Halleck

There is a gradually increasing number of specialists in psychology and human relations who are sufficiently concerned about the fate of American family life to discuss and write about divorce. These mental health spokesmen share many negative attitudes about divorce with journalists, educators and others whose views we discussed earlier. But mental health experts add a new twist: they use quasi-medical terminology to designate divorce as a symptom of emotional illness. Instead of calling divorce ridiculous, immoral or socially treacherous, they argue that it is the symptom of an ailment which requires prevention and treatment. Like many practitioners of social science in America, members of the mental health professions have "abdicated the intellectual and political tasks of social analysis" [1] and have substituted a set of quasi-medical value judgments to "explain" the phenomenon of divorce. What was once primarily a moral issue has become increasingly a clinical problem.[2]

Since it is fashionable in America to trust, even to revere, the judgment of specialists, and since so many Americans consult secular or religious experts during family upheavals, we think it is useful to scrutinize the theories and opinions on which influential specialists base their work. The most reliable picture of what helping professionals believe and do is contained in the books and articles they write. This material at least suggests what goes on behind the closed doors of the consultation room.

A reader searching the psychiatric literature for reliable data on why couples divorce and how divorce affects their psychological state is sure to be disappointed. The paucity of serious psychoanalytic and psychological writing on divorce indicates that therapists and researchers have largely ignored this important phenomenon.[3] But divorce has not been given the silent treatment because it is too trivial a subject for mention; quite the contrary. The relevance of divorce to American life is minimized because, as many mental health professionals see it, divorce represents not only the failure of marriage, and of a cherished American ideology, but the failure of treatment as well.

The lack of attention paid by clinicians to divorce is particularly curious since "divorce," "marriage counseling" and "family therapy" are now familiar household words, at least among the middle classes. But even before the recent popularity of marriage and family counseling, clinicians and ministers worked with people who were unhappily married and with parents and children in distress. As far back as the 1920's, a domestic counselor named Ernest Groves, who was also a sociologist, began working with married couples. He usually urged people to resign themselves to "mere" unhappiness because he believed that divorce was a searing and traumatic alternative.[4] He, like other early writers on divorce, took the gloomy view that divorce was usually a neurotic decision which the couple would later come to regret. Willard Waller, for example, argued that divorced people needed a complete "psychoanalytic overhauling" to prepare them for remarriage. For evidence, Waller cited a case in which the famous psychiatrist Wilhelm Stekel analyzed a man whose impotence was caused primarily by his repressed love for a former wife.[5] Without the benefit of extensive or sound research, writers in this field have always made dismal and dogmatic pronouncements on the grave evils of divorce. We have already shown, for example, how tenaciously the sacrosanct experts on family life cling to the invalid analogy between divorce and death (see Chapter 3).

The attitude of psychiatrists in divorce matters is particularly important because the general public prejudges the psychiatrist's activity with the same enthusiastic approval that they give to the practice of medicine.[6] But there are many dangers in an uncritical reliance on "experts." First of all, because of their medical training, psychiatrists are encouraged to view human unhappiness as a product of an individual disorder. "Even if he is exceptionally aware of the social forces that contribute to his patient's unhappiness," writes Seymour Halleck, "the psychiatrist's orientation as a physician tends to distract him from dealing with such forces."[7] Secondly, as psychiatrists reveal in their own writing, the practice of their craft is a social activity that consists not of benevolently diagnosing and healing illness, but of maintaining social control by giving guidance, education and personal consolation.[8] In the matter of divorce it appears that they use clinical data selectively to reinforce their negative personal attitudes.

The divorce literature written by professional clinicians now amounts to about a few dozen books and articles, containing broad conclusions, based on limited and ambiguous evidence. Usually the authors generalize from a biased sample, including only those people who have felt distressed or guilty enough to seek help. People who are joyous or who are simply contented and relieved about their decision to divorce and can take it in stride are a hidden population, rarely finding their way to the psychiatrist's couch or consultation room. Because clinicians often do see divorced people in treatment, it is easy for them to make the negative generalization that divorce is inherently detrimental to families and a peril to individual mental health. One of the points we are trying to emphasize in this book is that there is no reason to assume just because people seek therapeutic help during a time of stress that they are by definition *mentally sick*. There is a tendency in this country, with its ideology of rugged individualism, to associate any quest for help with either weakness, neurosis or social maladjustment.

More than a generation ago psychiatrists began to malign unhappy people who sought divorce. One doctor wrote that divorce, as a "disturbance of inter-human relationships," was a symptom of personal disease.[9] But the real champion of the negative psychiatric view was Dr. Edmund Bergler, whose classic work of 1948, called *Divorce Won't Help*, is often cited as the definitive psychiatric study on divorce.[10] This famous psychiatrist argued that people who were incapable of sustaining marriage relationships, and who preferred to divorce, had basic flaws in their character and personalities. Neurotics, he argued, are not "good material" for marriage; nevertheless, and "very conveniently . . . their underlying neuroticism is ignored and the institution of marriage is maligned." He goes on to characterize divorced women as unhappy, misunderstood, struggling neurotics who mistakenly think that divorce will resolve their inner conflicts.[11] Bergler assumed that people who divorce *always* have a persistent and underlying psychological illness which they cannot escape simply by changing partners.[12] It was Bergler who inspired the sociologists of his day, such as Willard Waller and Meyer Nimkoff, to believe that such flaws were best cured by psychoanalytic treatment.

Among contemporary psychiatrists, social workers, marriage counselors and ministers we find a similar set of negative attitudes. In her popular book about divorce, Dr. J. Louise Despert says there are two kinds of divorce: one that is based on "immature haste and impatience" and one that is based on "deep personal maladjustment." [13] Similarly suspicious of the emotional health of divorced adults, a marriage counselor writes that divorce seldom "solves the fundamental personality problems resident in a marriage situation." [14] A rabbi adds his negative judgment that "divorced people have never grown up to a sense of responsibility in family life. . . . It is not that they are incompatible—they're just irresponsible." [15] For writers of this persuasion, divorced adults are by definition psychologically unhealthy, an assumption that thinly veils a hostile moral evaluation. As Simone de Beauvoir aptly observed some years ago, "The defenders of marriage find support in the idea that conflict arises from the ill will of individuals, not from the institution itself." [16]

The bias built into the psychological literature on divorce is that emotional pathology and personal tragedy are an inevitable component of the divorce experience. The language that clinicians use to describe divorce and the way in which they perceive their own role heighten the potentially traumatic impact of divorce on families. Professional writing is weighed down with references to the failure, pain, anguish and tears associated with the end of a marriage.[17] For example, an often-quoted marriage and divorce counselor, Esther Oshiver Fisher, says that "divorce involves an admission of failure whatever the reason for the divorce, and it means loneliness, dating again [presumably an anguished experience!], the ghosts of an ex-spouse and often children." [18] She then envisions counseling as a means of preventing social maladjustment by helping divorced people "move away from egocentricity toward altruism and a desire to contribute to society." [19] The obvious implication in this hostile assertion is that people who divorce are adults chronologically but not emotionally. Infants are people who believe that the entire world revolves around their wishes and needs. That is why they are called "egocentric." Infants are people who cannot give selflessly to others, who have not yet developed what we call a social conscience. Fisher and others who argue a like point of view have *no evidence* to support the sweeping generalization that people who divorce are chronically immature.

Alas, Fisher's pessimism and moral judgments feel like a breath of sweet spring air compared with the writing of some other noted specialists. Haim Ginott, author of the best seller *Between Parent and Child*, wrote that divorce "like amputation, is a soul-shaking experience for all involved." [20] Contributing to another popular book, called *Explaining Divorce to Children*, psychiatrist Lawrence Kubie gives an equally maudlin account of divorce. "Divorce is always a tragedy," he writes. No matter how civilized the handling of it, "it is always a confession of human failure, even when it is the sorry better of sorry alternatives." [21] Dr. Despert describes divorce as an "abyss," filled with loneliness, despair, deprivation and economic hardship.[22] Although hardships often do follow divorce, they are neither inevitable nor insurmountable, and there are a variety of ways that families can try to mitigate them. What all these clinicians have in common is the failure to acknowledge the healthy, liberating and joyous aspects of being freed from conjugal misery.

Not only do many helping professionals write off divorced people as unlucky, maladjusted individuals who face a bleak future, but they reveal just how much anxiety and discomfort clinicians feel when they consider separation and divorce. Sometimes this attitude reflects the patient's feelings, and sometimes it "represents conflicts which are stirred up" in the therapists, despite "a rational consideration of the possible damage to result." [23] A therapist's status as either married, unmarried or divorced may considerably color his or her perception of the divorcing patient and may then influence the direction of treatment. There is little evidence that clinicians are aware of the extent to which their own personal lives are dictated by years of cultural indoctrination. One of our colleagues told us that in his supervision of therapists, he finds many of them emotionally threatened by patients who contemplate divorce because it reminds them, and in a way even forces them, to recognize that separation is one of the options available to themselves as well; if separation is a crisis for most patients,[24] then it is also likely to be a delicate and critical issue for many therapists as well. *This personal element in the treatment of divorcing and unhappy couples must be critically assessed by the therapist.*[25]

In an unusually candid discussion of how a therapist's biases influence clinical work, psychiatrist Seymour Halleck reviewed the case of one of his patients who was considering divorce when she first started treatment. Early in the therapy she developed some hope that her marriage would work out, and "she had sensed (probably correctly) that I [Halleck] did not approve of divorce." As time passed, her commitment to her children, her religious upbringing and her fear of being alone made her view divorce as impossible. Recognizing how he had subtly reinforced this woman's oppressed condition, Halleck began, in subsequent years, to tell his patients what his views were on such issues as divorce, sex, drugs, etc., before they started therapy with him. "Such revelation," he writes, "does not fully protect the patient from the political outcomes of therapy that he may not anticipate or desire, but it does give him a fighting chance to resist the potentially indoctrinating effects of psychotherapy." [26]

Many counselors and clinicians refuse to consider what Halleck calls the "politics of therapy" and continue to teach and profess an uncritical belief that marriage forms the healthiest and happiest basis for intimacy and family life. This is understandable since the Western world has long been dominated by the Judeo-Christian dogma that sexual relationships outside of marriage are sinful. But within the helping professions specifically, there is a tendency to shame people into abiding by conventional norms by suggesting that "deviant" life-styles are a barometer of emotional disturbance. When a doctor (or a lawyer) questions the propriety of our behavior we are much more likely to feel shame, guilt, or self-doubt than if the lady next door tells us we are crazy.

As a consequence of their own upbringing and their professional training, vast numbers of "helping" professionals believe that the nuclear family is the best possible environment for rearing children.[27] Implicit is the assumption that divorce is the precursor of a serious variety of social and mental illnesses. Anthropologist Paul Bohannan has observed how hostility to divorce has been broadened into a generalized theory in which divorce not only represents personal failure and illness, but is an index of social disorganization as well, associated with the future destruction of family life.[28]

While the community is likely to believe that psychiatric definitions of normality are based on medical facts, frequently all that psychiatrists do is echo the mores of the majority. There is no statistical or empirical proof that divorce is caused by or creates mental illness and social anarchy. In some cases anti-divorce indoctrination has a scientific veneer, but even psychologically sophisticated writers unwittingly reveal their prejudices. By portraying the traditional American forms of marriage and family as both good and necessary for people, mental health specialists further amplify common fears and misgivings about divorce. More than twenty-five years ago, a trained psychoanalyst wrote that "the normal family setting provides the young child the best opportunity to develop initial awareness of the nature of adults, their meaning to him and each other." [29]

Now, in the sixties and seventies, clinicians are still saying the same thing. Bernard Steinzor, a therapist and trained psychologist, maintains that "unquestionably, the bi-parental family is the best setting for raising children."[30] Psychiatrist John Millet writes that our future as a society lies in attempting to influence parents to be more patient and adequate with their children, and in creating more and better programs of "preventive education." Presumably, we could then "rescue matrimony from a declining reputation and restore it to its position as the most favored path to follow in man's search for self-fulfillment." [31] Theodore Lidz, professor of psychiatry at Yale University, and a well-known family therapist and author, claims that the stability of the nuclear family is essential to rearing secure and adaptable children.[32] He asserts that the family, formed by a marriage, serves to complete the lives of husband and wife, since "ideally" married people are "incomplete" alone.[33] Here is how Dr. Nathaniel Lehrman, a traditional psychiatrist, sums up *his* vision of the ideal marriage: The relationship of husband and wife, he says, should be like that of a king and a queen, where they are *not equal* but both are honored. There is a tendency now, he laments, to see the husband and wife as king and co-king or as two co-kings. "From where I sit, a two-headed family has as much chance of viability as a two-headed baby." [34] He perceives this analogy as an "accurate" conception which can help clarify things for the helping professions. There is no newfangled notion of equality or liberation for this writer, but instead a regal concept of subjugation. And, keeping perfect tune with her colleagues in the helping professions, social worker Emily Mudd wrote that since marriage is the core of family life, it seems appropriate to relate marriage to general family well-being and stability.[35]

If these typical remarks reveal the almost universal preference of the mental health professions for marriage, they also reveal their inevitable, if unconscious, hostility to divorce. This might not be the case if the experts were more careful in explaining which of their opinions were based on biological and social data and which were based on conventional moral norms.

Ostensibly the helping professions are committeed to the preservation and enhancement of emotional well-being for the entire population, using a skillful and nonjudgmental approach to human problems and relationships. Most professional counselors would agree that their proper task is to help patients and clients solve their problems, not to indict them for their conflicts or to redirect their life-styles in any specified channel. A psychiatrist learns that it is not his business either to try to save a marriage or to try to destroy it.[36] When mental health professionals fail to exhibit such restraint, they become spokesmen for conventional traditions and help support the cultural status quo. Ronald Laing, a pioneer of radical British psychiatry, once wrote that:

> When what we [psychiarists and social workers] think we do does not coincide with what we do do, we sink into assumptions that get pickled into our attitudes and we may find ourselves (if we ever find ourselves again) so pickled that we can no longer see what our assumptions are, nor that we are perpetuating practices we do not recognize.[37]

The fact that so many clinicians are committed to the preservation of marriage and the nuclear family can play havoc with their treatment of couples contemplating divorce. One California psychiatrist observed that as a result of advice and counseling, there is often an increase in one partner's adaptation to another, "along with a . . . diminution in the level of aspiration." [38] In other words, some counselors help people settle for mediocre marriages and expect less of themselves and each other rather than help them find the courage to achieve a successful and constructive separation. This is a common clinical problem, and we have seen psychiatrists give agitated marital partners tranquilizers to alleviate their tension "while they work through their problems." We recall the case of one woman who took pills and subsequently became less aware of her plight, or at least much less inclined (and able) to confront her unhappiness and struggle to do something about it. In conjunction with psychotherapy, sedatives and tranquilizers, muscle relaxers and anti-depressants, can be used as aids in keeping partners enslaved in unhappy unions. We can only guess at how often this kind of thing happens,[39] but we can take a clue from the expressed attitudes of many professionals toward the evils of divorce. It is tragic that when people find it impossible to live together, they are so often directed back to unhappy marital situations by counselors, therapists and legal advisers.[40]

While an anti-divorce ideology dominates much secular psychotherapy, counselors and social agencies with religious affiliations have an even more intense and emotional preoccupation with preserving marriage, supporting nuclear family life and condemning divorce. They are the people most likely to direct a couple back to marriage, rather than guide them toward divorce. We would expect many Catholic counselors to oppose divorce, but we were alarmed to discover that some have even tried to deny people who contemplate divorce any access to help. Psychiatrist John Cavanagh, in his book on marriage counseling, writes that "unfortunately the services of a marriage counselor are frequently sought by those who wish to . . . justify a divorce with remarriage." [41] Harshly rebuking people who desire divorce, Cavanagh argues that they show so little respect for the integrity and indissolubility of marriage that they abandon wedlock with even less thought than they give to the purchase of a new automobile. However, he offers us no clinical evidence to support this accusation.

Two generations ago, Protestants were arguing that divorce was a peril to our national life and that divorcees were "sub-normal, borderline, semi-criminal types." [42] By now it is probably safe to say that modern Protestantism has pretty well come to terms with divorce, although a distinction can still be made between modern and fundamentalist groups. The latter continue to reaffirm the exalted status of marriage and argue that God, who is the founder of the institution of marriage, still believes in it as firmly as He ever did.[43] There are millions of adherents to fundamentalist thought in America.

It seems, however, to be the Jews who are most panicked about divorce; they fear the loss of their ethnic identity. Contemporary Jewish professionals are calling for a heroic attempt to "plug the dikes of Jewish divorce." [44] The immensity of their fear is symbolized by the image of barriers against the lethal onrush of water. Prompted by the recent statistical increase in Jewish divorce, the Commission on Synagogue Relations of the Federation of Jewish Philanthropies held a conference on the problem in 1968. The participants wanted to study this "new affiliation" in the Jewish community. (The other three major afflictions cited were drug addiction, alcoholism and out-of-wedlock pregnancy.[45])

Their aim was not to help Jewish families cope sensibly with divorce, or live healthy and happy lives after divorce, but to *reverse* the trend with the help of social work agencies. Only one member of the conference perceived the dilemma created by their staunch adherence to traditional values. What should be the attitude of the rabbi, social worker, psychologist, or lawyer when faced with imminent divorce? asked Rhoda Simon. "Are we on the superhighways of community service traveling in an outmoded vehicle labeled 'Preserve the Marriage at All Costs' . . . or should we trade in that old antique for a more contemporary one . . . 'Divorce Is Here to Stay—How Do We Live with It'?" [46] This controversy still looms so large within the professional Jewish community that Rabbi Earl A. Grollman (editor of the anthology *Explaining Divorce to Chil-*

*dren*) cautions his colleagues not to take it as a "personal affront" if a couple decides to divorce even after they have received counseling.[47]

Whether they consult religious counselors or secular therapists, couples are usually so insecure that their intellectual and emotional judgments are clouded. They are unlikely to question or doubt the values of the professional expert. But as we can see, most therapists and social agencies have some preconceived idea of what is good for individuals and society, and they cannot avoid communicating and at times imposing their own values on their patients. Some clinicians are aware of their personal predilections and social values and openly acknowledge the relationship between their personal beliefs and the work they do. But how can we count the numbers who are blind to their own subjectivity?

For an example of the conscious and skillful integration of personal values and professional aims, consider the example set by Nathan Ackerman, one of the innovators of family therapy, whose recent death marked the end of a brilliant career. Ackerman acknowledged that professionally, as a psychiatrist, and personally, as a Jew, he was deeply distressed by the increasing rate of divorce among Jews. He was firmly committed to preserving and enhancing marriage and to keeping families intact because he believed that divorce was a sign of sociocultural decay. "When marriage fails," he wrote, "all else fails with it." [48] Wedded to the values of traditional family life, Ackerman believed that its very core was destroyed by divorce, so he put his clinical genius at the service of distressed families. For him, the fundamental therapeutic challenge was to prevent the breakdown of the nuclear family, in form and in essence. He did not believe there existed such a thing as effective divorce for parents, since they remain "permanently tied" by their joint responsibility for the care of children. In *The Psychodynamics of Family Life*, he warned that the bond between parents could not be neatly severed; the mere fact that they once had children together was destined to become a source of suffering for many years after divorce.[49]

Nathan Ackerman wrote with great authority, and was widely

admired as a humane man, a skillful teacher and an intuitive therapist. Nevertheless, he falls squarely within the tradition of conservative American thought, which deplores divorce, regards nuclear family life, based on marriage, as the healthy norm, and interprets parenthood as a permanently awesome and binding tie between two adults. But he differed from most therapists who write about divorce; while they simultaneously profess neutrality and scorn divorce, Ackerman recognized and acknowledged his biases (at least in his writing) and never adopted an untenable position of professional neutrality.

If bias is the omnipresent force that obscures our perspective on all human affairs, then therapists and researchers must heed Ackerman's warning that they are members of their society and culture first and scientists afterward.[50] It is as true of therapists as of any other "scientists" that they bring to their work a *culturally derived model of normal behavior* that influences the nature of their findings, their conclusions and their clinical work. "This model is a moral, not a scientific construct," writes historian Martin Duberman.[51]

It would be absurd to argue that in order to be effective in their work, clinicians must be "value free" as individuals. Obviously that is impossible; it is about time the myth of psychiatric neutrality was laid to rest.[52] But to the extent that professionals perceive marriage and nuclear family life as *the* normal and healthy aspiration for all people, they cannot help but perceive divorced families as either fragmented, neurotic, tragic, or socially destructive. Consequently, members of the helping professions compound the confusion and guilt of couples who seek help because they are not sure which way to turn.

Clinical literature on divorce has made a substantial and unfortunate contribution to the anti-divorce tradition in America. Subjective values continue to interfere with a rational understanding of divorce and an empathic approach to divorced families. It confirms William Graham Sumner's observation that there is little care or pity in our society for people who cannot adapt themselves to marriage, or who cannot adapt marriage to their own circumstances.[53]

We cannot claim that we have personally transcended our culture and professional training to emerge in a realm of pure rationality, but we do believe that rapid cultural change is creating an environment in which divorce stands out as a viable, healthy and liberating choice for many families. By the exercise of intelligence and the greater use of introspection, professionals can at least recognize their own fears, prejudices and personal conflicts, acknowledging them, and try to make allowances for them in their work.[54] We move closer to "objectivity" in clinical work if we understand that the negative judgment of divorce implied by the positive view of marriage can be a *cause* of emotional suffering to the people we are supposed to help.

# part two

# 5
# The Myth
# of the Damaged Child

> Every time we emphasize the importance of a
> happy, secure home for children, we are em-
> phasizing implicitly the rightfulness of ending
> marriages when homes become unhappy and
> insecure.
>
> —Margaret Mead

In the last fifty years the welfare of children has become the major justification for avoiding divorce and for preserving
the nuclear family. This has occurred partly because moral and
religious arguments no longer have the same effect on individual
behavior that they had a century ago. Furthering the interests of
anti-divorce forces in government and religion, influential members
of the mental health profession have defined divorce as inherently
traumatic and ill-advised for families with children. This clinical
indictment is the counterpart of society's moral disapproval of divorce and reveals a major means by which family organization is
controlled. Anti-divorce propaganda of this nature has increased

the fearfulness of unhappy parents who are worried about the ill effects of divorce and as a result often remain in unhappy marriages.[1] In some cases people find the anti-divorce position a comfortable rationale for avoiding the responsibility of extricating themselves from unhappy marriages.

In the psychotherapeutic community, concern over divorce and its effect on children has influenced the popularity of marital and family therapies. The increased availability of marital and court counseling during the last three decades illustrates, among other things, a professional desire to safeguard the security of children in "troubled" homes. We have found in our clinical experience that most counselors actively support the notion that the intact nuclear family is the ideal environment for rearing children. Psychiatrists and social workers frequently emphasize the emotional suffering with which divorced parents burden their children. Couples who do seek professional counseling find, in some cases, that their freedom to reach critical decisions exists only as long as it does not interfere with clinical prescriptions of what is best for the well-being of their children. One couple, after years of unhappy battles at home, finally sought marital counseling. Having reached the point where they thought they could separate without too much fear or bitterness, they were taken aback by their counselor's response. She advised husband and wife that such a decision indicated their irresponsibility toward their child, who would undoubtably suffer from such a decision.

A misplaced commitment to children is even more evident in the legal arena, where an elaborate court apparatus has been constructed with the supposed needs of children in mind. Family court judges, for the most part, view children of divorce as innocent victims of parental malevolence or malfunctioning. As a result the parents, who are often considered guilty of shirking their primary responsibility, are not granted sympathetic consideration of their needs. The behavior of judges and counselors supports Max Lerner's contention that "the greatest anxiety that Americans show about divorce is about the children of divorced parents."[2]

Contemporary attitudes toward divorce illustrate that serious attention is directed toward "protecting" youngsters, and away from the important task of providing encouragement and support for adults. Yet, it is parents' guilt and their vulnerability to society's negative indoctrination that ultimately determine whether or not the children of divorce can live happily ever after.

Professional literature on divorce is filled mainly with poorly documented clichés about children. Clinicians make the unsubstantiated claim that divorce inevitably creates serious adjustment problems for youngsters. Such assertions suggest to many parents that divorce will be more harmful to their children than even the worst marriage. Many professionals also claim that the "disturbed" children of divorce pose a danger to society in the form of delinquent behavior. Despite a lack of adequate evidence, both arguments against divorce—that it harms children and that they in turn harm society—have been the core of the anti-divorce crusade during the past fifty years. The late Nathan Ackerman employed both lines of reasoning in his discussion of family life. He considered divorce disastrous not only because he believed that it distorted the emotional development of children but also because it endangered the well-being of the community.[3]

With few exceptions, professionals like Ackerman view the child of divorce with great sympathy. At the same time, they blame the parents for inflicting the pain. One psychiatrist stated that divorce was a gift "which parents present to themselves," yet it "is complemented by the Trojan horse of unhappiness, involuntarily presented to the innocent children."[4]

Writers tend to focus so heavily on the trauma to children that they encourage avoidance of other important issues and conflicts that face divorced families. Overemphasis on the amount of hurt and deprivation children feel encourages those children to experience divorce as a morbid crisis and a paralyzing blow. Ironically, the designation of the child as "victim" was probably originally an attempt to alleviate the trauma caused to children. As it is now used, it represents a simplistic and punitive approach to parents and indicates a lack of true compassion for those families that defy tradition and public opinion by choosing the path of divorce. We

e that pity for children and censure of parents, whether public
ivate, can be far more destructive to families than the divorce
situation itself. Unhappily, the effect of such attitudes on divorced
families can never be objectively measured.

[ Because we think that common notions about divorce and its
effect on children are unproductive and biased, we have developed
a more positive analysis of the subject, based on our personal and
clinical experience with many divorced as well as intact families.
We have found no evidence that divorce is a danger to the welfare
of society or a psychological "inhibitor" of normal development.
Handled well, it is more likely to be a potentially liberating experience which restructures family life in a healthier way and provides
potential emotional gratification for all family members. We reject
the notion of divorce as inevitably "traumatic" and harmful for
children. This book reappraises common anti-divorce arguments in
order to minimize the guilt and confusion that plagues parents who
contemplate and go through with divorce.

Anti-divorce indoctrination affects all children, regardless of
whether their parents are married, separated or legally divorced.
Nondivorced parents tend to shield their children from the realities of divorce because they view the subject as anxiety-provoking
and inappropriate for young ears. Adults are generally careful to
discuss friends' and relatives' divorces in hushed tones. An aura of
secrecy surrounds this taboo topic, and children, who are very
sensitive to the nuances of parental conversation, inevitably assume
that their parents disapprove of or are ashamed of divorced families. One young man was trying to understand his upset over the
forthcoming divorce of his sister and brother-in-law. He suddenly
remembered that as a child the divorce of his closest aunt and uncle
was kept from him for almost two years. Another young patient
spoke about her inability for so long to ask her parents to tell her
what the word "divorce" meant. She knew it was something that
her parents did not like.

As one author observed, "We indoctrinate most people . . . to
feel that any person who gets a divorce is a horrible personal

failure or a dreadful sinner." [5] When children from intact families are exposed to divorced families, they are apt to view the young-sters as different or odd and to judge the parents as guilty of some meanness or wrongdoing. Evidence that these families may not be so different from their own only throws children into confusion. Children from "intact" homes are even more critically challenged when they are intimately touched by divorce. What happens to them if their own parents contemplate divorce or announce plans to separate? Surely greater confusion and bewilderment ensue as youngsters attempt to clarify the apparent inconsistencies between their parents' separation and the "messages" they had once received about "other people's" divorces from these very adults. Depending on how children resolve the incongruity between what their par-ents say and what they do, children of divorce will view themselves either as participants in a reconstructive event or as outsiders vainly watching their parents enter into an evil activity which threatens to shatter their world. Suzanne, aged eleven, reacted to her parents' impending divorce by withdrawing from them. They had always spoken of divorce as terrible, something that only parents who didn't care about their children contemplated. Suzanne needed months of help before she could understand that her parents still loved her; she had to grasp the meaning of their guilt before she could make sense of their abrupt attitudinal change.

This dilemma is by no means unusual. The prejudice of many married people against divorced couples characteristically dimin-ishes, as in the case of Suzanne's parents, only after they them-selves begin to contemplate divorce. But by this time their hostility to divorce has already been transmitted to their children. Parents can constructively help their children by educating them at an early age to the possibility of separation and divorce in their parents' marriage and in any other marriage. When children are falsely reassured of their parents' allegiance to each other, they are entitled to feel that they were lied to and dealt a lethal blow if their parents divorce. The shock of unexpected divorce would be diminished if the subject didn't get the silent treatment in so many homes.[6] It is nonsensical, moreover, and ultimately cruel to tell children that all or any marriages are forever.[7]

Anti-divorce indoctrination is heavily laced with the concept of the "broken home," which illustrates the societal and consequently the parental view that divorce is a destructive event in a family's life. Predictably, the idea of the "broken home" elicits tearful sentiments and creates in the public mind visions of unhappy, abandoned and desolate children actively being robbed of a secure, cozy two-parent home and thrust into a barren, unloving world which they can neither cope with nor understand. When children of divorce become familiar with the "broken home" ideology, they naturally react by feeling estranged from other youngsters. When children of intact homes learn about the horrors of the broken home, they begin to fear for their own security.

A sense of aloneness afflicts many children of divorce despite the fact that they are part of a vast number of children in similar positions. As of 1966, nearly one American child in ten lived in a one-parent home and about 1.5 million families were headed by unmarried adults.[8] There are ways of helping them develop a sense of community and personal optimism.

Some perceptive modern novelists have begun to break with the old tradition of portraying divorce as tragedy. In *Birds of America*, Mary McCarthy writes about a teen-age boy whose search for identity is embedded in the context of his relationship with his divorced parents. Neither his flamboyant and talented mother nor his predictable and scholarly father is devastated by divorce. The hero, Peter Levi, mocks the "public" stereotype that he is the miserable and deprived child of a broken home:

> Peter licked his lips. "My parents are divorced." Though divorce was as common as measles in the U.S., he could feel himself turning red. "So that I have quite a few step-brothers and -sisters. And a half-brother and -sister on my father's side. But I'm my mother's only child . . ."
> As he feared silence followed his revelation. Probably

his teachers were pitying him for his "broken" home . . .
The average American looked skeptical when he said he
approved of divorce for parents. They seemed to think
he had been indoctrinated. He decided to pipe down. If
he went on talking, he would be bound to disclose that
his mother had been divorced twice.[9]

The term "broken home" is actually a misnomer. The children of
divorce are really the children of broken marriages, not broken
homes. The divorced home may very well be healthy and whole,
though a marriage ends.

   Both lay and professional writers tend to emphasize the ways
that divorce ends family ties, and to ignore the ways in which
divorce positively restructures family relationships. Rather than
seriously gauging the positive dimensions of kinship alterations,
professionals who are in a position to influence public opinion
remain tied to a narrow, traditional, negative bias. While the notion of the "broken home" has come to symbolize the seamy side
of divorce, one-parent and multimarriage families are associated
with deviant and aberrant structures that cannot adequately transmit societal values from one generation to another. The intact
nuclear family, on the other hand, supposedly transmits to youngsters an abiding commitment to good values, such as marriage.
Clinicians, therefore, predict that youngsters deprived of a two-
parent home will either reject marriage for themselves or will
follow their parents' example by marrying "badly" and then
divorcing. Dr. J. Louise Despert has expressed her concern that
divorce causes children to become cynical about marriage.[10]

   With few exceptions, neither clinicians nor social scientists
question the desirability of the two-parent family. Therefore, they
do not adequately evaluate the alternative family systems that
grow out of divorce. They rarely consider post-divorce family structures to be secure or healthy. Social scientist E. E. LeMasters is
one of the exceptional researchers in this field. In an attempt to
compare the merits of various family systems, he specifically studied
the question of the proper number of parents required to socialize
a child.[11] After searching professional literature, he found no sup-

port for the belief in the one-parent family as either inherently "dysfunctional" or pathological. Moreover, since most societies involve more than two adults in the socialization of children, LeMasters could find no justification for the bias against the multiple-marriage forms of family life.[12] After a lengthy investigation, he concluded that "one good parent is enough to rear children adequately or better in our society." [13]

We cannot argue that divorce does not expose children to alternate life-styles, nor can we deny that children from divorced families probably question the advisability of marriage more than do their peers from intact homes. But more importantly, we can argue that because of the very nature of their life experience, children of divorce have particular advantages and opportunities that their peers may not have. Children of divorce may have greater insight and freedom as adults in deciding whether and when to marry. While this is considered by some experts to be a *negative* effect of divorce, it seems to us that these youngsters may be saved from the conditioning that leads most children to anticipate marriage as the only acceptable choice. If divorce is handled maturely by parents, their children can experience it as a relatively non-traumatic event: as adults they may then be able to accept with equanimity its possible occurrence in their own lives. Robert was eleven years of age when his parents divorced. He remembers the relief he experienced as the fighting ceased between his parents. After the divorce Robert's relationship with his father blossomed and he was able to enjoy his mother's more relaxed and less irritable behavior toward him. When Robert divorced his own wife twenty years later, he did so with the belief that, like his father before him, he would continue to have a meaningful relationship with his own children. In his experience and memory, divorce was not a shattering episode for the family.

Children of divorce have a unique opportunity to experience a variety of family styles, including the one-parent family and the multimarriage family. Exposure to new adults and the variety of post-divorce life-styles can enrich children's lives by providing them with a chance to break away from excessive dependency on their biological parents. Of course, the self-sufficiency of any child is determined primarily by the parents' strength and security, and not by their marital status. Most clinicians are familiar with the sad cases of small, isolated nuclear families in which the children have very little autonomy and are smothered by their ever-present parents. The wider availability or at best the potentiality for new relationships in the post-divorce home can be advantageous for children whose natural parents tend to be possessive, clinging and domineering.

Rhoda, a nine-year-old, was taken to a therapist because of severe anxiety that interfered with her daytime activities and her night-time rest. The only child of a divorced middle-aged couple, Rhoda was extremely overprotected by her anxious, fearful mother. Rhoda's father, with the help of his new wife and friends, was able to introduce her to many of the activities that she had been denied because of her mother's overprotectiveness. In her father's new home, Rhoda had a chance to discover that divorce was not synonymous with suffering. Her father, who did not need to cling to her, gave her a chance to explore the pleasures of childhood.

The lack of specific information and worthwhile clinical research on the adjustment of children to divorce and remarriage is surprising in view of the importance of children to the anti-divorce argument. Sadly, the conclusions drawn by clinicians about the child of divorce have not rested on substantial information. What has passed as major, definitive research on the subject is work that has actually focused on only a minute number of children who have been seen at particular mental health clinics or who have attended nursery schools which are "under observation" for research purposes. Using an absurdly small number of subjects, researchers draw conclusions that are then hastily applied to millions of children from divorced families, children who have not been professionally treated or clinically observed. For example, in one nursery school study, ten out of sixteen youngsters reportedly experienced a variety of negative reactions [14] that supposedly indicated a poor initial adjustment to divorce. Are we then supposed to infer that most children from divorced families experience similar responses? Dr. John McDermott ironically disqualifies his own conclusions when he suggests how difficult it is to measure the "real" causes of those observable "symptoms."

Research such as this may offer us some ambiguous information about ten children but it tells us very little about the half-million American youngsters who are involved annually in divorce.[15] In 1970 the number of children involved was six times larger than it was in 1922, and since 1950, the rate of divorce involving children has doubled.[16]

Clinicians like McDermott are quick to draw negative, actually meaningless, conclusions from inadequate research. But they fail dismally to raise pertinent questions about some of the visibly positive effects of divorce on children. One reason for the over-emphasis on divorce as a childhood trauma is that studies have been concentrated around the period of the divorce process— usually the time of greatest upheaval for the whole family. The actual legal divorce, when it occurs, may indeed be welcomed.

In our professional work, we have become familiar with numbers of children, for example, who experienced the actual divorce of their parents as a relief from tension and bitterness; many youngsters were able to come alive as the cloud of despair lifted from their homes. Case histories of such children are ignored in the professional literature of marriage and divorce.

It is characteristic of psychiatric literature to focus on abnormal development and problems of psychopathology. However, in the same way that research on normal behavior gives us a means of evaluating disturbed behavior, so research focused on the healthy adaptation to divorce would teach people how to handle the normal hurdles of divorce.

Furthermore, social scientists do not deal with the question of whether neurotic symptoms commonly attributed to the trauma of divorce may in reality result from the emotional turmoil that characterized the predivorce home. It seems likely that in the long run children will react more severely to constant bickering or other forms of emotional warfare than to a physical change in life-style, which may bring relief from tension. In order to make this distinction, researchers would need to focus on predivorce families and conduct longitudinal research that would pinpoint the actual factors that endanger the mental health of children.

It is a disheartening fact that because of society's prejudices in favor of marriage, there is little professional literature on the subject of why so many families who should divorce choose instead to coexist on the brink of disaster. In these truly "broken" families, where husband and wife continually bait each other or retreat into silence, the children are emotionally scarred by the silent and noisy hostility around them. When parents live amid confusion and pain, their children do too.

In many cases, when professionals attempt to analyze such families, they do offer lip service to the idea that emotional divorce can be more detrimental to children than legal divorce. Thus they establish their liberal credentials with the reader, and under the guise of speaking for the child of divorce, they usually proceed to crucify divorced parents for failing their children. We need less unsubstantiated opinion and more willingness at least to consider the potentially constructive aspects of divorce.

# 6
# Divorce Can Liberate Children

The child emulates unconsciously what the parents are, rather than what they pretend to be.

—Theodore Lidz

As long as love begets life no child is deserted, or hungry, or famished for the want of affection.

—Emma Goldman

It seems that few things occur in divorced families that do not also occur very frequently in intact ones. The crucial factor in a child's emotional well-being is not family *form*, but family *sentiment*. As a means of demonstrating that divorce, disentangled from its aura, is not inevitably damaging we must explore the validity of many of the specific warnings regarding divorce for children. It is only then that unsubstantiated mythologies can be laid to rest.

In both popular and professional anti-divorce literature, the major emphasis is on the specific disadvantages and problems that divorce creates for children. The theme reiterated over and over again is that of "loss" and the conclusion is somehow drawn that quantity is more beneficial than quality where parenting is concerned. Specialists inevitably argue that divorce means for the child the loss of one parent. The fact that a child may receive better parenting from one relaxed adult than from two bickering, upset adults is too glibly dismissed; preference is generally shown for the intact family, regardless of what atmosphere prevails in the home. Writers assume that the child (the victim) is inevitably plagued by feelings of loss, abandonment and rejection.

Mental health practitioners often assume that divorced parents have abandoned their proper roles and duties toward their children. Such views are apparently based on the notion that most divorcing parents are trying to absolve themselves of "real" parental responsibilities, or, even worse, that there is an inevitable abrupt cessation of all prior intimate ties between parents and children. Dr. J. Louise Despert presents a dismal picture of the father's post-divorce relationship to his children. She speculates that after divorce father and child are mutually ill-at-ease and unsure of how to approach each other in the best of circumstances.[1] Her view of the visiting father as a sudden stranger or as an expendable commodity to his children stems from the erroneous assumption that divorce occurs between parent and child, rather than between the married pair. This belief is not peculiar to Dr. Despert, and is not as unusual as one would imagine. Reputable authorities in the fields of medicine and sociology subscribe to the notion of the noncustodial parent as a "lost" parent.[2] Another writer, who also assumes that the parent-child relationship inevitably fails after divorce, advocated the cessation of visiting between young children and the noncustodial parent on the basis that such visits benefit only the adult, not the child.[3] Advice based on such an unsupported notion is cruel and absurd, especially if one is familiar with families where strong and loving ties remain between children and their divorced parents. Opinions of this caliber not only reflect a mistaken idea about child development, but more importantly, they stem from a powerful anti-divorce bias which serves the function of "punishing" divorced families. In reality, when strong, positive ties exist prior to divorce, and are thoughtfully preserved and cultivated after divorce, the actual parental separation can be a relatively minimal event in the child's emotional life.

In other words, a meaningful relationship between a parent and child can continue, unhampered, whether or not divorce occurs, and in the end feelings of loss and abandonment are unrelated to and unmeasurable by marriage and divorce. Children do not reject parents they love just because a separation or divorce takes place. The psychology of loss is far more complicated, and, if anything, children go out of their way to find signs of love and caring in their parents. One psychologist, who rejects the notion of the "lost" parent, has written that the child's tendency to experience divorce as loss is in direct proportion to the psychological distance between parent and child.[4]

Professionals, persistent in their efforts to "protect" children from divorce, have been known to amplify their arguments by equating the effect of divorce on children with that of the death of a parent (see Chapter 3). One social worker writes that in both cases there is "an interruption in the process of learning to love and be loved." [5] Even the most enlightened writers on the subject of divorce tenaciously link the results of divorce and death. Attempting to clarify the misconceptions inherent in this analogy, sociologist Jetse Sprey argued that divorced and bereaved families are not "incomplete" single-parent homes because the absent parent (usually the father) can remain a significant reference figure to a child.[6] We would add that an alive divorced father is certainly capable of being more to his children than a mere "reference figure"! Some experts have come to the perverse and bizarre conclusion that *the death of a parent may be more desirable than divorce* where children are concerned. They base their opinions on the assumption that the post-divorce home is characterized by such discord and unhappiness and that the death of the parent would surely be preferable. According to other sociologists, death is preferable to divorce because children are better able to integrate death.[7] These writers assume that children respond to both experiences with grief and mourning reactions. This apparent indulgence in morbid fantasy on the part of some clinicians and social scientists simply suggests how effectively the current generation of adults has been conditioned by the anti-divorce tradition.

Such gross suppositions about what children do and do not experience clearly disregards the clinical experience of countless practitioners who have worked with families of divorce. While traditional custody decisions do markedly interfere with the spontaneous relationship between father and child, both can express and demonstrate their love and concern through visits, telephone calls, letters, gifts and extended, shared vacations. (We have generally specified the sex of the noncustodial parent to be male *not* as an endorsement of the cultural and legal child-custody policy but with reluctant recognition of the present realities in American divorce practice.)

Ultimately a child's relationship with his or her parents, as we previously emphasized, does not depend on the parents' marital status. Ironically, in contemporary intact families, the father's primary link to his children is generally his wife, who has been delegated almost total responsibility for their upbringing. How many fathers "get to know" their children largely through the mothers' reports of the events of the day that occurred in their absence? *The New York Times* recently featured an article describing the absence of husbands and fathers in economically successful intact families. One woman was quoted as saying: "I almost exclusively bring up the children . . . I discipline them 100 per cent." [8] The fathers in question were preoccupied with other aspects of existence and subsequently became alienated from their children. According to one divorced father, the connection between a parent and a child is not based "on the amount of time—the dead weight of hours passed together in the same dwelling and some of them very dead indeed—but in the quality of time." [9]

Judging from our own clinical and personal experience, youngsters from divorced families generally fare no worse than their peers from intact homes where questions of time and attention from fathers are concerned. In fact, it has been our observation that unhappy fathers in "intact" homes gladly take on extra jobs in order to get away from their wives; this pattern of course cuts into their time with the children as well. A child may experience a more severe loss if he (she) lives in a family where the father is looking for excuses to get away from his wife; this hostility spills over into his relations with his children, who may misconstrue his absence as rejection of them. On the other hand, scheduled visitation, after divorce, commonly provides for a number of undisturbed hours in which parent and child may be left alone with each other, to share thoughts, feelings and experiences. Such reserved and uninterrupted time is very precious to children, and is not necessarily any more available to children who are considered fortunate to live in nondivorced families.

One young woman, a child of divorce, remembers her Sunday visits with her father as very precious. All through her youth her father never disappointed her and they enjoyed themselves so much that her friends would beg her for the privilege of joining them each Sunday. They grew more emotionally intimate as two individuals than they ever could have if the father had felt trapped in a bad marriage "for the child's sake."

The issue of divorced fathers and their children arouses in many people an intense concern that young boys will be denied an opportunity to model themselves after their departed fathers and that consequently they will fail to master important developmental tasks. William Goode has asserted that after divorce the child misses in the father an "observational model" and loses him as an "ultimate threat of punishment and misses out on the special skills that mothers cannot teach." [10] Goode's assumptions reveal a stereotyped set of attitudes about mental health, the proper sex roles for men and women, the general manner in which parents are expected to behave and the nature of post-divorce relationships. Social scientists typically assume that children of divorce rarely see their noncustodial parent and that children of both sexes are in danger of identifying with whatever sexual model is provided at home. Authors often imply that this "unhealthy" situation is one cause of homosexuality in males, and despite the fact that this idea is nonsensical, divorced parents often fear this very development in their sons. Though homosexuality has to do with the quality of parenting, not whom the child lives with, readers of divorce literature are asked to believe that children raised primarily by their mothers grow up "hermetically sealed from the realities of a heterosexual world." [11] When fathers are not available, friends, relatives, teachers and counselors can provide ample opportunity for youngsters to model themselves after a like-sexed adult. It seems to us that any child who can successfully be "hermetically sealed" from the heterosexual world is destined to grow up with much more severe problems than homosexuality!

Social scientists should be well aware that the mechanism of identification is affected primarily by the quality of relations between children and their "identification models." [12] Identification is more likely to be inhibited by parental rejection, anger and neglect, which, in many cases, are more prevalent in the predivorce home than in the post-divorce home. A child who must identify covertly, or who is torn, guilty and fearful, will have an emotional problem whether his parents are divorced or together. When parents are distrustful, hostile and competitive, they cannot allow their children freedom to identify with aspects of the other parent, and whether the parents happen to be divorced is largely irrelevant to this issue. Dr. Hendrik Ruitenbeek, a New York psychoanalyst who is interested in problems of male identification, concluded that fathers become estranged from their children not by virtue of divorce but by normal middle-class existence.[13] We would emphasize that the mere presence of a like-sexed parent in the home does not insure that positive sexual identification will take place. The process is influenced not only by contact between parent and child but also by the extent to which the child's needs are gratified by this parent.[14] Traditional ideas about the relationship between divorce and children having the proper role models have been based on the assumption that after divorce the noncustodial parent might just as well be dead as alive.

In addition to the issue of identification is the more general question of psychosexual development. According to psychoanalytic theory, only by the successful resolution of the Oedipus complex—sexual desire for the parent of the opposite sex—can lasting identification with the same-sexed parent occur. Clinicians generally consider this successful resolution to be inhibited by parental separation and divorce. The theory suggests that a youngster often wishes the same-sex parent (the rival) to be dead or gone. Any leave-taking by this parent frightens a youngster who may believe he was the cause. Presumably the child will be panicked because his fantasy has become a reality.

The obvious hitch in this argument is that marital discord can be a more lethal inhibitor of successful mastery at this stage than legal divorce, which may ease the tension in the child's environment. In order for a youngster to achieve healthy identification, and to resolve the conflicts of the Oedipal phase, parental competition for the child's affection should be at a minimum. There is *no evidence* that such competition is *more* prevalent in divorced than in intact homes. Adults who divorce do not necessarily have a need to use their children covertly as pawns in their battles with each other. J. C. Flügel, author of *The Psychoanalytic Study of the Family*, points out that general harmony within the family and particularly between the two parents is an advantage for the child, who is less likely to look upon the same-sexed parent as a tyrant or an intruder to whom the other parent must submit.[15] Flügel adds that divorce or separation of parents whose marriages are unhappy may therefore be of considerable benefit to the child.[16]

In spite of the fact that a parental decision to divorce may promote the emotional well-being of the child, clinical writers often assert that the danger of divorce lies in the greater propensity for delinquent acting out on the part of children. Some professionals go so far as to outline the specific danger signals in a child who is becoming anti-social. These supposedly indicate whether the child of divorce is in need of psychological help. The list of warning symptoms usually includes delinquency, truancy, sexual perversions, tics, etc.; all examples of the price children presumably pay for their parents' divorce.

Although most professional writing suggests that divorce causes psychopathological symptoms in children, there are a few serious articles suggesting that the children of divorce suffer fewer psycho-somatic ailments, are less inclined toward delinquency and have better relationships with their parents than children living in intact troubled homes. One writer on the subject of marriage and family stability suggested that the "chances of psychological dam-age to children resulting from the divorce of their parents is no greater than that for children in unbroken homes marked by con-tinued marital tension." [17] Lee Burchinal's research study on adolescents concluded that youngsters from divorced homes ap-peared no worse off than their classmates from intact families.[18] According to Burchinal, acceptance of his findings would require a revision of "widely held beliefs about the detrimental effects of divorce on children." [19] Research on delinquency, undertaken in 1947 by Sheldon and Eleanor Glueck, revealed what later research has confirmed, namely that the important dynamic of successful development lies in the quality of the relationship between parent and child. In other words, divorce in itself does not cause children to be emotionally damaged. Ivan Nye compared ninth and twelfth graders from divorced and unhappy intact homes. He concluded that "in the areas of psychosomatic illness, delinquent behavior and parent-child adjustment . . . children show better adjustment in broken homes." [20]

More recently, Parents Without Partners, an organization formed to assist single parents, also investigated the relationship between delinquency and one-parent families. The researchers found significantly less delinquency among children of one-parent homes than among those living in two-parent domiciles.[21] Chil-dren, we may add, who seemingly react to divorce with symptoms of disturbance are responding, more often than not, to the pain and hurt experienced, but not expressed, while they lived in a troubled predivorce environment.

Whether children live in intact homes or in divorced homes, the ingredient needed to avoid emotional disturbance is a high quality of adult empathy for children. Some unhappily married partners can remain empathic and loving parents, though this is probably more the exception than the rule. Most divorced parents are probably more available to their children after divorce than they were before. With the cessation of battle, parents can turn to their children and begin to pick up the pieces of their lives.

Neurotic symptoms that supposedly afflict children of divorce are thought to arise in part from the heavy burden parents place on them during and after the divorce. Assumptions about parental grief and preoccupation during the divorce process lead the public to presume that children will be deprived of adequate adult concern and care. Since adults who divorce are generally considered more unstable than adults who do not divorce, clinicians often shudder at the prospect that children will be dependent on such disturbed parents.

Mental health practitioners also bemoan the "fact" that children from divorced families inevitably face the consequences of intense loyalty conflicts. Much of the popular literature on divorce warns parents that a divorce pulls children apart and causes them to suffer extreme feelings of guilt and remorse because they are impelled to demonstrate their simultaneous allegiance to two hostile parents. However, *loyalty problems are not the exclusive domain of children of divorce*, because no one can grow up in a two-parent home, either happy or unhappy, without experiencing some split in affections and loyalties.[22] In unhappy homes, where parents are unable to cope with children's ambivalences and natural swings of emotion, parents will treat their youngsters as disloyal subjects.[23]

An example of such a loyalty problem occurring in an intact home may be seen in a thirty-five-year-old patient who has spent half of her adult life in therapy, immobilized by her parents' hatred for each other. Neither parent had the emotional strength to seek a divorce and each would exploit the patient, during her childhood, by using her as a private confidant. Perplexed and confused by the intimate details of her parents' life together, this woman was fixated at an early level of emotional development. Her inability to commit herself to relationships with either men or women was a sad reminder of her earlier life. Had the patient's parents separated or divorced during her childhood, there would have been a likelier possibility that she might have been spared this untenable role in her family.

The above case illustrates how some parents, devastated by unhappy marriages, have little "emotional poise" in relating to their children. Loyalty problems are especially common *because of* the nuclear family, regardless of the marital situation, for those within a family are inclined to develop intense loyalty toward those in the family and a lack of concern for those outside.[24]

( Unhappy parents are apt to lean on their children and burden them with daily expressions of hostility and pain. It is not unusual for therapists to have patients who felt "devoured" by their parents or who were led to believe that their parents could not survive without them to lean on. These individuals have also learned that their parents needed and depended on each other's hostility. For children raised in such an atmosphere, the normal tasks of separation and individuation become awesome burdens instead of normal growth processes. As one little eight-year-old girl remarked after her parents divorced and her mother moved out: "I like Momma better now than when she was living with us. . . . She's not so mad and angry all the time.[25]

We have described the means by which the mental health establishment and parents themselves have created the issue of the welfare of children as a deterrent to legal divorce. Emotional divorce, the estrangement between marital partners in intact families, cannot be as easily inhibited. Spouses who remain together for the "children's sake" impose severe penalties on their youngsters by inhibiting their chances for development of self-esteem, personal integrity and good judgment. The relationship between emotional divorce in parents and emotional shallowness and pathology in children cannot be overemphasized. Fortunately, evidence is mounting which sheds light on the effect of marital disaffection and alienation on youngsters. Child psychiatrists and family counselors are increasingly convinced that emotional divorce is more devastating to children than legal divorce. )

Parents who prefer married estrangement to legal divorce communicate a number of undesirable lessons to their offspring and to them a great disservice. Perhaps the most serious consequence is that healthy love, as opposed to neurotic attachment, between two adults is not reinforced. By their resignation to unfulfillment, parents lead youngsters to believe that they should not expect better for themselves. Children are thus taught to compromise their desires, to be untrue to themselves and to deny their innermost feelings. They are instructed by living example that it is preferable to abide misery and pretense or persist in a relationship one has outgrown than to divorce and "make a scene." Ultimately, staying married in order to give children maximum time with each parent erroneously teaches them that time spent together is inherently productive and can in itself compensate for other deprivations.

Parents who use their children as a rationale for avoiding separation or divorce burden their children with a terrible responsibility. Most children are well aware of the state of their parents' marriage, and where parents refuse to divorce, the children are laden with feelings of responsibility for their parents' pain. Often children expend (and waste) a great deal of energy attempting either to deny the reality of parental estrangement or to reconcile their parents. They may believe that they are guilty of causing parental fighting and that only they can save mother and father from hurting each other. This fantasy can appropriately be laid to rest by divorce.[26] Children have no stake worth protecting in a bad marriage, writes one perceptive attorney experienced in divorce cases. Those parents who remain together for the sake of the children are either advancing "false reasons" for not divorcing or are "guilty of underestimating the ability of children to judge correctly the atmosphere in which they live." [27]

Children are rarely deceived by superficial signs of affection that mark parental attempts to cover up hostile feelings. Children exposed to such sham become confused for they cannot be certain of the validity of their own perception and experiences; when their feelings are not validated by parental honesty, children lose the ability to associate feelings and behavior appropriately. Invariably, youngsters in such homes are expected to play a role in the intrafamilial battle. Usually they are forced to align themselves (at least overtly) with one of the parents and thus risk rejection by the other. Children in these situations are apt to experience inordinate parental hostility and rejection because they are the constant reminder of the adults' rationale for avoiding or postponing divorce. According to one research team, emotional divorce divides the entire family, "leaving the children torn between conflicting attachments and loyalties." [28]

Children are split asunder as they attempt to cope with the ups and downs of their parents' brittle relationship. When such parental conflicts are only partially exposed, children are often expected not to notice what is happening, and the pathological use of denial becomes reinforced.[29] Children may be unable to plead with their parents to separate and divorce, out of fear, but that does not negate the suffocation they experience in such tense, fragile environments. It is also not unusual for clinicians to hear their adult patients report that they wished their parents had separated or recall how they had even urged their parents to do so.

Staying together for the sake of the children is therefore fraught with difficulties and is rarely the healthy answer where children are concerned. Both adults and children require tension-free environments in order to express their individuality and to gratify their emotional needs. Divorce itself does not devastate children or inhibit their psychic development. Handled maturely by parents, divorce can offer children relief from chronic unhappiness and tension.

By emphasizing that stress is inherently bad for people, clinicians overlook the character-building aspects of living through a difficult experience. By underestimating the resiliency and capacities of children, writers often fail to recognize that divorce can teach many important lessons about marriage and about intimate relationships in general. What youngsters ultimately derive from their experience with divorce will depend largely on how their parents interpret the event.

# 7
# Reinterpreting Divorce
# to Children

Jeffrey, age 7, told his mother he was going to
get married when he was 17. She asked him
why he wanted to get married at 17, and he
replied, "So I can still be very young when I
get divorced."
—A New York family

The negative impact of anti-divorce indoctrination
on families does not diminish even after the decision to divorce has
been made. Parents are constantly misadvised regarding the correct
manner of interpreting divorce to children and the appropriate
form of expressing feelings toward one's spouse. Self-styled divorce
experts openly advise parents to be dishonest in their dealings with
children, the commonly expressed theme is that the parents are
obligated to shield their children from the true nature of the ongoing divorce situation when it is a hostile one, and from the negative feelings that ex-spouses may have toward each other.

With few exceptions, clinicians urge parents to reassure their
children that they "had nothing to do with" the parental decision

to split up. This simplistic advice ignores the complexity and variety of pre- and post-divorce parental relationships. In many unhappy marriages, children *have* been a focal point of parental disagreement; hence, to turn to children and inform them that they were "not involved" in the divorce decision denies the reality of their own memory and experience and merely confuses them. There is no reason why divorced parents shouldn't acknowledge when one major area of disagreement was the question of how the children should be raised. Children simply need to know that such problems were *examples* of why and how the parents were "mismatched."

The most outrageous advice that is offered to parents, however, is that which cautions them to *apologize* to their children for their decision to divorce. An apology implies that somebody has done something wrong, for which he or she should be sorry. Parents who apologize transmit the notion that they are "failures"; they also communicate to their children their own feelings of overwhelming guilt. Parents who apologize for ending their marriages give children ammunition for manipulation and emotional blackmail. Examples of this sort of advice are ample in the literature. Dr. J. Louise Despert, for one, openly advices parents to "admit" that they have erred.[1] Rabbi Earl A. Grollman urges parents to explain that they have blundered in their marriage.[2] Psychologist Bernard Steinzor advises ex-partners to tell their youngsters that their inability to find mutual love signifies a failure for both parents.[3]

Recommendations of this sort reinforce the widespread attitude that divorce signifies *failure* in two people who have *done something wrong*. When parents acquiesce to this conceptual model of divorce, they feel guilty and ashamed for "burdening" their children. We see no reason for parents to apologize to their children for deciding not to be married anymore. *Children would not feel so "wronged" if their parents did not feel so sorry.*

Instead of interpreting divorce as a good decision and a potentially happy, optimistic event in the life of the family, parents and others explain divorce to children as if it were a tragic affair, a destructive rather than a reconstructive process.

Divorce is a relief to many children and parents; but more importantly, it gives *all* family members a chance to achieve greater personal fulfillment. The psychology of apology stresses parental inadequacy. Thus children become hostile to their parents while they are subtly taught that it is wrong for people's needs and desires to change. By apologizing to children, parents exaggerate the role that divorce will play in causing suffering to their children. Self-deprecatory explanations have catastrophic overtones, especially for young children,[4] and may cause undue apprehension about what may be in store in the future.

As one clinician observed, we could condition children to feel that any change in their lives was tragic "providing we gave them the same kind of emotional reinforcement that we do on the matter of divorce."[5] If parents take divorce in their stride, their children, trusting of parental authority, would be reassured that divorce is not an awful crisis. Unfortunately, some parents project their own feelings of catastrophe on to their children, who respond with concern and fear.

Sometimes strong and independent parents are able to avoid projecting pain and tragedy with their divorce explanations and are able to present the divorce in a positive and hopeful manner. One young woman whom we worked with, who viewed her decision to divorce as the first in a series of steps toward greater happiness, offered this explanation to her two children: "Children, I have good news for all of us. There is going to be more happiness in this house from now on. Daddy and I have decided not to live together anymore, and we will all be happier because of this."

There are those parents who are unable to view or to present divorce as anything but disastrous. Victims of their own insecurity or of the pessimistic views propagated by popular media, their attempts at apology, self-flagellation and tragic drama often meet with surprising responses from their children; some youngsters react to divorce news by refusing to share their parents' grief and panic. One woman described to us how she went through weeks of anxious preparation in anticipation of her children's upset upon hearing the divorce tidings. She finally summoned up her courage and called her two daughters (ages nine and eleven) together. "Children, I have some very difficult news to tell you." The girls blanched. "Your father and I haven't been getting along and we've decided to get a divorce. This means that we won't be living together anymore." The nine-year-old heaved a sigh of relief and said, "Whew! I thought you were going to tell us that we had to get rid of the kitty!"

Such a reaction is neither atypical nor unexplainable. Although some clinicians might attribute this response to the girl's emotional denial of a painful reality, we believe that most children are amply prepared for such news by the nature of their prior experience with two tense and most likely angry parents. Judson Landis' important study of children's reactions to divorce revealed that youngsters who claimed ignorance about their parents' difficulties suffered more than those who admitted sensing that separation was on the way.[6] We can hypothesize that these "innocents" reflected the encouragement they had received from their parents to deny what they were actually experiencing prior to separation and divorce.

We recall one little girl who not only was able to tell her mother's social worker of her relief upon hearing that her parents would no longer fight in front of her, but also illustrated her diminished anxiety by coping more effectively at school and with peers. No longer forced to expend her energy blocking out or adjusting to parental tension, this child could now turn her attention to tasks far more appropriate to her age and begin to obtain much needed gratification.

Thus children are too often guided through divorce by parents who are misled and encouraged to be dishonest and self-effacing. In an often well-intentioned attempt to shield "innocent" children from the "harsh" realities of divorce, parents unfortunately yield to the temptation to fabricate. According to Jules Henry, it is a tradition in our culture to hide the "ugly" realities of life from children; while we expect children to tell adults the truth, "we take it for granted that adults will lie to children." [7]

Dishonesty with youngsters sometimes begins when the marriage ends. After parents have struggled to explain divorce, they struggle to maintain a "proper" and "benign" image of their ex-spouses, at least in front of the children. All hell may break loose when the little ones are presumably out of earshot, but post-divorce feelings between ex-partners, unless they are positive, are supposed to be hidden from children. Professionals often advise parents to emphasize some positive qualities in the ex-spouse, regardless of whether the parent wants to or even sees them there in the first place. Mrs. Jones, who would rather strangle her ex-husband than say a good word about him, tells Junior that his father is a good man and a loving daddy. Junior is understandably confused. If his mother is sincere, why did she leave his father? And what was all that fighting about before Daddy finally left the house? She didn't think he was so good before the divorce. She always used to accuse Daddy of hating her and him.

The following example of "benign" behavior comes from an expert who regularly writes for *Redbook*: "A twenty-nine-year-old divorced woman was crushed to learn of her husband's infidelities prior to her divorce. But she carefully and painfully conceals her true feelings from her children and tells them to 'Bless Daddy' in their prayers." [8] This is how divorced parents are typically urged to handle divorce with children on a day-to-day basis. The assumption that underlies such peculiar advice is that unless each parent presents a positive image of the other, children may become convinced that their own characters are impaired, since they are the biological and psychological offspring of both parents.[9] While we do not categorically dismiss this point of view, our own clinical experience has taught us that a neutral, more honest portrayal of one spouse's feelings about the other is not the same as a negative and angry portrait. We do not advocate that parents burden their youngsters with the complaints they have regarding their ex-spouses; but rather than compromise their own true feelings and be deceitful to their children, they can try to remain detached and neutral. In the case of divorce, there is considerable wisdom in the old adage that if you can't say something good about someone, don't say anything. In the long run, children are not so easily deceived that they blindly accept "image building" as a substitute for reality.

A truthful and accurate perception of parents, whether they are good, bad, or indifferent, is of overriding significance for a child's emotional growth; ". . . an honest negative image is superior to a false positive one." [10] When parents attempt deception, the consequences in emotional terms can be dear.

Mrs. W. tried to protect her eight-year-old son from the knowledge that his father had a violent and uncontrollable temper. Mrs. W. divorced her husband when Steven was an infant and the boy's visits with his father were infrequent and short enough so as not to tax this man's lack of control. Though this sensitive young boy had some suspicions about his father, Mrs. W. would quickly dismiss his questions with denials. One evening, Steven awoke to screams emanating from the living room. He ran into the room just in time to witness his father hitting his mother's boy friend over the head with a heavy object. Mr. W. had come to his ex-wife's apartment to demand that she return some child support money, and when the other man sought to intervene in the ensuing argument, Mr. W. lost control and became physically assaultive. After this incident, Steven was quiet, withdrawn and uncommunicative to his mother. In Steven's treatment it emerged that he was upset less by the incident itself than by deception that he felt he had experienced at the hands of his mother. Mrs. W. had demonstrated to Steven that he could no longer depend on her for the truth in important matters. Mrs. W., no doubt well intentioned, had sought to shield her son from the "ugly" facts about his father. Had she been more honest about her ex-spouse's frailty, Steven might have been spared a severe shock and would have had one less problem in his relationship with his divorced parents.

The incident described above may appear more extreme than most, since divorced parents are usually not as physically impulsive and angry as Mr. W. seemed to be. But the same processes of denial and dishonesty are rampant in even "average" families, whether they are divorced or intact. Parents take what they think is the easy way out—they either rant and rave about how beastly the other parent is or they "cover up" damaging evidence to "protect" the children. In neither approach is the child being treated with appropriate respect for his (or her) capacity to cope with honesty and reality, even if this is the way only one parent defines that reality. A sham atmosphere is created when parents concoct an artificial formula for handling divorce; on one level, the youngster is aware of the parents' real feelings about each other and of their individual strengths and weaknesses. By the age of three, most children know their parents' Achilles' heel. But when children are told what to feel, or when they feel different from the way one of their parents feels, they tend to conceal their real emotions. Though each secretly knows the truth, both parent and child act out the fraud. Therapists are confronted all the time with this "collusive" aspect of family pathology.

The "united front" tradition in the American family means that regardless of what disagreements exist between parents, they are bound to agree in front of the children. As the pretense of togetherness becomes more complicated and the web of deception grows, so does the gap in the trust between parent and child. Even when parents genuinely try to shield children from discord, the children often feel manipulated and deceived.

Divorced parents, as well as married ones, should enable children to form their own views of each parent, unobstructed by the other's smoke screen. It is difficult but crucial to choose between requiring one's children to see the world by one's own standards and allowing children to come to their own decisions by personal experience. When little eight-year-old Judy B. asked her mother whether she thought Daddy was the best man in the world, Mrs. B. bit her lip and answered: "Yes, Judy, Daddy is the best man in the whole world." This mother might have chosen honesty and neutrality, and thus handled the situation differently. Mrs. B. might have answered instead: "If you think Daddy is wonderful and he makes you so happy, that is fine." If Judy questioned her mother's lack of enthusiasm, Mrs. B. might have explained further: "Daddy and I do not agree on many things, and while I don't necessarily think

Daddy is wonderful, you may love him and have your own feelings toward him." In this way, Judy's mother, while not belittling her ex-spouse, has honestly offered an expression of her feelings that will allow her child to decide for herself what she thinks and feels about her father.

Sometimes a parent finds it necessary to tell a child that the other parent is not capable of showing love and concern for him. This usually occurs because the youngster is continually disappointed and rejected, or even abandoned, by one parent and needs some aid in dealing with this hurt. Dr. Richard Gardner, a child psychiatrist, stresses this point in his book *The Boys and Girls Book About Divorce*. He emphasizes that children should not be encouraged to seek love from those who cannot give it. If a parent tries to convince the child that the unloving parent is what the child knows he (or she) isn't, the youngster loses faith in the remaining adult.[11] Unfortunately, this advice can be sorely abused and misused by a bitter or neurotic parent who tries to *convince* a child that the other parent is unloving.

We are not suggesting that ex-spouses cannot maintain an amiable relationship. If they can, all the better, for both children and adults fare well under such circumstances. Unfortunately, this sort of post-divorce association is relatively rare in this society.

Regardless of the quality of post-divorce feelings, no emotionally stable parent would either ask or expect a child to renounce love for the other parent unless there were some drastically good reason to do so. Parents in divorce must make it amply clear to their children that they are in no way obligated to love or hate the people their parents love or hate.

That there are many troubled, angry, vengeful divorced parents who would like their children to renounce the "other parent" is not a problem that can be legislated away by telling parents what to say and feel or how to live. What we are discussing here is the question of what kind of advice is available and what healthy options exist for parents who are emotionally stable and have the best interests of their children at heart. The existence of "neurotic" patterns is a subject for study in abnormal psychology. While nonconstructive belittling is often characteristic of angry and/or disturbed partners, we are trying here to emphasize what we perceive as the healthy choices available to adults with normal self-control.

Of course, it is most desirable for youngsters to like their parents, custodial and noncustodial, but children must be given the freedom to love and to hate independently and without guilt. Whether the event is divorce, remarriage, or stepfamilyhood, children must be taught that they may love many people; such a lesson can best be transmitted by secure parents who are not overly possessive and who do not feel their own authority threatened by their children's ability to extend their affectional ties.

Our critique of contemporary anti-divorce indoctrination with respect to children brings us now to the broad question of what ingredients inherent in the divorce situation, if any, do tend to traumatize children. Having questioned many of the stereotyped associations between divorce and the well-being of youngsters, we have found that the manner in which divorce is interpreted to children helps perpetuate and reinforce their common negative misconceptions about it. They are encouraged to feel pity for themselves and contempt for their parents.

We have considered and subsequently rejected general attitudes and opinions about the inherent dangers in divorce and have substituted our thesis that divorce is in itself a "neutral" experience for children, which can be made into a "good" experience or a "bad" experience. As long as the larger society has a vested interest in preventing divorce, then those professionals who serve society will unconsciously work to preserve the harmful and traumatic aura that surrounds it.

It is clear that there is a destructive relationship between contemporary parental indoctrination on divorce and the handling of children in divorce. Most of the advice given to parents implies that divorce is not an honorable state, and parents in turn become the major determinants of their childrens' acceptance of it. Such contagion effects between parent and child have been noted in the literature on children's reactions to environmental disasters. A case in point is the London blitz, during World War II.[12] According to psychiatrists Margaret Mahler and Ruth Rabinovitch, tense mothers communicated their anxiety to their children in such a way as to create an actual neurosis in them, whereas relaxed mothers responded to the bombings in such a way as to reduce the potentially disturbing effects on their children.[13]

We can relate such information to divorce by inferring that when a youngster shows signs of not accepting parental divorce, it is highly probable that one or both of the child's parents is communicating the uncertainty and ambivalence in his (or her) own mind about the decision. A child's adjustment is heavily dependent on how the divorce "is lived."

In the end, observations by youngsters of the beneficial effects of divorce on their parents will enable them to conclude that for themselves divorce was a blessing, even if at first it was a blessing in disguise. A child cannot cope successfully with divorce, though, when a parent feels that something catastrophic has happened.[14] We are keenly aware that parents in contemporary society have a difficult time living a sane, happy divorce and cannot easily project images and hopes of unspoiled happiness on to their children. Adults still decide rather reluctantly to divorce when children are involved.[15]

While anti-divorce propaganda relentlessly badgers parents into feeling guilty and remorseful, the legal apparatus encourages post-divorce animosity by pitting men against women in custody, alimony and child-support struggles. Divorced spouses are often coerced into hostile interactions by mercenary lawyers. Inflexible legal precedents, set forth and adhered to by legislatures and courts alike, compound the misery.

Most divorced parents eventually decide to remarry. While this resolution ultimately may be welcomed by all family members, it means facing the challenge of incorporating the love of other adults into what was a closed system. Children of the isolated nuclear family, who prior to divorce have related intimately with only two adults, have an understandably difficult time of it until they can see for themselves that stepfamilies can be fun.

Trauma for divorced families, therefore, is not inherent in the process itself, but instead lies in the fact that our society scorns all alternatives to the conjugal nuclear unit and fails to sanction and encourage either divorce or family regroupings. The feelings of anxiety, depression and loneliness that divorced parents are conditioned to experience are directly transmitted to children, and thus the trauma of divorce is perpetuated from one generation to another. When divorced parents are particularly strong and independent, they are less likely to invite "pathological reactions" in their children.

For those families in which divorce is experienced as an opportunity for growth and greater happiness, major life patterns and parental role behavior remain essentially undisturbed. For example, women who have normally shared the role of breadwinner with their spouses can continue to work after divorce, and often welcome the chance to do so. Children who have lived with working mothers are not forced to cope with abrupt changes in their routine. Divorce will not be a disaster for those fathers who took a positive and active role in the care of their children prior to divorce. They will have an easier time maintaining close relationships with their children. If sexual roles in these primary areas were reorganized and equalized, parents could perceive in divorce a happier and plausible alternative to conjugal misery. Children, less awed by the changes that divorce brings, could retain the love of both parents and live with equal happiness in the "custody" of either parent.

We are sympathetic with mothers who would prefer to give up custody of their children but because of clinical and popular attitudes are unable to do so. We are sympathetic with fathers who are desirous of obtaining custody of their children but have little opportunity to do so. The myth of the mother as primary nurturer has been attacked by numerous women's liberation writers and progressive clinicians. We hope that ultimately "mothering" will lose its sexist connotations. When children are no longer pawns in custody battles and when mothers, in addition to fathers, can voluntarily relinquish custody to the other parent, children will be reassured that the custody decision was based on the needs of *all* family members. However, such a possibility depends almost entirely on societal sanctions and supports for women who will be self-respecting and courageous enough to be honest about their own feelings.

Children need to be prepared for the possibility of physical parental separation and divorce. Since the small size of the isolated traditional family reduces the number of people to whom a child can turn for love and security, youngsters should at least be exposed to a variety of outside relationships and become accustomed to being cared for by different people. Adults, apart from the child's own parents, should be welcomed as additional, meaningful people, because in the small family the roots of a child's emotional life are too dependent on and intermingled with those of the two parents.[16]

American society, rather than institutionalizing the restructured relationships that divorce brings to a family, fosters the disruption of pre-existing ties. For example, children residing with their mother, following divorce, are often deprived of prior relationships with paternal grandparents, aunts, uncles and cousins; this often results from the paucity of time legally allotted for visitation with the noncustodial parent. It is also not uncommon for divorced families to experience the withdrawal of companionship of friends and neighbors who look upon divorce with dismay or suspicion. Children are often left confused and upset by sudden reverses in prior friendships.

Until the nuclear family becomes just one of many alternative life-styles available to adults and children in this society, divorced adults will continue to live outside the accepted norm of family life. Until our familial relations and cultural norms are exposed and critically evaluated, by clinicians and the public alike, divorce will bring unnecessary guilt and despair to adults and confusion to children.

The mental health professions, which up to the present time have been guilty of bias and complacency where divorced families are concerned, have a unique opportunity and a major responsibility to legitimize divorce, whether or not children are involved. A particularly blatant example from the literature describes the all-too-typical professional intervention:

> A six-year-old girl had witnessed violent scenes between her quarreling parents. She had witnessed her mother suffer a fractured jaw at the hands of her intoxicated father. She had witnessed her mother waving a baseball bat, while threatening to "beat her father's brains in." And she had seen the police attempt to silence her parents after neighbors complained. When the family was evaluated at a social agency, the social worker cautioned both parents that a divorce should be avoided, as it was better for a child to have two parents rather than one.[17]

*Clinicians commonly view children as too fragile to cope with divorce, yet not too fragile to survive the effects of a violent environment.* Such skewed perceptions must be totally re-evaluated and eliminated as fast as possible. Professionals who recognize the ways in which the nuclear family limits and cripples the ability of children to relate to others outside their home should sanction alternate family styles that will pave the way for healthier and broader social development, regardless of whether divorce is involved. The mental health professional can at least attempt to clarify, once and for all, the fact that divorce in itself is neither good nor bad for children and that where the well-being of children is concerned, divorced parents as a group are no more destructive or hostile than nondivorced parents.

The role of the clinician is, in our opinion, as much a political and social one as a psychological one. Rather than merely exercising the narrow prerogative of helping a handful of families, professionals can establish guidelines to minimize the potential conflicts for families of divorce.

# part three

# 8
# High Jumping the Hurdles of Post-Divorce Life

> Many superficially intact homes may have an unhealthy impact on the children; . . . many homes with only one parent may be . . . successful in producing healthy and happy children.
>
> —William Goode

Like every life-style, divorce brings its own particular difficulties to families. The common aftermaths of divorce are essentially nontraumatic, though they may necessitate considerable adjustment by family members. Like the truck driver's family that must accommodate to the fact that the husband-father is away two weeks out of four, so the adults and children of divorce must jump the hurdles that emerge between ex-spouses and between parents and children. Whether divorced parents remain single, live in communes with friends and lovers, or remarry and form stepfamilies, certain typical problems may emerge which obstruct their attempts to lead gratifying post-divorce lives with their children.

Post-divorce problems usually arise out of the unresolved hostility between ex-spouses and usually involve the children, who are hauled into the battle arena whether they like it or not. While nobody *intentionally* hurts children in this way, the fact that many children are emotionally roughed up by their divorced parents is usually due to two factors. First of all, many aspects of American divorce encourage the continued animosity between ex-spouses. Second, many parents consider their children a measure of their success or failure and therefore value them as important pieces of property. For this reason, children become the pawns in their parents' competitive struggles.

When Michael and Ann divorced five years ago they did so in a storm of anger and mutual accusation. The post-divorce life for this family was initially colored by parental attempts to vie for the children's loyalty. When the younger child began to have school problems, his guidance counselor recommended family counseling. In an effort to find satisfactory solutions to difficulties, many adults like Michael and Ann seek counseling from mental health professionals. They do so not simply because they and their youngsters are neurotic, but because they find themselves facing many new and difficult real-life situations. It is important to make a distinction between severely disturbed families that need long-term psychological intervention and those that in the beginning need some advice and guidance in helping themselves and their children deal with divorce more effectively. In other words, the divorced family that seeks psychological aid is not necessarily a sick family; parents are often merely confused and uncertain about how to guide their children and how to conduct themselves in the new situations that occur.

Because of the frequency with which divorced parents and children express their concern over particular issues, it might be helpful to discuss some of these issues in detail. Divorced parents often report to their therapists that they feel they must somehow "make up" to their children for the divorce. Filled with guilt and worried about the effect of divorce on their youngsters, adults often bribe their children with toys and clothes or spoil them in other ways. In fact, as much as the realities of divorce create a greater need for all family members to pitch in with household tasks, some custodial parents shrink from imposing these on their children. Emily, aged twelve, faced a situation common to many children of divorce. After her parents announced their intention to divorce, her mother immediately took over Emily's chores, which at the time included making her own bed and helping with the supper dishes. When Emily's mother went back to work she found herself resenting her daughter, who by this time did not participate in any household chores. Once the mother recognized her own anxiety over Emily's reaction to divorce, she was able to re-establish her prior expectations for Emily.

Children usually welcome the opportunity to partake in household tasks because they want to feel valuable to the family. In fact, divorce offers parents and children the chance to tap hidden areas of competence. Children who before separation and divorce were pampered by their parents may need extra time to assume new responsibilities. Children who spend time visiting the homes of their noncustodial parents should also be required to share some household tasks. To avoid chores, children may resort to the "I'm a poor unfortunate child of divorce" routine, which plays on parental guilt. This ruse should not be indulged.

Most noncustodial parents (who usually happen to be fathers) find that in their early visits with the children, following divorce, they treat their children as if they were special guests. Joe, one divorced father, described his initial visits with the children as a series of outings—to movies, puppet shows and ball games. He found that at the end of each visiting day he barely had an opportunity to sit and talk with his youngsters. After a few months, visits settled down and Joe and his children began spending more time at his apartment, talking, playing games and listening to music. The children were especially fond of participating in the preparation of meals. What was initially an awkward and artificial situation between Joe and his children eventually became a natural and relaxed one.

Children visiting their noncustodial parents for longer periods of time may have a difficult time meeting other children their age. Because fathers usually work during the day, their contacts with other families are often not very extensive. In this situation, other complications emerge. Eddie, a divorced suburban father, whose young son, David, was visiting him for a month, noticed that his neighbors were uncomfortable around him. The neighborhood mothers eagerly offered to have David play with their children, in their homes, but turned down Eddie's reciprocal offers. They generally felt that caring for a child was not a man's role and they did not want to "burden" Eddie with their children. Moreover, when they invited David to come to play with their children, they openly tried to discourage Eddie from coming along. These mothers were reluctant to participate in a relationship that had "sexual overtones," despite the fact that Eddie's behavior and manner did not indicate any desire for involvement with these women on a sexual level. The illegitimacy of friendships between married women and divorced men (and vice versa) affected Eddie and David by isolating them from meaningful relationships in the community.

Noncustodial parents who desire to maintain a full relationship with their children must possess wisdom and forbearance. If they are lucky enough to have ex-partners who recognize the importance of such relationships and refrain from sabotage, certain problems may not arise. On the other hand, there are many ways in which post-divorce bitterness between ex-spouses may interfere with happy and healthy post-divorce relationships.

Perhaps one of the most common situations that parents worry about is the effect their face-to-face arguments will have on their children. While many people expect that children will have heard the last of their parents' fights by the time separation takes place, this is not always the case and parental friction is often revived in front of the children. Many youngsters are quite resilient and able to tolerate such scenes without ill effects. One eight-year-old child interrupted a loud disagreement between his divorced parents and said, "Aren't you two tired of arguing? You're acting like two babies." Understandably, both parents were stunned and not a little embarrassed. Other children take parental fights harder and parents of course should try to control themselves in front of their children. There are always opportunities to discuss problems privately without involving the youngsters. If face-to-face battles take place when the children are present, parents should at least reassure the youngsters that they cannot be involved in their settlement. This may dispel children's fantasies that it is their responsibility to rectify the situation between their parents.

Post-divorce parental bitterness also takes on a variety of less direct forms. In some divorced families, one parent persists in telling the children nasty things about the other. Ellen reports to her mother that her dad called her mother immature and irresponsible. Madeline's mother responds to her daughter's request for a new dress with the disparaging remark, "Your stingy father doesn't give me enough money to buy you the things you need." Grapevines and children being what they are, father soon learns what mother said. Ellen's mother and Madeline's father, as the maligned parents, may understandably be outraged and be tempted to defend themselves and lash back at their ex-spouses with equal vigor and with whatever ammunition is available. Madeline's father may decide to respond by showing his daughter his budget, his bills and his canceled checks. However, the best defense in these unhappy situations is *no defense*.

Recrimination and mutual accusation are costly games. "Accused" parents who *can* control their anger communicate to their children that they are not interested in what their ex-spouses say because they are no longer dependent on them as sources of love and self-esteem. Granted, the technique of passive resistance to a barrage of criticism may chronically place one parent in the role of "bad guy." But children will ultimately judge their parents *not so much by what they say as by what they do and how they live*. In treating the children of divorce, we have repeatedly seen the tactics of overt accusation backfire against the parents who tried to "win" the children.

While mother's or father's image might have to suffer a bit in the short run, to follow one's impulse and react with anger merely forces children to take sides with one parent against the other.

Parents tempted to take revenge would do well to consider what it feels like to be in the middle of two angry parents. Ultimately, denigration of one parent by another undermines a child's self-esteem. Even if a parent and child team up against the other parent, the child will feel ambivalent and guilty. When one parent confides to his child about problems with the other parent, he or she burdens the child, who must then be careful not to betray the maligned parent. In effect, this cripples the child's capacity to relate and to love.[1]

This does not mean that parents must turn the other cheek in the face of provocation, but they should confine their anger and outrage to an appropriate time and place. In general, it is wise to discourage children from carrying tales from one house to the other. It is only human for parents to be jolted and peeved at the nasty things other people say about them, but the unpleasant aftermath creates an unhappy tension in each home. Moreover, parents feel impotent in their inability to control the behavior of their ex-spouses. Parents must eventually come to terms with the fact that they cannot control what others say to their children.

At least one of the motives for actively denigrating the other parent is to derive pleasure from the power to be able to provoke him or her. When parents refuse to listen to tales and insist that their children keep such stories and remarks to themselves, the pleasure the other parent derives from being hostile is considerably negated. Either the stories that children bring home should be ignored or parents should try to communicate decently to clarify distortions. If one parent deliberately and consistently provokes the children to defy the other parent, the latter can petition the court to either alter visiting arrangements or custody. Finally, before seeking to avenge difficult and provocative ex-partners, it might be helpful for parents to remember the reason they chose to divorce in the first place. They probably wanted in part to spare their children painful involvement in the home-front battles and hostilities.

Often children attempt to use their awareness of parental competition to gain sympathy and favors. By repeating that "Mommy doesn't make me eat vegetables" or "Daddy always lets me stay up to watch *The Brady Bunch* on television," the child hopes to maneuver the other parent into granting a variety of privileges. Parents who compete for their children's love and loyalty by playing this game are being led on a merry chase by clever youngsters who will escalate their demands as they see fit. The wise parent may have to state firmly a number of times: "In this house, you will follow my rules, and in your father's [mother's] house, you will follow his [her] rules." Chances are that children exaggerate their other parent's cruelty and permissiveness as it suits their momentary aims. They, like all other children, need to be taught that emotional coercion and blackmail are not healthy ways of getting their needs met.

When children bring dreadful horror stories to one parent about ill treatment by the other, some investigation should be initiated, but minor complaints surrounding food habits, bedtime, baths, etc., are not the same as child abuse. As much as parents may welcome this opportunity to intervene on the child's behalf and be the "good guy" to the rescue, they are better off controlling the temptation and letting their children work out minor problems with the other parent on their own, even encouraging them to do so. The proverbial apron strings are hard to untie, whether or not divorce is the excuse for overprotection. Since the mother is usually the custodial parent, she is more inclined to interfere with the child's small, daily struggles. We have had years of contact with one divorced mother who persistently acts as her child's savior and spokesman through phone calls to her ex-husband. "Stuart is afraid to tell you but he doesn't like to go to the zoo." "Stuart didn't want to mention it but he would rather you not come every week." This mother emasculates her son by talking for him and reinforces whatever belief the child has that he is incapable of working things out alone with his father.

There are those divorced parents who, in spite of hostile feelings for each other, maintain "friendly" relations for the sake of the children. Parents who feel pressured to be overtly friendly to ex-spouses minimize their own chances for emotional emancipation and feed their children's fantasies of reuniting the parents.[2] Parental separateness may in the long run increase the child's capacity to love. This same principle operates on special occasions, when parents often partake in artificial reunions. On children's birthdays and at Christmas, parents often get together and act as if the intact nuclear family existed for a day. In general this practice simply makes it harder for children to understand that they must build separate lives with each parent. Ultimately the divorced parents' aim should not be to achieve agreement or disagreement with the former spouse, but instead to support the child's painful steps in learning how to reconcile differences among people.[3]

Sometimes one parent finds himself (or herself) in the position of protecting the children from the other parent. In one case, Steven, a seven-year-old boy, constantly accused his mother of stopping him from seeing his father. In reality, the father was a heroin addict so self-absorbed that he was unable to understand his son's needs or to keep grandiose promises he perpetually made to the boy. The mother, who felt that she was doing the best she could, was hurt by her son's false accusations and angry at her ex-spouse for disappointing the child. At the same time, this mother was well aware that her son could not understand the reasons for his father's unpredictable behavior. By seeking counseling for herself, she found an empathic therapist who could recognize her rage and frustration and could help her to look for positive and aggressive means to relieve her anguish and Steven's confusion. She learned that she could help her ex-spouse recognize their son's hurt. She began to offer Steven more opportunity to contact his father by phone and gradually relinquished her urge to protect him from the inevitable disappointment he would suffer. This mother learned how to take a more active role as a "buffer" against Steven's pain by acknowledging and talking to him about his sadness. Most important, she learned to accept the fact that she might have to be the "bad guy" in her son's eyes, at least for the time being. Too young to understand his mother's refusal to let him live with his father or to analyze his father's strange behavior, Steven needed a mother who could absorb his anger without seeking revenge or threatening to abandon him.

The common situation where one parent reluctantly assumes the role of "bad guy" becomes more palatable when the parent realizes that eventually most children gain considerable insight into the realities of their situation. If children are given enough opportunity to act like children, rather than being forced to reason like adults, they will know in the long run who has really acted in their behalf. In Steven's situation, there were clear reasons why he was unable to live with his father, but there are other circumstances in which children express a desire to live with the other parent who is *not* troubled or withdrawn. Sometimes these requests arise after fights between the custodial parent and the child. In one divorced home, Jimmy announces after a heated argument with his mother, "I want to live with Daddy. I like him better than you." It would be most unwise for Jimmy's mother to allow him to resolve his conflict by running from it or to permit him to use his father as a means of avoiding confrontation with his mother.

On the other hand, when a child consistently demonstrates a desire and need to live with the other loving and available parent, such a request should be taken seriously. Most custodial parents are emotionally threatened by the question of custody transfers because they tend to believe that such a request is a symptom of their failure as a parent. Moreover, negative feelings toward the other parent often deter the custodial parent from agreeing to what might be a healthy change for the child. Parents who cannot let go of their youngsters communicate that they are frightened of losing their children's love, and the youngsters, in turn, may feel burdened and exploited.

One of the advantages of divorce for many children is that it opens up the possibility of having two homes in which they are loved and wanted. When difficulty arises between the child and one parent, an option exists within the family to make a change. In intact families, when children and parents feel that they cannot live together, they must solve their dilemma by a variety of less satisfactory means. The child may run away or may have to be placed in a special school. The parents and children of divorce have a real choice when both parents are amenable.

Parents would probably be wise to seek therapeutic advice in resolving custody transfers, especially if they are uncertain about its benefits or have extremely ambivalent feelings about their ex-spouses. It is most beneficial that such changes, temporary or permanent, be effected with the good will of both parties.

Post-divorce problems are often exacerbated by the legal and economic realities of American divorce. Often the antagonism between ex-spouses is perpetuated by how divorce must be lived. For many people, divorce is a long-drawn-out experience having repercussions for the participants and their children. In the aftermath of divorce, custody, visitation and financial arrangements are constantly tested and adjusted. Were custody and financial arrangements worked out in a humane way, not based on guilt or innocence, but on the welfare of all family members, angry feelings between ex-marital partners might be diminished. There are as many variations in post-divorce life as there are sets of parents and children. But it has been our experience that most of the problems are in some way variations of the broad themes we have described.

Divorced families must be receptive and open to both the joyful and the difficult experiences that lie before them. In spite of the number of problems that they will face, for those willing to participate, exciting family adventure awaits them, in stepfamilyhood, communal living arrangements, single parenthood or nonlegalized "marriage."

# 9
# Stepfamilies: Extending Trust and Love

Second marriage is the victory of hope over experience.

—Oscar Wilde

Remarriage and stepfamilyhood have become part of the fabric of American life. As of a few years ago, one American child in nine had a stepparent.[1] This figure has increased along with the rising divorce rate. The remarriage of one or both ex-spouses means that a host of new relationships has to be created, while old ones are juggled.

There is intense psychological pressure on divorced people to remarry. The likelihood of remarriage is increased by the fact that it is still easier in America, economically and socially, to live in marriage than in any other arrangement. One of the few positive aspects of divorce, according to many writers, is that it paves the way for a "good remarriage." That seems to be the major redeeming virtue of an otherwise scorned institution.

As stepfamilyhood becomes more common, the ambivalent and contradictory attitudes of professionals become increasingly apparent. On one hand, they have encouraged remarriage on the ground that single parenthood is psychologically destructive, culturally unacceptable, temporary and an inherently unstable way of life.[2] The mental health profession has helped to convince parents that remarriage will give their children a "reconstituted family," also known as a "normal home life." The position of children, explains one famous sociologist, is "regularized" by remarriage because the structure of the family approaches the norm of the nondivorced family.[3] Parents are, by and large, convinced that they need partners and that their children need two parents in the home. A custodial parent who does not remarry may be accused of being insensitive to the children, of being unable to become intimate, or of going through a phase of cynicism and adolescent rebellion. On the other hand, the divorced parent who marries too quickly may be suspected of re-enacting an earlier, neurotic relationship or of rushing headlong into remarriage out of deep-seated fears and insecurities. It is hard to escape guilt in this game of psychological one-upmanship.

As if to confuse the issue even more, some professionals are as pessimistic about the effects of remarriage as others are optimistic. Psychological articles often imply that children pay a dear price for parental remarriage; writers persistently warn parents against abruptly or selfishly altering their children's familiar patterns of family relations. When it comes to the question of remarriage, many divorced parents feel guilty if they do and guilty if they do not.

Professionals are most apt to describe stepfamily problems in terms of children and adults resenting one another, or of children feeling abandoned by their natural parents. Writers do not usually focus on the creation of new and potentially meaningful relationships. In a society where children are often viewed as possessions, or as symbols of fecundity and virility, neither clinicians nor laymen recognize the possibility that biological parents and step-parents can comfortably and equally share the experience of raising children.

Professional and popular writers have described the stepchild as helpless, "desolate and hopeless." [4] Some writers even claim that stepchildren are never happy,[5] while others predict the inevitable trauma that awaits these youngsters.[6] The lay public has been taught to be wary of remarriage; it comes as no surprise, therefore, that stepfamilies are often regarded with suspicion and disapproval.

Actual proof that the remarriage of one or both parents is traumatic for children is as negligible or nonexistent as data substantiating notions about all the other negative effects of divorce. In fact, one authority on remarriage, psychologist Jessie Bernard, has suggested three reasons why remarriage is not inherently injurious to youngsters. First, youngsters generally look favorably upon the remarriage of parents; second, the new parent may be a positive force in the child's life; and third, there is a "reservoir of resiliency" in children that positively affects their adjustment to such changes in their life.[7] Dr. Bernard's positive statement on remarriage may appear to be a bit defensive and apologetic; perhaps the cautious reserve of most other clinicians has affected her presentation. One such researcher who studied divorced and nondivorced homes found that a child's self-esteem is lowered by remarriage.[8] He explained this conclusion by speculating that divorce encourages mothers and children to become very dependent on each other, out of their "common plight." [9] When the mother remarries, her interests are refocused, her attention must be shared and she becomes less dependent on her child, who then feels less significant.[10] This researcher fails to recognize that what he has labeled as self-esteem is really the child's narcissism and his or her inability to individuate from the mother. Remarriages, in fact, often bring to an end the unhealthy closeness that sometimes develops between children and their custodial parents and therefore becomes a positive aid to a youngster's future development.

Our own clinical experience has furnished us with a positive view of remarriage, and also of family life in which one parent continues to live alone with a child or chooses instead to have a lover living in the home, without remarriage. Rather than causing trauma or doing violence to children, abiding relationships with new adults frequently offer them an opportunity to extend their trust and affection, to develop a broader, more humanistic concept of "family," and to enrich their own lives by exposure to new habits, tastes and life-styles. The ties that cement members of a family, after all, are not always the result of blood relations, but are also formed by intimate sharing. The more troubled the relationship between child and biological parent, the greater the need for new satisfying bonds and the greater the rewards for an empathic stepparent.[11]

In our work, we have known children who have escaped severe pathology because of the positive and strong ties they formed with their stepparents. Johnny, an eleven-year-old boy, was brought in for treatment by his father, who had been divorced from the boy's mother for a year. He feared that Johnny's relationship with his mother was inappropriate and detrimental to the child's emotional growth. The boy's mother, a weak, helpless and ever-complaining woman, constantly seduced her son into spending his time with her by flattering and cajoling him. The boy really believed that she couldn't get through a whole day without his assistance, and that he was responsible for taking care of her. The mother, unwilling (and psychologically unable at the time) to see how destructively she was coping with her loneliness and dependency, could not be drawn into the boy's therapy. Because this youngster was devoted to his mother, and did not want to hurt her, or deprive himself of her attentiveness, it was difficult to help him initiate a more suitable relationship. Therapy progressed very slowly until the father began living with a woman who had a teen-age son by a previous marriage of her own. Although Johnny visited his father's home only once a week, he could not help but notice how this other woman "never seemed to need her son for anything." Her demands on Johnny were likewise very minimal, compared with what he was used to. Although it took many, many months for Johnny to recognize that his mother was hurting him, even though she loved him, he gradually began to use his new relationship with his healthy and independent stepmother as a guidepost for growing up.

Contrary to popular folklore, we have found in our experience with divorced and reorganized families that the strongest impulse of stepparents and children is to have warm feelings for each other and to find areas of mutual interest. When this opportunity remains unrealized, most likely the natural parent's own ambivalent reactions to the remarriage have been transmitted to the child and to the new stepparent, restraining both of them. Youngsters require the remarrying parent's affirmation that remarriage does not imply any severing of ties with either biological parent; this reassurance is easily given by parents who believe that divorce does not mean the loss of a parent. Successful remarriage may, in fact, help a youngster relinquish the fantasy of reuniting his biological parents.

Sometimes children persist in rejecting their parent's new spouse, regardless of attempts to ease the adults and the children into their new relationships. This may be understood as the child's way of expressing anger and upset over the inability to control the parent's life. The parental decision to divorce and the subsequent decision to remarry, when they are made without the child's approval or permission, can create a feeling of "impotent rage" in the child. This is understandable since, in many contemporary American middle-class homes, youngsters are granted too much pseudo-decision-making authority. This teases them into assuming that all family resolutions of importance will be arrived at via some "democratic" process. Subsequently, when children balk at not having their opinions polled on the subjects of divorce and remarriage, they are reacting with understandable confusion to their parents' lack of consistency.

On the deepest level, children welcome the opportunity to be treated as children, especially in those areas where it is inappropriate, because of inexperience and immaturity, that they play a role in the decision-making process. As much as children may complain, their sense of security depends in part on their parent's strength in the face of protestations about an impending or already consummated remarriage.

In other situations, children sense the disapproval and doubt that others feel toward their parent's remarriage. They may be afraid to commit themselves enthusiastically to something that feels so flimsy.[12] One nine-year-old boy in treatment spoke of his doubts about the wisdom of his father's forthcoming remarriage. His grandmother's negative attitude toward the remarriage frightened this youngster and compelled him to avoid and mistrust his father's fiancée. Before he ever had a chance to form an independent opinion, his grandmother had already let him know that his new stepmother was "no good."

We have seen some youngsters readily support their parent's remarriage, as a means of re-establishing the familiar two-parent family. Because of their past experiences and their exposure to the notion that only two-parent families are "normal" families, children often promote the remarriage of their own parents or the remarriage of their parents to others. Adolescents, who are particularly vulnerable to societal pressures to conform, may feel that the parent who fails to remarry is the one who was negatively responsible for the demise of the prior marriage.

Professionals reinforce such narrow attitudes when they encourage parents to remarry for their children's sake. One psychologist actively promotes remarriage as the best means of countering the "pessimism" children may have developed about the possibility of good relations between adults.[13] Pressure to remarry quickly, based on the assumption that children will otherwise become wary of intimacy and wedlock, furthers the myth that *only* in marriage can adults have loving relationships. This particular psychologist also assumes that divorced parents are not perceived by their children as healthy and mature people. The persistent emphasis on remarriage in the literature of divorce illustrates the extent to which both professionals and laymen have succumbed to cultural indoctrination on the subject.

Cultural conditioning on the virtues and vices of stepparents has been less complicated and ambivalent than indoctrination for remarriage. Basically, stepparents are considered uptight outsiders who will resent the children they "inherit," while stepchildren are viewed as the victims of unfeeling and hostile adults. In our society, the word "stepchild" is applied to anything that is "mistreated, neglected and mismanaged." [14] For centuries we have lived with the myth of the wicked stepmother. Almost all children are introduced to the stories of Snow White and Cinderella. This hostile stereotype, so much a part of their informal education, is very important in molding attitudes toward stepfamilyhood.

In professional and popular literature, stepmothers have long been depicted as narcissistic, poorly adjusted and unaccepting of their stepchildren.[15] When problems with children erupt in the stepfamily, the stepmother is usually blamed by friends and family for their existence. Countless women in this position are forced into defensive postures when their devotion and concern toward their stepchildren are questioned. This is complicated by the fact that stepmothers themselves have been indoctrinated in the evil-stepmother tradition; they may feel demoralized and therefore be less effective as parents or guides because they do not anticipate positive appreciation. Obviously, not all stepparents are warm, loving and devoted to their young charges. But then again, there are lots of biological parents around who don't have much feeling for their children either. There is no evidence that either of these two groups is inherently more loving or better able to raise children.

When children accuse their stepparents of unfairness, cruelty, or favoritism, they are, intentionally or not, touching on some of the latent anxieties of these adults. Half believing the evil stepparent myth, the stepparent often erroneously looks to the child for reassurance that he or she is doing a good job. When this confirmation is not forthcoming, the stepparent may defensively battle with the child. The most benign stance for a stepparent to take if accused of cruelty and unfairness is to acknowledge the child's anger without being devastated or defensive. Perhaps the adult can ask the child to specify his (or her) grievances; when they are warranted, adults can strive to become more aware of their shortcomings. A thoughtful evaluation of the child's accusations will reassure the youngster that the stepparent respects him (or her) and is optimistic about the future.

To succumb blindly to criticism, especially when it seems irrational, frightens children who may be feeling guilty for not loving their stepparent as much as they think they should. Honesty, self-confidence and patience on the part of stepparents are important assets in developing long-term, meaningful relationships between stepparent and child.

The lack of institutionalization of the stepmother role does little to ease the potential difficulties; the culture fails to provide any norms that would educate the stepmother to recognize if or how her role differs from that of the biological parent.[16] Many stepmothers do not know whether they are supposed to "take over" child rearing or stay loose and neutral. They are often accused of trying to "replace" *real* mothers. Obviously, each situation is unique and the proper role of the stepparent is determined largely by whether the biological parents have close and warm ties with each other and the children or whether they are all severely alienated from each other. We have met some biological parents who are healthy and secure enough to encourage and respect the relationship between their children and the new stepparent. Other parents will be more threatened by their children's outside relationships. In the latter case, children will have to struggle harder to extend and receive love from the outsider because they have to overcome their fear of hurting their "real" parents.

Saul Bellow's insight into the psyche of a divorced father and the fears that accompany divorce is beautifully described in his novel *Herzog*.[17] Anguished by his wife's rejection, Herzog struggles to preserve his sanity. In one touching scene he peers into his wife's bathroom window to catch a glimpse of his children before bedtime and sees them being bathed tenderly by the "other man." This experience fills him with ambivalence which is resolved when he finally relinquishes the fantasy that neither he nor his children could cope with the ordeal of divorce.

Stepparents, often anxious for their stepchildren to love and need them to the same degree as they do their biological parents, may try to compete with the child's own parent. This dilemma derives from two common mistaken notions: first, that there can be only one set of meaningful adults in a child's life and, second, that the stepparent has to play the same kind of role for the child as does the biological parent. In reality a youngster can derive different kinds of gratification from new family relationships; in fact, this very possibility in stepfamilies is an important advantage of this life-style. Where biological parents are alive and actively involved with their children, the stepparent may play a more auxiliary role with the child though not necessarily a less important or less satisfying one. In the early days of the stepparent-child relationship the adult would be wise to take a "wait and see" position in determining what kind of relationship the stepchild will need and desire. Such a posture reassures biological parents who may be anxious and competitive where their children are concerned and, more importantly, shows respect for the stepchildren's need to take stock of their new family and find their own comfortable place.

Both professional and popular writers are less critical of stepfathers than of stepmothers, but at the same time, they ignore the challenge of this role. The position of the stepfather is peculiarly vague and ill-defined in America. Legally, he has no obligations to his stepchildren, and while clinicians describe fathers as "crucial" to the normal development of children, they never go beyond the banal observation that stepfathers are male figures with whom children can identify.

While assumptions about the inevitable disturbance in stepfamilies are aired in the literature,[18] role definitions for all stepparents remain undefined, poorly articulated and negatively tinged. We almost expect to learn that a stepchild has been emotionally abused and rejected by a stepparent, and hearsay and gossip frequently fulfill this anticipation.

The lack of clearly defined roles in multimarriage families is nowhere more obvious than in the connection between half siblings. The common designation of a person as "stepbrother" or "half sister" illustrates the myth that stepsiblings are not considered to be "regular" siblings, but nobody has outlined any formal set of expectations or obligations that would set these relationships apart from those of "pure" biological brothers and sisters. The importance in our society of who one's biological parents are puts additional emphasis on the difference between a natural sibling and a stepsibling. Because biological ties take precedence over other kinship relationships in our society, nonblood ties are typically considered less intense, less rewarding and less permanent. A friend of ours who is a sociology professor asked his students about their attitudes toward stepfamily relationships. Most of them assumed (and not from personal experience) that stepsiblings would be more competitive and jealous of each other than would "real" siblings. They could not back up their assumptions with any evidence, but had been indoctrinated by the media to believe that stepfamilies were less wholesome and more hostile than biological ones.

Other cultures have been far more successful in integrating stepchildren with each other, regardless of parental relationships. The Kanuri Eskimos, for example, established kinship associations whereby the offspring of any kind of marital arrangement would be considered sibling to one another.[19] Ties of kinship in that Eskimo community were permanently established, continuing through generation after generation regardless of the form of marriage initially involved.[20] Because of this institutionalization of stepchildren into the total extended family, one source of potential emotional upheaval was eradicated. In our society such protection does not exist, for a stepchild's relationship with new siblings is dependent on the current state of emotional warfare between the ex-partners and on the marital status of the new parents. Relationships between stepsiblings are apt to suffer because of the premium Americans put on the nuclear family.

Sibling rivalry may be universal but it is magnified in the small nuclear family where emotional relations and sensitivities are greatly intensified.[21] Social scientists predict that youngsters in this society will reject stepsiblings and will jealously view them as a threat to their security. With the small number of "nuclear" adults available to each youngster, children would presumably vie to protect the relationships they already have. But in our experience, which we do not think is unique, children do not respond in the expected sinister fashion. We have found that the children of divorce do not feel that stepsiblings are "robbing" them of crucial sources of love, any more than stepparents "substitute" for or rob them of biological parents. They are, instead, proud of and fond of their half siblings; these children can enrich each other's lives and become friends and companions for life. When youngsters are actively encouraged to broaden their ties rather than to regard newcomers with suspicion, they are able to appreciate new relationships without feeling that they have violated older ones. This is true of children in or out of divorce.

A more sophisticated rationale for the anti-stepparent bias derives from the clinical assumption that a child separated from its biological family cannot progress through the normal stages of emotional development.[22] Specifically, some professionals speculate that the absence of the incest taboo in stepfamilies leads to incestuous behavior or at least to a disruption in the resolution and inhibition of normal Oedipal feelings. Some clinicians further argue that the forbidden sexual attraction between stepfamily members gets converted into an inevitable hatred between stepparent and child.[23] We can find no evidence to substantiate that hypothesis, based on either research data or clinical experiences.

By means of such propaganda, the stepparent-child relationship is sullied before it even begins. The biological hierarchy, with its consequent "pecking order" of love and authority, encourages children and their stepparents to suspect each other's motives. When stepparents are kind or gracious, friends and relatives suspect that they are trying to "take over" the "real parent's" place. When stepparents discipline, they are often accused of hostility, are ignored, or are warned "You're not my real mother [or father]!" When stepparents do occasionally become exasperated, arrive at a point where they've "had it," and express some resentment, there are always people around ready to draw a sigh of relief and happily add "I told you so!" In this circular fashion, negative folklore is constantly reaffirmed.

In stepfamilies where stepparents live with their own children in addition to stepchildren, other concerns often arise. Stepparents may feel guilty over the fact that however they try to overcome their feelings they still prefer their own children to their stepchildren. This anxiety is especially prominent in new stepfamilies, where stepparents and child have not as yet shared a variety of intimate experiences and where stepparents are worried about how effective they will be in their new roles. It is important to keep in mind that preference for one child over another is not uncommon, even in intact nuclear families. For a variety of reasons, one child's personality may be especially gratifying to a parent in comparison to the other children. This may, but does not have to, spell disaster for a child, and in stepfamilies of divorce, stepchildren have their own biological parents to whom they are usually considered special. Each youngster's needs are different and an empathic adult will in time come to understand these needs. To expect to love a child automatically because you love his or her parent is nonsensical and not necessary for a healthy and happy adjustment.

In spite of all the dismal statements issued by professional writers on the subject of stepfamilyhood and remarriage, extreme and special problems need not exist in such families. Clinicians have, by and large, failed to account for those positive aspects of the stepfamily relationship that often overcome initial barriers to closeness. In terms of successful mastery of Oedipal feelings, for example, stepchildren are offered a unique opportunity to re-experience these particular sexual feelings and to resolve conflicts they may have been unable to resolve in their original unhappy homes. Furthermore, it has been our experience that normal "incest" taboos are transferred unconsciously and automatically from the biological family to the stepfamily.

Stepparents can frequently offer children invaluable assistance with some problems that natural parents, because of the intensity of their involvement with the children, are unable to furnish. Because the stepparent does not perceive the child as an extension of "self," the way a natural parent might, he (or she) may have an easier time encouraging and permitting youngsters to develop and nurture new ties outside the family and to develop independent opinions of the outer world. The multimarriage family offers children a second chance to resolve many conflicts and frequently gives them a broader and more sophisticated view of people.

The multimarriage family can be seen as an extended kinship system that provides relief from the suffocating relationships children often encounter and endure in the intact nuclear system. Finally, there is often less strain on stepparents in dealing with troubled and difficult youngsters than there is on natural parents. They feel less motivated by guilt because they can always reassure themselves with the comforting notion that they "inherited" a troubled child. "His parents made him that way, not I." In this way, stepparents do not always have to compensate for their mistakes with children as biological parents often find themselves doing.

We do not deny that remarriages involving children demand special adjustments from all family members. Indeed they do. The ease of that adjustment depends on the maturity and flexibility of the stepparents and the expectations and attitudes of the biological parents. It is not the easiest thing in the world to marry into a ready-made family. Newlyweds who are also parents have to compromise their desire for privacy and often have to postpone honeymoons and pinch their pennies due to financial responsibilities. Furthermore, the stepparent role is vague and ill-defined, especially when the child is in the other parent's custody and just "visits" with the newlyweds. We have known many women who worked for years at figuring out how a "part-time mother" should behave.

Sometimes hassles between biological parents persist well beyond the remarriage of one or both partners. Economic pressures in multimarriage families are a typical consequence of the necessity to support two households on one salary. Visitation between children and their noncustodial parents may result in broken, changed, confused and last-minute plans. There is, in a sense, no end to the number of issues the stepfamily can complain about. But intact families face crises of other sorts and somehow learn to weather their troubles and to make the most of their shared joys and intimacies. It has been our experience that multimarriage families in which people adopt the attitude that in some way life is complicated for most people are at least as happy as other families.

When divorce is followed by remarriage, or when one parent just lives with another adult, children have the opportunity to learn how to extend trust and love. At the same time, stepparent and stepchild are *not* parent and child, certainly not while the biological parents are alive. Therefore, what arises is a new kind of relationship, based on separation and independence, that is also potentially intimate.

For many stepparents, the situation is aided by the fact that ex-spouses are sometimes amicable and can share the work and rewards of co-parenting their children. The remarriage of one partner need not be a threat to such amicability, though the American loyalty fetish to the nuclear family plays havoc with this alternative. We have been fortunate in knowing and working with divorced families whose members have maintained respect and friendship for each other despite the fact that they have all gone their separate ways.

Many other difficulties that supposedly characterize stepfamilies are not necessarily more extreme in intensity than those in the biological nuclear family. Children who are severely troubled are likely to be so whether or not their parents divorce or remarry. Anti-stepfamily propaganda frightens adults into feeling that they will not be able to handle new family relationships; nobody encourages young people, or older married people, to throw themselves into new life-styles with vigor and enthusiasm. Most people are either potential stepparents or stepchildren, and there is no need for them to succumb to the mythological pitfalls and horrors of those two roles.

In our opinion, remarriage and stepfamilyhood should be looked upon as processes of addition rather than of substraction. The potential for creating new and loving ties after divorce is most seriously undermined by the assumption that children cannot (or should not) experience love and personal loyalty toward more than two adults at one time, specifically their biological parents, or to children who are not their "real" brothers and sisters. Motherly, fatherly, sisterly and brotherly feelings are born out of love and shared experiences, not out of blood.

# 10
# The Challenge
# of Divorce Therapy

Individuals seeking help have no way of knowing what to expect in the way of attitude
biases in the professional to whom they will be
entrusting high hopes and a great deal of
responsibility, time, and money.
—William J. Lederer and Don D. Jackson

While the decision to divorce may mark the beginning of an important stage of emotional growth, at least for one
partner, clinicians frequently misconstrue the motives of their
patients. Often, without realizing what they are doing, therapists
attribute greater maturity, health and wisdom to the spouse who
is *more reluctant* to part and more committed, verbally, to "working at the relationship" and "preserving the marriage." The ability
to stand alone, to face uncertainty and to strive for greater fulfillment is not as highly valued as the determination to struggle and
stoically accept life's hardships. Therefore the flight from pain
becomes associated with neurosis and immaturity.

In light of the fact that it requires intense effort in our culture to achieve a healthy separation from one's spouse, even when it is long overdue, couples seeking divorce sometimes require the empathy, talent and skill of clinicians who are intellectually and psychologically prepared to deal with the process in all its phases. The courage and vision of therapists to go beyond the limits of their own upbringing and often narrow professional training will have to be based on a serious reconsideration of the connections that exist between marriage, divorce, emotional sickness and emotional health.

Since most therapists are products of the same Judeo-Christian tradition as their patients, there may be a considerable tendency, from the outset of treatment, to help couples resist divorce and counterculture life-styles in favor of marriage. Competent counselors try to encourage mature human intimacy and healthy family life, but as we have shown (see Chapter 5), some of them mistakenly believe that these goals can be achieved only in traditional marriage. Although large numbers of people are now "afflicted" with marital unhappiness, many practitioners still believe, as Nathan Ackerman did, that a corrective approach to marital discord means therapy for the problem of "husbanding and wifing," [1] an attempt to patch up, salvage, or resurrect a dying relationship. But in reality it is the stubborn American tradition of "husbanding and wifing" that needs to be overhauled.

For example, clinicians can help parents re-examine the entire process of rearing a daughter; for every middle-class girl a "normal" upbringing has meant learning to place love of husband and children before any personal ambitions and strivings.[2] The identity crises and the economic deprivations that sometimes follow divorce, especially for women, seem to us proof that the safety and security of *wifehood* and *motherhood* are paltry substitutes for personal achievement and at least potential economic independence.

The numerous decisions and changes in life-style occasioned by our rapidly changing and mobile society, in which divorce is increasingly prevalent, suggest some urgent new tasks for the helping professions. Clinicians now have to respond to a myriad of new and relevant problems, some of which have been generated by the vitality of the women's liberation movement. Helping parents guide their children through divorce, and cope with its aftermaths, is one of them. The elimination of traditional sexist expectations in marriage is another. For example, would the man who angrily complains that the house is messy think of cleaning it up himself? In addition, many people come for treatment struggling with their conflicts and uncertainties about the risks of living together and having children outside the framework of legal marriage.

But at least as important, and perhaps even more crucial, is the problem of separation anxiety in adults, which seems to us the crux of the psychic "trauma" associated with divorce. The dilemmas and complexities of pre- and post-divorce life cannot be separated from the task of helping people derive the courage to sever ties that are deep but often unhealthy. Thus, one dangerous corollary of a commitment to preserve marriage is the tendency of therapists subtly to reinforce the excessive dependence that many couples have on each other and on legal marriage.

Before a therapist can help a patient achieve a successful divorce, he or she has to be convinced that divorce is not solely the consequence of a neurotic inability to "adjust" and "struggle," but is a legitimate, valid, moral, creative act, and an orderly and respectable instrument of change.[3] The mere fact of whether people stay married or get divorced is no index of psychological health; it is a mistake to assume that people who divorce are people who *couldn't* sustain marriage. More likely, they are people who could have stayed married if they had wanted to, but who preferred separation. Moreover, divorce does not necessarily mean that a marriage was a *failure*. It may have been quite successful, for a time, in giving the couple warmth, friendship, love and intellectual stimulation. Until the helping professions carve out a broader and more empathic role for themselves in divorce and family counseling, domestic misery will be engendered and intensified by the very people who are committed to relieving it.

Very few patients, when they start treatment, have a clear and unequivocal commitment either to marriage or to divorce. Under certain circumstances, therefore, marriage counseling may shade imperceptibly into divorce counseling, but the distinction is still an important one for couples seeking help. One marriage counselor suggests that the new title "marriage and divorce counselor" be used to allay the fears of couples who might otherwise feel trapped.[4] However, much more important than what counselors *call themselves* are their ability and willingness to state their own values without intimidating or prejudging their patients.

In all fairness to the helping professions, it should be pointed out that the understanding and treatment of divorced families is a badly neglected aspect of professional and graduate training. One author who has closely surveyed the field of marriage counseling finds, for example, that the majority of people who take up this specialty have very little formal training or supervised experience,[5] with either intact or divorced families.

Graduate schools of social work and psychology and post-graduate psychoanalytic institutes pay no systematic attention to the complexities of divorce. As far as we can discern, clinicians are not even taught the rudiments of marriage and family law. Increasingly confronted by patients who are engrossed in the confusing legal skirmishes that surround divorce, they are often at a loss to evaluate which of their patients' fears and anxieties are realistic and which are unwarranted.

Legal questions frequently arise in the treatment of single and divorced parents. The therapist cannot artificially separate, for example, a divorced mother's emotional concerns from the legal "danger" she may be in. How is a professional to help a lesbian mother decide whether to live with or just date her lover? Will her lesbianism threaten her right to custody? (see Chapter 17.) Should she hide this aspect of her life from her children, her lawyer, or her ex-husband?

A woman patient insists that until she gets her final divorce decree she cannot live with her male lover because her husband is still trying to prove she is an adulteress. She has been legally separated for fifteen years, dating one man for ten years, and both her children are grown. Is she using what she thinks are legal impediments to justify and rationalize her preference for living alone? Or is she exercising sound judgment and wisely protecting herself against a notoriously punitive tradition?

We are not recommending that therapists dispense legal advice, but simply that they be well informed about their state laws and keep abreast of important judicial and legal trends. Therapists should at least have more accurate and reliable information than their patients, lest they do some grave damage in the name of treatment.

We can envision professional training and services that are more adaptive and responsive to the needs of the community. For example, the American Association of Religion and Psychiatry, in cooperation with the American Academy of Matrimonial Lawyers, recently established a course on "Divorce, Remarriage and the Law." [6] An academic course of this nature should be a mandatory part of clinical training in social work, psychiatry, psychology, and marriage and pastoral counseling. In addition, mental hygiene clinics and family-serving agencies should have qualified matrimonial and divorce lawyers available for professional consultation, in the same way that they enlist the aid of a panel of medical specialists.

Our clinical experiences, which are similar to those of many other therapists who work in urban agencies, show that the culturally approved denial of divorce as a part of everyday life is a subtle but significant handicap in treating families. When patients are merely directed back to their own lawyers, they often ask the wrong questions, distort information and unwittingly hurt themselves; what is worse, they sometimes have incompetent lawyers, and the therapist is ultimately misinformed and misguided as well. Therapists sometimes resort to calling their own lawyers or to "asking around" for information. Procedures such as these are inconvenient and often unreliable.

The kinds of families seeking help have changed radically in recent decades. The patient population used to represent intact first marriages, with strong family, religious and community ties. Now therapists work largely with extended and single-parent families, including children of his, hers and theirs.[7] Social agencies are beginning to acknowledge (though reluctantly) that couples increasingly come to them seeking advice, justification and professional approval in their decision to divorce.[8] We think it is a positive and healthy sign that more and more couples are beginning to reject emotionally barren marriages and search instead for new and more satisfying lives. It is increasingly "unprofessional" for counselors to use their status and authority in such cases to shore up the institution of marriage.

In anticipation of the work their students will eventually do, graduate schools and training institutes should teach them how to evaluate the relevant research and literature on divorce and new life-styles. During their years of field work and internship, in which they are closely supervised, students should have as much exposure as possible to families whose lives do not follow traditional patterns. Therapists are more likely to examine and confront their own prejudices when they are students and trainees than later in their careers when they work privately and more autonomously.

In addition to giving their students practical experience, schools should offer new types of academic courses. For example, they might give ongoing seminars on divorce or specific courses in divorce counseling. It has been our personal experience that the understanding and treatment of divorced families is not implicit in courses and workshops in the philosophy and techniques of family therapy.

There seems to be some movement in this direction, but it is still on a very small scale. For example, at a recent meeting of the American Orthopsychiatric Association, held in New York City, there was one workshop on divorce and one on the special problems in treatment of children in separated and divorced families. In the spring of 1973, the New School for Social Research offered a series of six lectures on the subject of "Marriage Reconsidered," including extensive discussion of the alternatives to nuclear family life. It also offered a three-lecture series called "In and Out of Marriage."

In our opinion, it is both a privilege and a serious responsibility to be trusted by another human being who is in emotional pain and wants help. Patients who seek advice and guidance are often people who are victims of grave social injustices and are often passive recipients of the myths perpetuated by gossip and the mass media. It is the job of the therapist not only to make them conscious of their plight, but also to help them derive strength from the therapist's own courage to understand and deal creatively with the rapid and far-reaching social changes of our era.

# part four

# 11
# Hebrew and Roman Divorce:
# A Comparison
# of Two Ideologies

> For the Lord, the God of Israel, saith that he hateth [divorce] . . . therefore take heed to your spirit, that ye deal not treacherously.
> —Malachi 2:16–17

> Seldom do marriages last until death undivorced.
> > On a stone erected to a certain Turia
> > by her husband
> > in the early days of the Empire.

The ancient Hebrews and the Romans during the early days of the Empire developed markedly different marriage and divorce customs. Although the contrast between these two societies in their practice of divorce was extreme, each tradition has had a strong and lasting impact on contemporary attitudes and legislation.

The ancient Near Eastern pastoral tribe known as the Hebrews exhibited a patriarchal kinship pattern characteristic of nomadic desert herdsmen. The head of each family exercised life-and-death control over a two- or three-generation household which contained conjugal units in addition to concubines, their children

and servants.[1] Matrimonial customs were characteristically patriarchal. The fathers of the prospective bride and groom would
arrange the marriage without considering the question of free
choice, which was not relevant to that society. Wives were simply
purchased by the groom's family. After being dominated by their
fathers throughout childhood, women in marriage were subordinated to the authority of their husbands. A double standard of
morality was enforced in which men could have many wives while
women were severely punished for any hint of interest in other
men.

Among the Hebrews, marriage was considered necessary for
group survival. Everyone was expected to marry and to produce
children. The Bible (Genesis 1:22) taught the Hebrews to "be
fruitful, and multiply," and bachelorhood and spinsterhood were
not acceptable social roles for adults.[2] Marriage gave both men
and women social approval and economic stability, and assured
men of legal heirs.

While marriage was deemed a necessity in ancient Judea, provision was made, in the Old Testament, for divorce. In Deuter-
onomy 24:1 we read: "When a man hath taken a wife, and
married her, and it come to pass that she find no favor in his
eyes, because he hath found some uncleanness in her: then let him
write her a bill of divorcement, and give it in her hand, and send
her out of his house." In accordance with this teaching, divorce
could be obtained easily by men, but women could not initiate
any formal steps to end marriage. A woman could probably provoke her husband to initiate divorce himself if she were determined
to be rid of him. By contrast, all he had to do was literally throw
a divorce document at his wife and she was divorced. The major
deterrent to casual divorce was negative public sentiment, articulated by the prophet Malachi, who condemned it in Malachi
2:16–17 in the following way: "Let none deal treacherously against
the wife of his youth."

In the middle of the twelfth century B.C., Hebrews began to
take possession of Canaan and in time settled in agricultural communities. As towns and cities began to grow, tribal life gave way

to urban living. Wealth increased and new laws were enacted to protect private property and to insure that inheritance would be passed on along the male's line. Women were propertyless and were cemented in their inferior status. The woman was her husband's chattel; he could live with or love any woman he desired as long as he did not violate another man's property.[3] Women were guarded strictly, and if they were found guilty of adultery, they were stripped naked and were publicly stoned to death.[4] The original law that permitted the husband to divorce his wife without considering her opinion remained in force.

Beginning in the sixth century B.C., the Kingdom of Judah was overthrown by a succession of foreign powers; as a result, a large number of Hebrews were forced into exile. With the Roman conquest in the first century A.D., Jews were further scattered throughout the Mediterranean world. As Hebrews began to live in close proximity to other peoples, they strove to maintain group identity by solidifying themselves around family and synagogue. The Hebrew family system remained patriarchal, with polygamy and concubinage continuing until the Talmudic era.

Though divorce rules and practices remained essentially unchanged until the later Talmudic period, controversy flourished among leading Hebrew sages. A few years before the birth of Jesus, Shammai and Hillel, two of the most influential teachers of antiquity, debated the question of divorce.[5] Shammai believed that infidelity on the part of a wife was the only ground justifying divorce. Hillel maintained the ancient practice of interpreting the Scriptures in a looser way, and supported the right of a man to divorce his wife for any reason. Rabbinical leaders later concurred that while the teachings of Shammai and Hillel were equally inspired by God, Hillel's views would be put into practice.[6]

The Talmudic period of Hebrew history began during the latter stages of the Roman Empire. The Talmud is a written collection of decisions and discussions by Jewish sages who tried to explain the meanings of God's messages. A highly complex document, the Talmud expressed a "cross-section of the heart and mind of the Jewish nation during the rise and fall of the Roman empire." [7]

Talmudic rabbis generally censured divorce. Rabbi Eleazar wrote that the "very altar sheds tears" when a man divorces his first wife.[8] Other rabbis warned husbands to be patient and to maintain their marriages. Since the Jewish family was the major institution necessary to preserve group identity, these rabbis viewed divorce as a destructive event. Furthermore, these men considered Hebrew contact with Roman liberal ideas as potentially dangerous to Jewish tradition.

Patriarchal privilege continued in the area of divorce until about the eleventh century A.D., at which time a modification was introduced by Rabbi Gershon ben Yudah. Rabbi Gershon (965–1028) was the earliest notable West European Jewish scholar and his legal decisions were accepted as binding by European Jewry. Along with a ban on polygamy, he ordained that a woman could not be divorced except by her own consent.[9] Here then was a major shift in the authority that men had exercised over their wives since ancient times. Both the Talmud and later rabbinical law established the wife's right to request divorce; if the Jewish court could compel the husband to grant his wife a divorce, all was well. There was one hitch, however, to female emancipation in divorce matters. Biblical law specified that the act of divorce had to be voluntary on the part of the husband.[10] In other words, regardless of which spouse wished to divorce, the decision ultimately rested with the husband. Though a woman supposedly had to consent to a divorce, this contradicted Biblical law, which in practice reigned supreme. The Mishnah, a portion of the Talmud, anticipated one of the practical difficulties of this Scriptural teaching and ruled that if a husband became mad the only chance of divorce was to hope that he was willing to grant it during his lucid intervals.[11]

Hebrew scholars during the medieval period urged that women be granted further privileges in divorce. Maimonides (1135–1204), the great medieval sage, suggested that a woman should not be forced to remain married to a man she hated. But such views did not alter the fact that the husband still exercised the *final* and *only* authority to divorce and all privileges that women gained were dependent on their husbands' good will. This situation persists today among some Orthodox Jews, and has become a severe problem for many women, not only in Israel.[12]

The right of the husband to divorce his wife at pleasure is central to the entire system of Orthodox Jewish law.[13] While rabbis gradually modified the severity of patriarchal privilege, they could not set the law aside. While we do not know how much social pressure tempered the husband's "right" to divorce at will, we do know that women under the Hebrew laws and practice of divorce were never treated as legal equals with their husbands. The paternalism characteristic of Jewish divorce customs [14] was not unique in the ancient world; the early Romans designed a similar divorce system based on the supremacy and privilege of men.

As in ancient Judea, family life in republican Rome was essentially partriarchal. The head of each family was a male who owned and controlled all family property and enjoyed the absolute authority to direct the lives of family members, which in later centuries also included slaves.[15] Marriages were arranged by the fathers of the bride and groom and it was not necessary that the betrothed couple be fond of each other. Within the family, women were totally subordinate to their husbands. Married women were legally minors and marriage itself merely transferred them from the hands of their fathers into the hands of their husbands, who could whip, chastise and even kill them.[16]

Marriage in early Rome was a private affair, terminable at will. But "within the family, traditional mores exercised strict control making divorce relatively rare." [17] Essentially divorce was a family matter and the privilege rested with the husband or his father, who could even divorce his son and daughter-in-law without the consent of either party. The law permitted divorce as a means of ridding a man of his wife without having to murder her.[18] The wife, by contrast, had neither the authority nor the right to request a divorce. The only controls over the male's power to divorce were public opinion and family pressure.[19] Judicial (government) involvement in such family matters was deemed unnecessary.

During and after the Punic Wars of the third century B.C., Rome accumulated great wealth; changes in marriage and family life came rapidly.[20] Because husbands were away at war for long periods of time, women assumed additional responsibilities and experienced a great deal of freedom from male domir ition.[21] A more egalitarian pattern of family life emerged as a r iddle class grew in wealth and Rome acquired more territory. The leisure classes began to live off the proceeds of land rent i and slavery rather than work.[22] There was less of a need for the family to function as an economic unit; women were no longer essential to farming, child care, or domestic work.

"When the Republic finally gave way to the Empire, extravagance, conspicuous consumption and domestic intrigue were widespread in the upper classes." [23] Fathers were now able to give their daughters large dowries, but did not necessarily want their property to pass into the hands of their sons-in-law. Older forms of marriage were avoided, and under a more equitable form of marriage, women remained under their fathers' guardianship even after marriage.[24] Freed of the traditional dependence on husbands, women began to experience greater freedom in questions of divorce.

With the rise of this more balanced form of marriage, divorce was permitted by mutual consent and also at the will of either spouse. Both men and women could divorce by sending their spouse a written notice; divorced women usually returned home to their fathers with their dowries intact. As a result, divorces grew common, the marriage rate decreased, and people ceased to regard marriage as a sacred obligation.[25] When couples did marry, they often dissolved their unions for trivial reasons; men with political ambitions often married four or five times in acts of self-advancement.[26] Because of the high divorce rate, childbearing became less desirable to women and abortions and contraception were widely practiced among the wealthy.

It is difficult to estimate how high the Roman divorce rate actually was because the tremendous publicity given to the divorces of the socially prominent has obscured the total picture. Although Cleopatra married four times and Ovid married three times, the common people probably did not indulge in marriage and divorce with such frequency. The independence found among upper-class women did not extend into lower socioeconomic levels.[27] However, the Punic Wars dramatically changed Roman society from a patriarchal republic, in which women were subjugated to men, to a free and open culture in which women, at least wealthy ones, were offered virtual equality.

The rise and triumph of Christianity brought an abrupt halt to the liberal tendencies in Roman divorce practices.[28] Early Christians, along with Stoic philosophers, introduced concepts of "fault" and "guilt" that now permeate the institutions of matrimony and divorce.

# 12
# The Catholic Church
# and the Protestant Revolt:
# Power Against the People

> The Pharisees also came unto him, tempting him, and saying unto him, Is it lawful for a man to put away his wife for every cause?
>
> And he answered and said unto them, Have ye not read, that he which made them at the beginning made them male and female,
>
> And said, For this cause shall a man leave father and mother, and shall cleave to his wife: and they twain shall be one flesh?
>
> —Matthew 19:3–5

> Ofttimes the causes of seeking divorce reside so deeply in the radical and innocent affections of nature, as is not within the diocese of law to tamper with.
>
> —John Milton

> Of all actions of a man's life, his marriage does least concern other people. Yet of all actions of our life 'tis the most meddled with by other people.
>
> —John Selden

As Christianity spread among the people of the Roman Empire, it began to transform not only general moral attitudes but domestic customs and values as well. Early Christians held in contempt what they considered to be the corrupt and worldly practices of the Roman nobility, the Hebrews and other groups in the Empire. As Christianity gradually grew in power, before it became the state religion in the fifth century A.D., it wrought a vast change in matrimonial customs.

The early Christian attitudes toward matrimony are ambiguous. While the beliefs of the early Christians are recorded in the Scriptures and in the writings of Church fathers, much less is

158

known about how, in fact, the masses lived.[1] The teachings of the Apostles indicate that the Christians accorded marriage and family living a lower status than the Hebrews and even the Romans did. While they often spoke of the purity of matrimony, they did so with tones of apology and deprecation.[2] Wedlock was deemed holy, but celibacy was even more holy. Paul, in his First Epistle to the Corinthians (7:2–9), said: ". . . to avoid fornication, let every man have his own wife, and let every woman have her own husband. . . . For I would that all men were even as I myself [bachelor]. . . . But if they cannot contain, let them marry: for it is better to marry than to burn." Thus, marriage was tolerated in order to avoid the greater sin of fornication. Virginity and celibacy were considered states of higher purity, even though the early Church teachers were well aware that families were necessary to produce more virgins and more celibates.[3]

Early Christian teachers held a low opinion of women, which was related to the low esteem in which they held marriage. The Genesis account of temptation in the Garden of Eden clearly stated that women were the source of original sin. The teachings of Jesus and Paul were invoked to support the concept of female inferiority, which was ultimately based on the impurity of sexual relations.[4] St. Augustine, a fifth-century theologian, taught that women should look upon their marital chores as "indentures of perpetual service" and should "joyfully endure the debaucheries and ill treatment" by their husbands.[5] Paul, centuries before, had spoken about the role women must play in the Christian family: ". . . to be sober, to love their husbands, to love their children, to be discreet, chaste, keepers at home, good, obedient to their husbands . . ."[6] Christian teachings reversed the emancipation some women had achieved in Roman society and insisted on their inferior status. The Church attacked sex as vile and lashed out at all expressions of immodesty and vanity.[7]

During this same period, before Christianity had become the official state religion, the Roman government was growing concerned with high divorce and low marriage rates; in response, the government imposed penalties on unmarried adults and offered privileges to men and women in proportion to the number of children they had.[8] At the same time these measures were instituted, Church fathers were praising those who avoided matrimony.[9] Only a small number of Christians actually succeeded in suppressing their drives and leading lives of abstinence; the rest continued to lust, love, fornicate and marry.[10]

Early Christian teachings on divorce derived from two statements attributed to Jesus in the Gospel of St. Matthew: "What therefore God hath joined together, let no man put asunder" (Matthew 19:6) and "Whosoever shall put away his wife, let him give her a writing of divorcement: But I say unto you, that whosoever shall put away his wife, saving for the cause of fornication, causeth her to commit adultery: and whosoever shall marry her that is divorced committeth adultery" (Matthew 5:31–32). These two texts were highly ambiguous and were debated for centuries; some Christians believed that Jesus forbade divorce on all grounds while others argued that Jesus permitted divorce when one spouse was adulterous.

The early Christian fathers probably would not have paid much attention to divorce if it were not so frequent, casual and notorious among the upper classes. While Christian opposition to divorce wavered for a number of centuries, Church leaders eventually crystallized and formalized a Church position. In about 306 A.D. the Council of Elvira declared that a woman who divorced her husband for any reason and then remarried would be excommunicated. In 407 A.D. the Council of Carthage definitively laid down the doctrine of the indissolubility of marriage. Yet Christianity had still not succeeded in becoming the official religion of Rome and the government continued to permit divorce.

In the fourth century, the Church gained enormous influence in Roman government and marriage and divorce started to come under clerical domination. In the fourth century the Emperor Constantine, a convert to Christianity, tightened the divorce regulations of the Empire. In the sixth century the Christian Emperor Justinian revoked the ancient Roman privilege of divorce by mutual consent except in cases where a husband was impotent, had been in foreign captivity for five years, or either partner wished to enter a monastic order. Though divorce penalties were imposed by Constantine, Justinian and other emperors, divorce was always valid and private, for no court decree was ever required in Rome.[11]

With the fall of the Roman Empire, the Church finally succeeded in taking power in many matters—spiritual and temporal—and its decisions superseded Imperial law. The popes exercised jurisdiction over all marriages and forbade divorce.

The Dark Ages descended on Europe and Roman sophistication merged with various primitive cultures of the Franks, Normans, Goths and others.[12] Life, during this time, became "grossly sensual, harsh and sinful with penance easily and cynically performed as often as required."[13] By their vilification of sex and marriage, the Christian fathers had made impossible the union of sex, love and marriage; even sex within marriage was, at best, considered disgusting and shameful.[14] Marriage was tolerated as suitable for those weaklings who could not control their passions and yearnings.

Christian contempt for women fused with Oriental, Hebrew and barbarian ideas of women as inferior and inherently sinful.[15] Centuries of gains that women had achieved during the zenith of Roman civilization were wiped out; women were again demoted to the status of domesticated animals and pieces of property without status in the eyes of the law.[16] The clergy was also affected by the fusion of barbarian morality and ascetic values; "the more the Church fought against clerical marriage, the more the clergy turned to simple concubinage."[17]

Despite the Church's prohibition on divorce, ecclesiastical authorities in the Dark Ages were able to separate couples and even dissolve marriages. Following Jesus' teachings, the courts permitted separation on the ground of adultery; but remarriage of either spouse was forbidden—the partners either lived in celibacy or reconciled.[18] The Church permitted annulments on three grounds: (1) if some impediment existed in the original consent or will of the parties to the marriage, an annulment was permitted, as if the marriage had never actually taken place; (2) if a Christian convert was abandoned by his infidel spouse, the convert could remarry; and (3) if a marriage was unconsummated it could be annulled by papal dispensation. According to Christian doctrine, a marriage did not exist "until man and woman had been one flesh." [19]

Church dispensations, which served the purpose of obtaining revenue for the Roman Church,[20] were basically the only means of escaping an unhappy marriage. The liberty to divorce during the time period that began with the fall of Rome and ended with the Protestant Reformation existed only for those wealthy enough to pay for a way out of marriage.[21]

The doctrine of the indissolubility of marriage was never practiced by the Roman Church except where the partners were too poor to pay their way to freedom or when women sought to divorce husbands who were powerful or wealthy enough to stop them. According to ecclesiastical officials, the husband was considered head of the family, to whom the wife owed obedience and from whom she could expect chastisement at his will.[22] Therefore, the courts generally preferred the husband's evidence over that of the wife in divorce cases, and since women were not supposed to inquire into their husbands' behavior, they often were denied the right to leave their husbands.

The abuses of the Roman Catholic Church,[23] in its almost complete usurpation of individual liberty and its negation of family authority, were unacceptable to growing numbers of people. When the feudal era began to pass, challenges to the undisputed hegemony of the Roman Church, including its authority over matrimony, became insistent.

The Protestant reformers who revolted against the Roman Church gained support from Renaissance kings and parliaments who were no less anxious to strip the Catholic Church of its excessive power and authority. While the Renaissance had resulted in increased trade and accumulated wealth, the Roman Church continued to treat business as a shameful activity[24] and thus earned the disfavor of an increasing number of merchants. Moreover, the Renaissance revival of learning weakened the hold of medieval theology on men's minds [25] and they were amenable to the ideas of the Reformation.

Despite Protestant claims that they were merely restoring Christianity to its pure apostolic state, rescuing it from the corruption of the Roman Church, novel matrimonial practices began to develop in the sixteenth century. Martin Luther, the first reformer, condemned the Roman Church's scandalous abuse of power, which permitted, for example, the rich and powerful to obtain divorces for frivolous reasons, while the poor and powerless were forced to circumvent the law.[26] Luther also attacked the lustful lives of monks and priests who lived in open sacrilege with their concubines without interference from higher Church officials. The reformers looked upon their own movement as a moral alternative to the hypocritical Church.

The break with Roman doctrine was initiated by people whose quarrel with Catholicism was, in part, due to matrimonial issues. Luther considered that the Roman prohibition of divorce forced unhappy partners into illicit sexual arrangements. Luther found in sex an ideal weapon in his war against the Roman Church.[27] He sanctioned the marriage of priests and advanced the view that marriage was not an unbreakable contract dominated by religious concepts but was an institution ordained in heaven and yet subject to the civil authorities of city and state governments.[28] Furthermore, the reformers devalued celibacy, praised marriage without qualification and viewed marital sex as wholesome. They considered marriage a necessary antidote to promiscuity, but also as a higher good than mere celibacy. Luther himself envisioned wives as affectionate companions, although John Calvin later stressed the repression of sensuous enjoyments in marriage. The average Protestant, a practical and businesslike person, preferred Old Testament patriarchism to romanticized notions of love and marriage.[29] With the rise of capitalism, a rigid anti-pleasure ethic developed; the reformers were obsessed with making people good and righteous.

Despite claims to have broken with the Roman Catholic Church,

Protestant reformers retained many of the medieval practices and doctrines concerning divorce. Jesus' teachings as set forth in the Gospel of St. Matthew provided the basis for both Catholic and Protestant pronouncements. While Catholics interpreted the Scriptures as forbidding divorce, the reformers interpreted them as permitting individuals to divorce on the grounds of adultery and desertion.[30] However, only the innocent party to a divorce action could remarry. Since divorce was based on marital fault, one party was deemed guilty and was forbidden the privilege to remarry, while the other spouse was considered innocent and was permitted to remarry.

The Protestant notion of patriarchy was as severe as was the Roman Catholic concept. Women in Protestant lands remained subordinate to their husbands and were expected to tolerate marital abuse without redress.[31] The woman's legal position was summed up: "husband and wife are one, and the husband is the one." [32] The identity of a wife was submerged in that of her husband. At the same time, Protestant wives, unlike early Christian and medieval wives, "were not subordinated because of their vileness and frailties, but because of their adaptation to child-rearing and home-making." [33]

An increase in respect for women did not necessarily affect their position in matters of divorce. Since women were regarded as their husband's property, desertion or adultery was considered an offense against the husband.[34] *Legally*, Protestant women were no better off than were women in Catholic jurisdictions.

While the Reformation was intentionally a movement in the direction of greater religiosity, the Protestants obliquely contributed to the secularization of marriage and divorce. Capitalism and the Protestant ethic contributed to the liberalization of matrimonial law and divorce provisions. By emphasizing the authority of the family and the state in matters of marriage and divorce, civil control eventually increased as secularization took place. With the acceptance of Luther's teaching that marriage was not a sacrament, the power and authority of ecclesiastical courts diminished.

In the early years of the Reformation, Luther and his followers advocated self-divorce; when an adequate cause (adultery or desertion) existed, a marriage was automatically dissolved without any intervention by magistrates.[35] In some German lands at the time, the only purpose judicial action served was the determination that a marriage was actually dissolved, so that a remarriage could proceed.[36] Even this rather minor intervention planted the seeds for later public jurisdiction in divorce cases, and while practices were uncertain and informal for a while, eventually all cases were taken before various officials; these secular judges, in time, decided whether a divorce should be granted at all.

The reformers considered the Scriptures as the sole basis for divorce decisions and theologians were often called in by civil jurists to answer difficult religious questions. In this way the Church steadily gained greater control over divorce cases. Eventually the divorce doctrines of the Roman Church were revived by court officials in Protestant countries, who found a "ready-made machinery which they adapted to their own use."[37] Regardless of the increased religious orientation of the courts, divorce decisions were often more liberal than either the ordinances or the dogma of the Church.[38] By actually conceiving of divorce as a civil matter, the reformers had planted the seeds of secularization and increased liberalization of the divorce laws.

The fathers of English Protestantism were essentially more conservative than their colleagues across the Channel. King Henry VIII severed the ties between the English Church and Roman authority after the Pope refused to annul his marriage to Catherine of Aragon. In spite of this maneuver, Henry permitted Roman doctrine on divorce to remain in force in England. Because he disliked the idea that papal authority superseded his own power in certain areas he appointed a commission to compile a new body of matrimonial law. This commission recommended the adoption in England of what was rapidly becoming standard Protestant practice on the Continent — most importantly, permitting divorce on a variety of grounds. But even such moderate reforms were blocked as Parliament refused to adopt the commission's recommendations.

After Henry VIII, England's matrimonial practices exhibited a kind of Catholicism, without papal authority. Ecclesiastical courts under the Church of England continued to have authority over divorce, often granting divorces leniently on what were frequently rather casual grounds. Clergymen who retained their loyalty to the traditional medieval Catholic commitment to the indissolubility of marriage were angered by what they considered heretical departures from Scriptural teachings. After Elizabeth's reign these clerics successfully lobbied for the cessation of divorces for adultery or desertion. For many years after, all exits from marriage, except by death, were closed, for no divorces or annulments were recognized by the English ecclesiastical courts.

Not every Protestant thinker supported the practice of basing divorce actions on Scriptural teaching. During the Puritan revolution, John Milton published a forty-two-page pamphlet, "The Doctrine and Discipline of Divorce" (1643), that urged Parliament to authorize divorce on the ground of "contrariety of mind." While Milton's divorce tract is full of hatred for women, his views on marriage were rather idealistic and romantic. His own marriage to a woman much younger than himself was not a happy one, yet he believed in an affectionate basis for matrimony. Though Milton was chaste and puritanical he considered sexual activity between two loving partners as natural and healthful.[39] Milton considered loving companionship as the most important goal of marriage.[40] He recommended that where a deep-seated inability of a man and a woman to be happy together existed a divorce should be granted.[41] Milton's ideas were considered heretical by his contemporaries and Parliament completely ignored his recommendations. Later modifications of the English divorce law came nowhere near Milton's "radical" position.

English divorce law,[42] which had a strong impact on early American divorce customs, was essentially conservative. By and large, the anti-divorce doctrines of Roman Catholicism were adopted and then transplanted to America with the founding of the colonies in the seventeenth century. Americans thus inherited a divorce tradition that rested on the subordination of married women, a guilt-innocence approach to divorce and the state's interest in preserving marriages. The same oppressive religious forces at work in English matrimonial and divorce practice remained influential in the American colonies and persist into the present.

# 13
# Historical Perspective
# on American Divorce

[People] make their own history, but they do
not make it just as they please; they do not
make it under circumstances chosen by themselves, but under circumstances directly found,
given and transmitted from the past. The tradition of all the dead generations weighs like a
nightmare on the brain of the living.
—Karl Marx

The planting of colonies by what one historian calls
the "vexed and troubled" Englishmen of the seventeenth century
was in great measure a migration of families. With this movement
of population, beginning as a trickle and reaching thousands each
year by the era of the American Revolution, came the transplanta-
tion of traditional matrimonial practices. The overwhelmingly
Protestant, white colonists brought with them not only New
Testament hostility to divorce but also Old Testament patriarchal
values that supported stable family life.[1] But often the practices
and convictions brought from England were modified in America.
Puritan settlements in New England relaxed strict American prohi-

bitions on divorce, but in the southern colonies, legal restraints on marriage dissolution remained as severe as in Old England.[2]

Despite sectional variation, certain legal concepts relating to divorce were common to all the American colonies, especially the ancient distinction between *absolute divorce* and mere *separation from bed and board*. Absolute divorce, unavailable in the South, was granted in New England after one spouse was found guilty of adultery or some serious crime, and the innocent party was permitted to remarry.[3] In 1680 Elizabeth Stevens of Plymouth, Massachusetts, obtained a divorce from her husband when it was proved that he had three other wives, one each in Boston, Barbados and England. But a decade and a half earlier, another Plymouth wife won only separation from her husband, who had persisted in a long series of "abusive and harsh carriages" toward her and had even declared "his insufficiency for sexual converse with women." She was not permitted to remarry.[4] A third legal alternative was annulment, more common in the southern colonies, where absolute divorce could not be obtained. An annulled marriage was legally void and either party could remarry. Discovery of "blood" relation between spouses or of impotence provided the usual grounds for annulment.[5]

Religious ideas played a major role in shaping the tradition of early American divorce, even when applied by secular officials in civil courts. The canon law concept of matrimonial "fault" threw a quasi-criminal aura over divorce and separation. Two main effects were fairly obvious. Since "guilt" and "fault" would be determined by legal proceedings, partners to divorce actions faced each other as courtroom adversaries, with harmful consequences that will be detailed in subsequent chapters. Also, since wives and mothers were considered to bear major responsibility for family stability, women bore the brunt of whatever guilt was associated with divorce.[6]

These anti-divorce attitudes, going back at least to New Testament doctrines, were moderated somewhat by the early American environment. Frequent death of women in childbirth, especially in isolated frontier communities, contributed to the tolerance, and even approbation, for remarriage of the surviving spouses. Some of this attitude carried over to divorce, contributing to the relative American liberalism on this matter. The looseness of a wilderness society, in which men often escaped marriage by desertion and flight to the west, reinforced this tendency. It was also possible for the runaway spouses to get divorces in their new domiciles.[7]

But there were strict limitations to the liberalization of divorce in early America. The subordinate status of women continued, despite struggles of feminists.[8] Such subordination usually locked women (who could not as easily flee out west) into marriage. Conservative practices were strengthened as courts even before the Civil War began to take over divorce jurisdiction from the more liberal state and territorial legislatures. Even though divorce came to be granted in some southern states during the same period, the South generally lagged behind the rest of the nation in this as well as other liberal reforms.[9] New York State too remained a bastion of anti-divorce tradition under a law drafted in 1787 by Assemblyman Alexander Hamilton. Permitting adultery as almost the sole ground for divorce, this law made New York notorious for fraudulent legal procedures, where courts came routinely to accept perjured testimony to issue divorce decrees.[10] In addition, conservative polemicists, especially from Connecticut, where divorce was relatively easy to obtain,[11] kept up a drumfire of propaganda. For example, Yale President Benjamin Trumbull fulminated in 1785: "If matters are suffered to run on in their present channel shall we soon become like the nations of the world before the giving of the law when marriage were only for moons or years as suited the party? Or will it not be as it were in Rome after divorce grew into fashion that married people will separate at pleasure?" The implication was that easy divorce would represent either a lapse back into savage barbarism or Roman decadence.[12] Without any extensive historical argument, an early-nineteenth-century successor of Trumbull's, Timothy Dwight, roundly condemned liberalization of divorce in 1818. "It is incomparably better," Dwight announced, "that individuals should suffer, than that an institution [marriage], which is the basis of all human good, should be shaken or endangered." [13] (We have seen that such sentiments are still current in the mid-twentieth century.) These anti-divorce propagandists, unable to halt the rising divorce rate, nevertheless won a partial victory. Allying themselves with hallowed religious doctrine, they managed to associate divorce with sin and scandal, bequeathing to later generations of Americans the legacy of guilt and shame that this book in a small way attempts to reverse.

The nineteenth-century struggle between conservative anti-divorce forces and their liberal opponents thus resulted in a kind of stalemate. Divorce was increasingly permitted, and in some places even encouraged. But dire predictions about the impending collapse of both the family and civilization generally were not fulfilled. In fact, the rising divorce rate turned out to be perfectly compatible with, and even necessary to, the development of the standard nuclear family system. Historians Christopher Lasch and William O'Neill have clarified this connection.

> When families are large and loose, arouse few expecta-tions, and make few demands, there is no need for divorce [they argue]. But when families become the center of social organization, their intimacy can be suffocating, their demands unbearable, and their expectations too high to be easily realizable. Divorce then becomes the safety-valve that makes the system workable. Those who are frustrated or oppressed can escape their families, and those who fail at what is regarded as the most important human activity can gain a second chance. Divorce is not, therefore, an anomaly or a flaw in the system, but an essential feature of it. When the modern family came to dominate society in the nineteenth century, divorce became common.[14]

It is only necessary to add that tradition-spawned guilt helped to keep divorce from getting out of hand and was thus also necessary to the "system" that Lasch and O'Neill describe.

The growing public acceptance of divorce was therefore not based upon the belief that divorce itself was good; rather, advocates of easier severance of marriage ties could justify their cause as a means of preserving the sanctity of marriage. Henry James, Sr., father of the novelist and of the philosopher-psychologist, gave classic, if stilted, expression to this liberal viewpoint in a letter to the New York *Tribune* in 1852. Defending himself against charges that he was hostile to the institution of marriage, James contended that he had "invariably aimed to advance the honor of marriage by seeking to free it from certain obstructions in reference to divorce." [15] By the mid-nineteenth century many, although by no means all, Americans agreed.

The opinions of feminists constitute an interesting variation on general attitudes toward marriage and divorce. Some favored freer divorce, going even farther than Henry James. The radical feminist Elizabeth Cady Stanton wrote in her newspaper *The Revolution* in 1868: "The widest possible reform we could have on this whole [divorce] question is to have no legislation whatever. The relations of the sexes are too delicate in their nature for statutes, lawyers, judges, jurors, or our public journals to take cognizance of, or to regulate." [16] But few feminists were ready to endorse such a radical conception of free relationships between men and women, unencumbered by state intervention. Most took a more conservative position, including Lucy Stone and Julia Ward Howe. They believed that easy divorce only made women more vulnerable to cruel and harsh treatment and they welcomed the protective cloak of the law. But the advocacy of radical ideas by some feminists drove ultraconservatives to equate any divorce liberalization with the supposed horrors of "free love." [17] A remnant of this viewpoint survives in the legend of the "gay divorcee," a woman who just because of her divorce is automatically considered promiscuous.

This fear of "free love," along with the development of "Puritanical" ideas in the late-nineteenth century, brought about a veritable legal counterrevolution on the divorce question. Liberal legislation enacted early in the century was repealed, legislative divorce became unavailable as courts and judges took over this jurisdiction,[18] and judicial decisions were alarmingly conservative. America's elite became more and more concerned about the rising divorce rate. Echoing his New Haven predecessors, Theodore Dwight Woolsey (yet another Yale president) launched an ultimately successful attack on Connecticut's easy divorce laws. Divorce, thundered Woolsey in 1867, was a sure sign of corruption: "Whether we are to be a thoroughly Christian nation, or to decay and lose our present political forms, depends upon our ability to keep family life pure and simple." [19] Such sentiments would soon issue from the "bully pulpit" Theodore Roosevelt thought the presidency to be. Roosevelt roundly denounced "dangerously lax" divorce laws as heralds of a more general social decay, saying: "When home ties are loosened, when men and women cease to regard a worthy family life, with all its duties fully performed, and all its responsibilities lived up to, as the life best worth living then evil days for the commonwealth are at hand." [20]

These conservative spokesmen were particularly incensed that certain states and localities, especially Nevada and the city of Reno, where marriages could be easily terminated, operated as virtual divorce colonies. Under the federal Constitution (Article IV, Section 1) states were required to give "full faith and credit" to the proceedings, including divorce decrees, of other states. Conservative efforts to weaken the "full faith and credit" clause brought about what one Supreme Court justice called "a tortuous course of constitutional adjudication relating to dissolution of the marriage status." [21] But despite these efforts to stem the tide, the divorce rate rose fairly steadily (see graph p. 174). People were willing to travel to distant places and even to resort to fraud, collusion and perjury to circumvent toughened divorce laws.

Not only people but statistics proved the conservative antidivorce advocates wrong. Strict statutes were not effective barriers to spouses determined to break out of confining marital bonds.[22] Nor did the rising divorce rate contribute to any decline in marriage. On the contrary, as Hugh Carter and Paul Glick conclude in their 1970 study, *Marriage and Divorce*, "for every unit of increase since 1940 in the proportion of divorce among adults in the United States, there have been five units of increase in the proportion married." [23] Rather than falling off because of more frequent

DIVORCE RATE PER 1,000 MARRIAGES IN THE UNITED STATES *
BETWEEN 1860 AND 1963 BY FIVE-YEAR INTERVALS

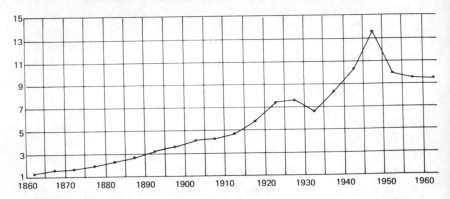

SOURCE: Computed from annual rates, by permission of the author, from Paul H. Jacobson, *American Marriage and Divorce* (New York: Rinehart, 1959), p. 90, Table 42; and Alexander A. Plateris, *Divorce Statistics Analysis (United States—1963)*, Department of Health, Education, and Welfare, Vital and Health Statistics, Series 21, No. 13 (1967).

divorce, marriage has actually increased! The most recent data reinforce the conclusion that divorce enhances marriage by providing a way out of some of the worst forms of connubial misery. But if the divorce rate continues to climb, and alternatives to traditional marriage become prevalent, the present legal labyrinth of divorce may prove to be a serious obstacle to the creation of new social institutions.

* From Bert N. Adams, *The American Family: A Sociological Interpretation* (Chicago: Markham Publishing Co., 1971), p. 333 (by permission).

# part five

# 14
# Prejudice Enshrined in Law

> By elevating fault to the level of legitimate
> consideration in making alimony and property
> awards, injury in divorce is compensated and
> fault in destroying a family unit, which the
> state is interested in preserving, is penalized.
> —Joseph Winslow Baer and Muller Davis,
> in the *Illinois Bar Journal*, June, 1972

> There is very little difficulty in framing laws as
> regards divorce, because whatever the laws
> may be, judges and juries will be governed by
> their passions, while husbands and wives will
> do whatever may be necessary to circumvent
> the intentions of the legislators.
> —Bertrand Russell

For most people, the law is the final, awesome source of authority. It defines right and wrong behavior, distinguishes social from anti-social acts, and shapes public attitudes on questions of justice and morality. Its hovering presence has a powerful impact on the way people judge themselves and one another. When the law itself, by irrationality, inconsistency and undue severity, implies that divorce is a dishonorable act, it not only casts a long shadow over unhappy families but also strengthens the anti-divorce tradition. In divorce matters, harsh laws condition the public to believe that divorced people deserve no compassion. "The law of divorce," wrote one judge, "seems to be less civilized than the criminal law." [1]

American courts have been hesitant in granting divorce because the marriage relationship involves more than strictly legal considerations. The sole exception to this policy has arisen when one partner commits some flagrant marital offense which puts an unreasonable burden on the other partner. As a result, the *adversary process* became an integral part of divorce litigation.[2] Such proceedings fall into the legal category called *tort*, which refers to a civil wrong that the law compensates by awarding "damages" to the innocent party. Although the divorce laws were once overtly brutal and savage in almost all states, in some areas they are now milder and more benign; it is possible for many couples to make the transition from marriage to freedom with a minimum of legal subterfuge. But even the most liberal laws retain a lethal dose of hostility, powerful enough to poison the lives of couples who are poor, ignorant, or unable to agree to separation.

The "no-fault" divorce law, now operative in twelve states, was designed to facilitate divorce without the traumatic burden of legal guilt. This statute permits husband and wife to plead that "irreconcilable differences" have caused the "irremediable breakdown of the marriage." *With the mutual consent of each partner*, a judge may grant a divorce without considering the "guilt" or "innocence" of either party. Unquestionably, the no-fault concept is a substantial improvement over the traditional adversary system, still in effect in several states, but in our opinion it is *not* "the key to divorce reform"[3] because it has not solved the basic question of whether divorce is an individual "right."

In most states, couples who mutually agree to divorce can do so fairly easily, especially if they have money. At the moment, for example, wealthy people go to Haiti or the Dominican Republic for "quickie" divorces. Or one partner can still establish "residence" in one of the "easy states," such as Nevada, and obtain what is called a "migratory divorce." It costs by a conservative estimate at least a thousand dollars to buy such a divorce. Nevertheless, migratory divorce is a popular method, satisfactory for affluent people who can neatly circumvent the unwieldy, time-consuming and repressive laws of individual states by temporarily changing their residence. The legal power behind the migratory divorce is the aforementioned Article IV of the Constitution, which says that "full faith and credit shall be given in each State to the public acts, records, and judicial proceedings of every other State."

In uncontested cases, where both spouses agree to divorce but haven't much money, there is a more modest variety of slower but still reliable techniques for obtaining a divorce. In New York, for example, each partner retains a lawyer and eventually husband and wife agree to a legal separation, which verifies that they are living apart and specifies the details of child-custody and financial support. The lawyer files the agreement with the County Clerk and a year later the couple can be granted a divorce. In many states, however, the mere fact of physical separation for a year is not sufficient ground for divorce.

In those states that still require specific evidence of "fault," couples and their lawyers can engage cooperatively in collusion and fraud. A "collusive divorce" is a divorce obtained by mutual consent but dressed up to look like a divorce for "cause." In other words, the partners are told how to go about staging the kind of domestic drama that can be used as evidence in court. Usually only one party appears in court for a procedure that may take only five minutes. Since the facts can be changed, stretched and invented, the law silently condones perjury.[4] The need to conjure up admissible evidence encourages husband, wife, and lawyer to feel personally degraded and hostile to the law. In most divorces both husband and wife eventually consent,[5] although the official law of every state still frowns on the frivolity of a mere request for divorce when it is not based on *some* "ground." Even the no-fault law demands an explanation of why the couple wants to divorce. Tragically, some of our state laws are so destructive that even when the man and wife are *willing* to end the marriage gracefully and quietly, the law perversely sets them against each other.

In those cases where divorce is a *contested* issue, that is, when one spouse wants a divorce but the other refuses to grant it, the brutal obsolescence of the law becomes apparent. For people who cannot finance a collusive or migratory divorce, the vision of a humane and therapeutic divorce court is still an unrealized dream. In a large number of cases the law transforms divorce into an emotional massacre, while the courts and their judges tenaciously cling to power, exercising tight and sometimes arbitrary control over who may and who may not divorce.

Every time a judge grants a divorce begrudgingly, or refuses to grant one, we are reminded sharply that the state is the third party to every marriage contract. Most states maintain a steadfast interest in holding partners to their obligations; therefore marriage goes beyond the bounds of a mere civil contract.[6] It is the only form of contract requiring personal services which may be specifically ordered by the court to be upheld.[7]

Sometimes the attitude of the judge, who has broad, discretionary power in divorce, coincides with the state's aims and a couple will find no legal way out of marriage. Recently, Diana DuBroff, a New York lawyer, cited the decision of a New York judge who refused to disturb the "status quo" and denied a woman a divorce although she had demonstrated that violence and cruelty had existed in her marriage for thirty years. The judge concluded that the wife's health and life were not actually in danger because she had obviously learned to cope with the antics of her brutal alcoholic husband.[8]

In addition to demonstrating an instance of judicial insensitivity, this case shows how the court can arbitrarily tighten the Gordian knot of an unhappy union. Judges themselves have admitted that the court purposely places obstacles in couples' paths to dissuade them from separation.[9] Consequently, lawyers who simply want to facilitate divorce without becoming embroiled in warfare characteristically scout around for "easy judges" who have "good" reputations because they ask and probe little. Some lawyers count on the fact that judges are often so bored or overworked that they simply want to speed up the process and get the day's work over with.[10]

Other judges, like Paul Alexander, of Toledo, Ohio, may carry a burden of personal guilt for the couples they have divorced. He once described himself as a "faintly glorified public mortician" who had buried more than thirty thousand marriages. In retrospect, he worried about having interred "many a live corpse." [11] Almost as a symbolic penance for what he evidently perceived as *his personal errors*, Alexander helped institute a family court system in Toledo in which a team of experts studied each case to determine whether the marriage was viable. "The final decree would be issued," wrote Alexander, "only if the investigation . . . compelled the conclusion that the marriage could no longer be useful to the spouses, the children, or the state." [12] Although he never explained what criteria were to be used to determine what makes a marriage useful, it is clear that marriage stability, at least in form, is inherently good in the states' eyes. Although Alexander talked a lot about a "therapeutic approach to divorce," he argued that a way had to be found to stop divorces that *should not be granted*. He at least conceded that if a divorce were to be granted, it should be done without public trial. [13]

While the law cannot physically compel people to live together, it can effectively prevent them from divorcing, delay their divorces indefinitely, make remarriage difficult, or discourage partners from parting when they are unhappy together. [14] Under the liberal guise of "conciliation," the courts can harass man and wife. For example, the state of Wisconsin requires compulsory appearance before a judge or counselor to explore reconciliation, and the court can decide to grant only a legal separation, even when an absolute divorce is requested *and* grounds have been established. [15]

A woman who is unhappy can always decide to pack up her children and leave. But what if she has no place to go and no way to earn a living and her husband does not consent to her departure? If she is guilty of abandonment, whether or not she has been abused and neglected, she can be denied financial support from her husband. The courts can refuse to grant her a divorce, and unless she becomes a public charge, her husband may never be required to provide her any financial support at all. Even if she is "guilty," however, the husband is required to provide for the children. When one partner refuses to leave the house, the economically dependent spouse may physically be trapped. It is much easier for the man, who is customarily the main wage earner, to leave the marriage and offer to pay for his liberty. But if a woman desires divorce, she usually has nothing to offer and therefore has less leverage in demanding her legal freedom. A friend of ours (living in New York), who had been separated from his wife for a year, was frustrated by the fact that she refused to grant him a divorce. He had been supporting her and their children handsomely on a voluntary basis. He finally had to rely on the one speedy and effective weapon at his disposal: money. He withheld the usual amount until she agreed to a legal separation and divorce, and they both knew that if she took him to court, she would be awarded less money than he was giving her voluntarily each month. She then "agreed" to give him a divorce, which he obtained in Mexico a few weeks later.[16]

Repressive divorce laws give married people extraordinary power to coerce and blackmail each other and to act beastly in ways they would probably never even dream of if such behavior were not fostered by "the system." One patient of ours, a woman in her forties, was horrified to discover that there were detectives spying on her every morning at eight as she left her apartment. This woman, who has two teen-age daughters, has been dating one man steadily for ten years and has been legally separated for fifteen years. Her lover occasionally stays in her apartment overnight. One day her husband decided that he wanted a divorce and he preferred not to pay her support as he had been doing in the past. If he could convince the court that she was an adulteress, he would be in a better "bargaining position" when the time came for a financial settlement. In New York State, this woman could be denied alimony on the ground of adultery, and it does not matter whether she is caught once or a hundred times; nor would it matter if her husband has had dozens of affairs during the last decade. Our warped legal system is saying to this woman: "Too bad. You may be a hard-working and successful mother, and have raised two fine children, but if it looks as though you are having sexual relations with a man who is not your legal husband, you do not deserve support, and you are a branded woman in the eyes of the law."

In another situation, a friend of ours, recently separated from her husband, was "warned" by her lawyer to "play it cool" in her new romance. She was advised that she would jeopardize her privilege of custody if her lover stayed in her new home in the presence of the children. For the next year, until her divorce decree becomes final in New York, her freedom to live a spontaneous and private social life will be severely curtailed because the law can interpret her affair as evidence that she is an unfit mother, even if the children know and like the man and are being well cared for. The law sanctions the accumulation of evidence that one partner is "morally" unfit to rear children, yet it simultaneously denies people the opportunity to divorce quickly so that they can remarry if they want to. Its stance on adultery is particularly hypocritical, since thousands of Americans are technically "living in sin," with and without children, and the law does not routinely try or convict them. Adultery is a weapon held over the head of divorcing couples and is a powerful tool in the hands of a vindictive spouse.

As adversaries in divorce proceedings, plaintiff and defendant accuse and sue each other back and forth, effectively making divorce complicated, costly and ugly. The spirit of each partner can be broken thoroughly before there is even a divorce decree, since husband and wife try to amass evidence of each other's lying, immoral, or vicious conduct. Couples in conflict are at the mercy of their lawyers and the judges who happen to hear their case. One divorce lawyer recently remarked that even our domestic relations judges presume their clients are hopeless liars, therefore "an awful lot depends upon whether the judge is an artist or a hack." [17]

This observation is repeatedly borne out by our contact with divorced families. We have talked and worked with many intelligent divorced people whose tales of woe confirm our thesis that the emotional traumas commonly associated with divorce and post-divorce life are largely *created by* the judicial system. In one fascinating, grotesque situation, a man, whom we shall call Larry, went through the following experience. He had been separated from his wife, by mutual consent, for more than a year. After a decade of marriage, they agreed to separate and arrived at a financial settlement with the help of their accountant. Larry soon met another woman and the new relationship became serious. His wife, upset by this new turn of events, expressed her own unresolved conflicts by accusing him of mental cruelty and desertion of the family. He was then faced with the onerous task of proving that they had separated amicably and that he was innocent of her charges. In the preliminary papers to the court for the purpose of establishing interim alimony, he succeeded in convincing the court that he had not unilaterally abandoned his wife and children. Although, or perhaps *because*, he was found "innocent," her rage intensified. She hired a gunman and a photographer and arranged to raid a vacation cottage in which Larry and the other woman were spending a night. If his wife could prove he was "living in sin," she could exploit his "guilt" to her financial advantage in the final divorce decree, and could jeopardize, or at least tightly control, his visiting privileges with their children. She wanted him to pay exorbitantly for the legal freedom to remarry. At this point he had already borrowed three thousand dollars in cash to retain a lawyer who was skilled enough to help him defend himself against her onslaught. Using "proof" of his adultery as leverage, his wife persisted in her refusal to grant him a divorce unless he paid her off. Larry never did succeed in New York in legally detaching himself from this manipulative and vengeful woman. Ultimately, following the clever and devious scheme outlined by legal strategist Louis Nizer,[18] Larry went to Mexico, paid for a unilateral divorce, took that decree to a state which accepted it as valid, and remarried there. In New York he was technically a bigamist, because he still had a wife in that state. However, courts prosecute in these matters only upon complaint of some aggrieved party. The only person who would want to prosecute Larry for bigamy would be his first wife. If she went to the New York district attorney, she would get little satisfaction because the bigamous marriage was contracted in another state, out of the jurisdiction of the New York courts. Since the state in which Larry remarried recognized the Mexican decree as valid, his ex-wife would have no success in suing him there for bigamy.

While Larry and his new wife were living happily together vaguely within the confines of the murky law, his first wife became more fiercely determined than ever to exert control and power. Using the law as an accomplice in her vindictive struggle, she embarked on yet another scheme. She appealed to the New York State Supreme Court for an increase in payments, arguing that Larry was lying on his income tax statements and was earning twenty thousand dollars a year more than he was declaring. He, the "defendant," maintained that his stated income was his real income and that the monthly payments he had been making were the largest he could reasonably afford. So the judge had to decide on a "just" course of action. What evidently happened was that the judge said to himself, "They are both lying. I will presume his income to be precisely in between what each of them claims, and therefore I will set a new monthly allowance based on a compromise figure." A new settlement was imposed on Larry, considerably higher than what he had been paying. But he could not afford the new payments because he really was not earning the alleged twenty thousand extra. It just happened that the judge didn't believe him. Larry could have borrowed money to comply with the new order or he could simply have continued to pay the previous sum. Since he could not start a new life if he gave so vast a portion of his earnings to his ex-wife, he decided to pay only what he could afford. (During an interim appeal to the New York State Supreme Court he was able to get a partial reduction, but he still felt the amount requested of him was an unreasonable percentage of his income.) His ex-wife, a professional woman who was earning at least fifteen thousand dollars a year on her own, then sued him for contempt of court, since he was defying a court order.

Larry again had to make a choice. He could leave New York and be pretty certain that no extradition proceedings would be carried out against him.[19] However, he didn't want to forfeit his right to see his children. His alternatives were to make up all the accumulated arrears and follow the court ruling or to fight for what he believed to be a just settlement based on the needs of each family. He fought for what he believed was right, was convicted of contempt of court and spent six months in civil jail. At no time did he comply with the order of the disillusioned, cynical judge who mistakenly presumed that he was a perjurer and a thief. Larry's ex-wife, perhaps weary, and probably stunned by his fortitude, ultimately accepted the amount he had originally agreed to pay. He is still paying, and is now living happily with his second wife and their new children; he has also managed to maintain a good relationship with his children by the previous marriage. Larry's story is a frightening testament to the judicial hostility that can legitimately be unleashed on unhappy couples, and to the outrageous behavior that is sanctioned by law.

Many lawyers have tried to caution people that the average judge is not sitting on the bench conducting a search for truth. Judges are civil servants, political appointees, full participants in the moral ambiguities of American society, and they too have been indoctrinated in the anti-divorce tradition. We can only imagine how many men and women passively surrender to unfair settlements because they fear, with good reason, the judge's power to make matters worse. Things have changed very little in American family law during the forty years since Isabel Drummond wrote that the power exercised by judges in the United States in matters of divorce parallels that of emperors, popes and ecclesiastics.[20]

The discretionary power of judges, in coordination with the adversary system, not only curtails personal freedom but shapes the outlook of the entire community. It is no wonder that most people attempting to arrange divorce become cagey, suspicious and hostile to each other, and that they come to regard the law as their enemy. It is natural for people to suffer when they are subjected to investigation, prying and blackmail. Divorce will continue to be degrading, expensive and humiliating as long as the law converts one of the most important decisions of a lifetime into a grotesque masked ball attended by sadists, adulterers and thieves.

In light of the pain and injustice that it inflicts on people, the American compromise of strict divorce laws coupled with endless practical schemes for circumventing them is an entirely unsatisfactory approach to the reality of divorce. The agreement of spouses, lawyers and judges to disregard the intent of the law (which is to prevent divorce) gives preferential treatment to the wealthy, the clever and the hardhearted; simultaneously, it encourages angry and neurotic adults to torture each other. It makes families excessively dependent on the chance laws of a given state, and it has a confusing and demoralizing effect on the legal profession, as we shall soon show.

# 15
# Modern Efforts
# to Resist Change

Reform is in order for our divorce procedure;
reform not simply for the sake of reform, but
reform to protect the institution of the family.
—Lee Hawke

Man does not always need bars for cages.
Ideas can be cages too. Doors are being
opened in mental hospitals as chemical restraints become more effective. The doors in
our minds are the most difficult to open.
—Ronald Laing

The lack of uniformity among the states in American divorce law magnifies the difficulty people experience when they wish to end marriage. Since the laws vary so much from state to state, some people have relatively quick, painless, equitable divorces. A friend of ours, recently divorced in California, received a call from his ex-wife who said to him: "You know, we had a really lousy marriage, but at least we had a great divorce!" It cost them $37.50 and they did it by mail. On the other hand, there are many couples who argue and suffer for years and never reach an equitable settlement or even get a legal divorce. In some states, women automatically get a share of all the family property. (There are five such community property states: Iowa, Florida, Colorado, Oregon and California.) In others, such as New York, family assets are not automatically divided. When divorce is contingent upon a mutually agreeable property settlement, hostile spouses can hold out against each other indefinitely. This kind of interstate diversity encourages fraud and migratory divorce, which in turn create a shady "underground" divorce system. The frantic tactics of desperate couples who try to circumvent locally restrictive statutes reinforce the popular belief that divorce is a sinister, dirty and unhealthy business.

Therefore we feel that it is necessary to create new and more uniform state laws, although we recognize that state differences rest on a historical basis. At the time of the framing of the Constitution, the individual states were unwilling to let the federal government encroach upon family or other matters deemed appropriate for local jurisdiction. This prohibition on the federal government was written into the Bill of Rights, in the Tenth Amendment to the United States Constitution, which effectively prohibits Congress from enacting uniform federal divorce laws. However, action by the federal government is not the only way to bring uniformity and sanity to the chaos of present-day divorce law. (See Chapter 17.)

Although it is easy to visualize divorce as a nonpunitive, inexpensive,[1] fairly simple process, there is massive resistance to legal changes which some people fear would threaten or undermine the institutions of marriage and family. More than a century ago, when conservatives began to worry about the breakdown of family stability, they advocated a harsh legal system as a means of preventing divorce. In the nineteenth century, many people argued in favor of uniform national divorce legislation, which they hoped would be strict enough to protect family life and put an end to the abuses associated with the "divorce racket" in easy states like Nevada.

The traditional anti-divorce position has been enunciated most recently by Max Rheinstein, emeritus professor of law at the University of Chicago. He argues that young people should learn to endure and to preserve their marriages and prepare themselves adequately for the "fateful decision" to marry. He specifically suggests that the schools make a positive contribution to the perpetuation of marriage and family life, since contemporary parents seem unable to handle that task. Since it was Rheinstein himself who demonstrated that nowhere in the world have harsh divorce laws prevented or even reduced the incidence of marital breakdown,[2] it was inevitable that he should turn to education and counseling as the only other possible antidotes to divorce.

Liberal reformers have simply tried to substitute sophisticated psychological schemes for simplistic legal ones. Legislators and social scientists have not generally disagreed on basic value commitments but merely on the best way to achieve the common aim. It is only the radical critic of society who would dare to question the anti-divorce tradition and argue that divorce should be a constitutionally guaranteed personal right. The kind of liberal legislation that is now gaining in popularity is mainly a reaction to the failure of harsh legislation to "stem the tide of divorce." The use of new as well as traditional forms of social control to keep partners in marriage shows that the anti-divorce tradition is still potent. Even under liberal auspices, American governments are as dedicated as in earlier conservative epochs to the prevention of divorce. In recent years, the law has reaffirmed its commitment to holding families together. Lawyers are still protesting that we should not allow the nuclear unit to be easily dissolved.[3] One of the major reasons why contemporary federal and state legislatures are hostile to divorce is that these governments want to insulate themselves against the economic claims of divorced people. The women and children of divorce often become public burdens, to the distress of taxpayers and voters. Swelling welfare rolls are augmented daily by middle- and lower-class mothers who have custody of dependent children. At least 42 per cent of all Aid to Dependent Children (ADC) payments are made to children from divorced homes.[4] Separated families are "the nut of the welfare problem." In about 12 to 15 per cent of the ADC cases, absent fathers make support payments, but these rarely amount to more than $100 a month for entire families. The public outrage against deserting fathers effectively obscures the fact that even if these fathers lived at home, and worked, they would usually be so outrageously underpaid that their families would still need supplementary assistance. Even among the middle classes, when divorced men reliably pay as much as they can, the amount is usually not enough to support the mother and children on a minimal basis.[5] It is therefore in the states' interest to dissuade families from splitting up. Of course divorce would not be nearly as financially costly as it often is today if the government took responsibility for meeting more of the basic needs of families. For example, legal fees, medical bills and education expenses place an extreme burden on lower- and middle-class families in divorce.

Another possible factor that motivates legislators to suppress divorce is that our capitalist system depends heavily upon the traditions of marriage, nuclear family life and the sexual division of labor. In most middle-class American families, men work outside their homes all day for salaries which are supposed to support their families; women work inside the home, without payment for their labor, and are not *obligated* to support themselves and their children. Since capitalism thrives on the exploitation of workers, those who own and monopolize the means of production recognize greater profits by keeping wages as low as possible, while simultaneously encouraging families to consume a great deal. While women are urged to stay at home and "buy" things, men are forced to work even harder to meet the demands of their families. Even if a worker is a white male, his wages alone may not be enough to support a family in the governmentally defined "modest" manner. Women are now forced, in increasing numbers, to take on at least part-time employment, but because they earn so much less than their male counterparts, they contribute even more than men to the profit of the few. The definition of women as primarily child raisers and homemakers rather than skilled laborers or educated professionals is used to perpetuate this reserve of cheap labor.[6]

These oppressive distinctions threaten to break down after

divorce, and in fact often do. Women begin to compete with men for full-time jobs and men are devastated by the burden of trying to support two households. The law, the capitalist economy and the American family tradition conspire to deny women equal pay for equal work, access to the most lucrative jobs and the freedom to relinquish custody after divorce. Both in marriage and in divorce, the law helps perpetuate their dependence on men and their inferior social status.

Even while divorces are being granted more liberally, the state is still energetically pushing marriage and discouraging divorce. It has managed to by-pass the needs and the interests of divorced families by conspicuously failing to find an effective means of enforcing and insuring support payments for women and children. It has been quite resourceful, on the other hand, in facilitating marriage and perpetuating the myth that nuclear family life is the most noble and proper life-style. Marriage is accompanied by a bare minimum of governmental intervention and is made attractive by economic benefits, such as joint income tax privileges and inheritance and property benefits. The state also declares as "illegitimate" those children who are born out of wedlock. This negative incentive to marriage is a vast and significant legal force. Furthermore, couples who desire to marry do not routinely have to justify their behavior, prove their innocence, or explain their motives. Mutual consent is good enough as long as they are legally of age.

We raise the above issue because proposals for tighter regulation of marriage are part of the contemporary movement for divorce prevention. Many legislators, social scientists and lawyers pin the blame for the divorce upsurge on our loosely structured marriage licensing laws. Hasty, ill-advised alliances, they argue, can be prevented by rigid regulations and stricter marriage laws aimed at inhibiting marriages between young people.[7] Two lawyers who head an Albany, New York, firm specializing in divorce cases recently called for a three-month minimum waiting period between obtaining a marriage license and getting married. They also favor sixteen hours of *mandatory* premarital counseling during the waiting period. In their view, all states should adopt this "enlightened legislation." [8] Julia Perles, an often-quoted attorney, suggests that premarital counseling be required beforehand just as a blood test is required.[9] In his book on sex and marriage, author Havelock Ellis called for questionnaires and prior investigation of "intimate attitudes" in order to single out people who are "unmarriageable." [10]

It seems that the state of California has been particularly worried about the high rate of marital failure. The California legislature passed a law, effective November 23, 1970, now known as California Civil Code 4101, which is the *first* of its kind in the nation. It empowers the superior courts in California to require premarital counseling for any couple applying for a marriage license if either party is under eighteen and the court deems such counseling necessary. In Los Angeles the court has made such counseling a mandatory requirement. All minors have to meet with a Conciliation Court counselor for a final evaluation interview; the counselor then makes a recommendation to the judge regarding the couples' "readiness for marriage." [11] In our view, this proposal, which is winning support among growing numbers of influential people, is just another attempt to legislate divorce away.

Such a scheme is objectionable on many grounds. It suppresses personal freedom and encourages punitive state intrusion into the private lives of citizens who have not done anything anti-social or criminal. It is based on a naïve assumption that some fixed and arbitrary period of mandatory counseling with young adults will be an effective antidote to the strains and pressures that accumulate after marriage. It neglects the important fact that the divorce rate has doubled since 1960 not among newlyweds but among couples who have been married fifteen to nineteen years.[12] Furthermore, harsh legislation, instead of deterring a determined couple from getting married, will encourage them to find ways of circumventing these requirements in a manner similar to the extralegal tactics of couples who seek divorce. It is basically irrational for the government to try to discourage divorce by discouraging "potentially bad" marriages since it is that very same government that simultaneously makes marriage financially attractive and uses marriage to legitimize sexual intimacy and parenthood.

Many state legislatures support other strategies as well for bolstering the institution of marriage. Court-affiliated reconciliation services are a good example of another "therapeutic" approach to divorce prevention. This scheme has gained considerable momentum during the past ten years. Designed to complement the "no-fault" reform provision, mandatory counseling is based on the *assumption* that the decision to divorce is often made in a fit of anger.[13] Catholics in the various state legislatures have been special champions of this cause.[14] They regard conciliation as a positive alternative to divorce and believe that mandatory court-affiliated counseling will be so effective that it will render looser legislation unnecessary.[15] Many lawyers are convinced that conciliation procedures are incorporated into state laws only to pacify the Catholic Church.

The distinction between coercive and voluntary counseling is so vague as to be almost nonexistent. Using the pioneering Los Angeles Conciliation Court as a model, one author describes how the court "constructively" uses its authority to surround a collapsing marriage with structure. The judge signs the original appointment letter, which contains the following sentence: "We trust you will keep this appointment voluntarily, and avoid the necessity of requiring the Court to issue a subpoena." [16] This letter is *not* intended to harass, punish, or embarrass the couple or to "coerce them into a reconciliation!" [17] The distraught couple is simply supposed to benefit from help which is aimed at avoiding the "tragedy of the unnecessary divorce." [18]

Emily Mudd, one vocal advocate of compulsory court-related marital counseling, insisted that couples could still be helped even if they *were* coerced into treatment. She predicted that counselors could help many couples stay together if the courts would require that they discuss their problems with a counselor before being permitted to file a divorce petition. Mudd cited the example of patients in mental hospitals who can make remarkable progress and "constructively" use help even when they are incarcerated and treated against their will. She also observed that delinquent children who are wards of the court can be helped to mature by having counselors assigned to them.[19] The same two Albany attorneys who advocated mandatory premarital counseling recommend forty-eight hours of mandatory reconciliation counseling and a six-month waiting period before a divorce action can be carried out so that counseling can have a chance to take effect.[20]

Many clinicians believe that it is useless to undertake psychotherapeutic treatment unless a person wants help; Dr. Thomas French, for example, who argues that therapy and compulsion do not go well together, is skeptical as to whether a "therapeutic approach" can be associated with compulsory agencies, such as courts.[21] In reality, emotional "help" is forced upon people all the time as the lines between "criminal," "sick" and "different" behavior grow hazier.[22] (Many people who have committed crimes are "being treated" in mental hospitals, while countless people designated as mental patients are locked up in hospitals.) It is likely that most people would protest being referred for help which they have not requested, and their resentment would negatively prejudice the chances of their becoming closer to each other. It is also unlikely that they would want to discuss the intimate details of their personal life with a court-appointed counselor.[23] While lawyer Max Rheinstein calls for counselors who are "mature . . . patient, sympathetic, open-minded, vigorous, as well as modest, experienced and wise," [24] it is doubtful that the courts will find enough professionals of this description to serve all the families that seek divorce, unless the Girl Scouts are pressed into service.

One patient recently brought in a copy of the conciliation form she was required to fill out. Ominously stamped with a New York State Supreme Court label, it asked a host of personal questions, including one about her sexual relationship with her estranged husband. Horrified and indignant, she had absolutely no intention of filling out that form so that some official, whom she did not even know, could decide whether her sex life was so hopelessly unsatisfactory that conciliation was out of the question. This form is simply one example of the kind of pressure and stress that the law can impose on couples seeking divorce.

The state of Iowa has also been concerned with the problem of high divorce rates and therefore set aside a period of ninety days during which reconciliation counseling is mandatory. No divorce may be granted until that reconciliation process is completed.[25] Legislators apparently believe that mandatory counseling can anticipate and overcome the danger that the no-fault concept will result in an upsurge of hasty divorces among people whose marriages are actually viable.

The entire constitutionality of mandatory counseling is still very much in doubt [26] apart from the purely pragmatic question of whether it does any good. One attorney writes that he would consider it "an invasion of privacy if the counseling were mandatory." [27] The question of whether potentially effective counseling is an appropriate and desirable impediment to place in the path of a divorce litigant has not yet been decided in the courts.[28] Under the liberal guise of divorce law reform, the law still tries to preserve marriage and prevent divorce and constantly finds new ways to exert authority over families. The modern trend is for the law to assume *greater, not less*, responsibility for the preservation of the nuclear family and to expand its role beyond the narrow consideration of grounds for divorce.[29]

Since the purpose of court-affiliated conciliation schemes is to preserve marriage, it is relevant to ask whether such mandatory procedures have accomplished their aim. The New York State legislature, for example, supports a Conciliation Bureau that is supposed to oversee all divorce cases. From the moment it was proposed, lawyers and psychologists attacked the New York scheme as an unworkable farce, a patronage ploy and a waste of money.[30] In New York, the conciliation program is little more than an outrageous, if ineffectual, invasion of privacy. Even if couples have no desire to be reconciled, they can be told that they must appear before a counselor, and pressure can then be put on them to air the personal details of their lives.[31]

Periodically, the New York State legislature evaluates the effectiveness of its reconciliation program. But it does so in a statistical vacuum since there are practically no studies of whether reconciliation proceedings *anywhere* in the United States have been effective in rekindling charred or burned-out marriages. Figures on "conciliations achieved" are meaningless because there are no longitudinal studies that follow through on the fate of reconciled couples.[32] We have no idea how many marriages end after the alleged reconciliation; even worse, we have to wonder whether reconciled couples *should* have been encouraged or coerced to stay together, given the easy perpetuation of too many destructive and hate-filled marriages. The fact is that less than 3 per cent of divorce cases brought before conciliation bureaus have resulted in reconciliations, and in most of New York, the figure is closer to 1 per cent.[33] These figures suggest that in spite of enforced counseling, people who have decided to divorce are not easily maneuvered out of their decision. Seldom in divorce actions do both partners genuinely want to continue "working at" the marriage. Their determination in pressing for their freedom indicates that divorcing adults are not as flippant, impulsive, or neurotic as the anti-divorce tradition supposes. These data bear out William Goode's finding that the majority of divorced people do not express later regret over their decision.[34]

Not only are such court-related schemes as conciliation caught up in the ambiguities of divorce in modern America, but lawyers themselves are often confused. At the center of the "adversary system" of divorce jurisdiction in most divorce courts, lawyers usually try to steer their clients through the legal shoals of marriage dissolution. A minority of attorneys is going further, trying to clarify and simplify the confused legal machinery of divorce in America.

# 16
# The Ambiguous Role
# of the Divorce Lawyer

> There are countless lawyers, doctors, analysts
> and marriage counselors who happily proclaim
> their success in saving marriages which are
> later either dissolved without their knowledge,
> or which continue to subsist in such a trou-
> bled state that the temporary respite offered
> by the "cure" was scarcely worth the effort
> and expense.
> —Norman Sheresky and Marya Mannes

Since divorcing couples are usually dependent on
lawyers, it is helpful to know what lawyers think about divorce,
how they perceive their own role in the divorce process, and how
they are affected by prevailing laws. At many stages of the process,
attorneys play a vital role in shaping the nature of the divorce.
For example, in states like New York, the entire conciliation process can be short-circuited if the lawyer is convinced the marriage
is hopeless. Worried and confused couples turn to lawyers for
help, but they usually don't know what to expect any more than
the patient who goes to a therapist knows what to expect. In addition, the proper role of the lawyer has been the subject of considerable disagreement among members of the profession.

198

Many lawyers advocate mingling the tasks of psychotherapy and legal counsel for the express purpose of preventing divorce. The general bias of the American Bar Association is reflected in its quarterly journal of family law, which is subtitled "To stabilize and preserve family life." John Mariano, who is both a lawyer and a marriage counselor, coined the term "psychotherapeutic jurisprudence" to refer to the work of divorce lawyers.[1] He argued that a lawyer should act like a psychotherapist, search out the real causes of marriage breakdown, and save clients from themselves.[2] Since the therapeutically trained lawyer "stands in the position where he can strengthen a marriage or doom it,"[3] he must not advocate "purely legal" remedies for emotional problems. Lawyers can try to save marriages by *compelling* clients to talk about their shortcomings as marriage partners.[4] Nester Kohut, who is also a marriage counselor and a lawyer, writes that before proceeding with a separation agreement, the *lawyer must be convinced beyond every doubt* that the partners cannot be reconciled.[5] Kohut practices matrimonial law with the explicit philosophy that lawyers should try to preserve and enhance marriage.[6] Max Rheinstein, in his massive study *Marriage Stability, Divorce and the Law,* also advocates that conscientious attorneys be "reluctant" to file petitions for divorce and urges them to send their clients for marriage counseling.[7] Divorce lawyer Haskell Freedman insists that lawyers should challenge their clients to consider the certain ill effects of divorce on children.[8]

Adding a popular new twist to the same argument, other lawyers propose that clients be pressured into counseling and conciliation. The two Albany attorneys referred to in Chapter 15 recently wrote that since divorce is all too often a "cop out," legal reform should be undertaken to save as well as to end marriages; the step they recommend is mandatory conciliation counseling.[9] Henry Foster, one of the country's outstanding draftsman of divorce laws, is concerned that the courts will just "rubber-stamp divorce decrees." He therefore argues in favor of mandatory counseling to serve the needs of children.[10]

Encompassing the views of his colleagues, attorney David Merder takes the position that if a lawyer is confronted with a client who refuses to follow through with voluntary counseling or a formal conciliation procedure, the lawyer "should not hesitate to do his utmost to provide the necessary counseling." The alternative, he writes, "would be to proceed with the divorce, although there could possibly be a chance to save the marriage." [11]

Beneath the "therapeutic" advice of lawyers such as these, there lurks subtle hostility to divorce. Since many professionals try to temper extreme and dogmatic positions when they write, it is probably safe to speculate that lawyers who mildly disapprove divorce in print are more harshly judgmental in the privacy of their consultation rooms. It is at least clear than many matrimonial lawyers share the assumption that marriage is good, that divorce is bad, and that a therapeutic approach to divorce is synonymous with an aggressive effort to prevent it.

Among all the people who get divorced each year, it is probably true that some would be happier if they had sought help in staying together. Sometimes couples feel driven to divorce although they still feel considerable love for each other. We are not saying that once people are miserable enough to consult lawyers they are automatically better off divorced. But once they have gotten that far, the time for effective counseling is usually past [12] and the chances of a happy reconciliation are very slim. Divorce is not an all-purpose remedy for marital conflict, but divorce is now so widespread that *the traditional institution of marriage is more suspect and inadequate than are the couples who reject it*. We do not believe that married adults should be pressured into counseling or obligated to convince some lawyer or judge that divorce is warranted. Defenders of this approach believe in a legal apparatus that Isabel Drummond accurately described in 1931 as a "paternalistic exercise in coercion." [13]

Although there is a tendency among many professionals to mourn divorce and to view divorcing couples as people in need of protection from themselves, neither lawyers nor judges are warranted (nor should they be permitted) to stop divorce. They are not personally accountable for the high divorce rate; they are "enablers" in a process they do not initiate. The only people who can be held responsible for errors of judgment in divorce are the couples who seek it. In our opinion it is arrogant, untherapeutic and irresponsible for lawyers to impose either counseling or their personal ideas on clients who come to them for legal help. It is reasonable to expect that lawyers with perceptivity and common sense will volunteer information about counseling services in the community, especially if they sense that a client is notably confused or ambivalent.

Donald Cantor is one of the outspoken attorneys who is worried about the destructive impact of compulsory legislation and personal pressure on both clients and the legal profession. He argues that reconciliation and counseling procedures that are forced on people are usually exasperating and exhausting and have the net effect of destroying all hope of renewing a marriage. It is more humane, he writes, to recognize and respect a couple's need for privacy and time to think, free of coercion and probing.[14] Instead, people fall after marriage from the field of free choice into the dank, fetid, subterranean pit of divorce law, where they are treated as semicriminal types or as obstinate, troubled children.

It is just as hard to establish broad guidelines of proper conduct for lawyers as it is to establish them for mental health professionals. In both of these areas, people often work privately, without any supervision, and are guided largely by the dictates of their conscience. Therefore the significance of their personal attitudes cannot be overstated.

At present, the Code of Professional Responsibility, which guides the legal profession, does *not* require the divorce attorney to undertake extensive counseling. Once a lawyer asks a client whether he or she has considered conciliation or counseling, the lawyer's ethical duty is fulfilled (Canons 8, 22). But some lawyers now argue that the legal canons should be broadened to "pick up the slack" of inadequate conciliation systems. In other words, instead of considering themselves above all as "advocates" (Canon 5), lawyers should assume the complementary responsibility of clinical counselor as well. "He will not necessarily move immediately towards the initiation of divorce proceedings," writes Merder, but will provide his client "with a much broader type of service." [15]

In our judgment this is a careless, unwarranted and repressive interpretation of the need for divorce reform and the ethical duty of the matrimonial lawyer. Not only is it *not* their duty to *save* marriages, as Merder suggests,[16] but even if lawyers had professional preparation for counseling, which they don't, they would be encroaching on the privacy of their clients. Furthermore, it takes years of intensive training to become a competent therapist and to help couples identify the sources of their problems. It is absurd to presume that rigorous training in this area can be combined with thorough legal training through the mere inclusion of a few courses in counseling techniques. If lawyers feel the need to refer clients for therapy, they should have a complete and accurate picture of what public and private resources are available to their clients.

Of course, whether they are recognized matrimonial experts or not, some attorneys, like Louis Nizer, will be fascinated by the traumatic psychological impact of divorce laws and will be poised for battle. Some professionals revel in the opportunity to wield power and to play an omnipotent role in their clients' (or patients') lives. According to Nizer's own account, "shrinking a client's anxiety" may be in the psychological or even psychoanalytic realm, but the sciences cannot be separated into neatly labeled compartments. "It is essential," he writes, "that the client emerge immediately from the depressed atmosphere of fear and defeat which envelops him, or he will not be able to function in the legal struggle ahead. I consider this my first problem and deal with it directly." [17] Nizer's plea for "reason and compromise" in favor of inflammatory litigation falls limply against his flamboyant descriptions of the notorious cases in which he brilliantly rose to the challenge of a good courtroom battle.[18] He falls neatly into that category of lawyers who inflate their own importance and justify outlandish fees by arguing that they are combination psychiatrists, detectives and bookkeepers.[19]

Since divorce law is riddled with irrationality and corruption, it is reasonable to expect that at least some lawyers will take advantage of the clients' vulnerability and confusion. Because the legal machinery of divorce is inconsistent throughout the United States, people often feel compelled to find lawyers who are shrewd, politically connected, or famous for their ruthlessness. The public has been conditioned to believe that a good lawyer has to use fraud, and use it well, to combat a fraudulent legal system.[20] Given our present system of divorce, good lawyers have to be ruthless in behalf of their clients. The growing hostility of the public toward divorce laws, lawyers, and judges who administer the law is a healthy sign that a basis for change may be at hand. People are becoming justifiably suspicious of the "high priests" of the law who are supposed to be objective, professional and competent.[21]

Among the divorced people we have treated and interviewed, there is widespread feeling that a brotherhood of lawyers profits handsomely from divorce by exploiting the terrific public pressure on couples to "get legal advice." Lawyers depend on the popular belief that ex-partners are ignorant and helpless and need protection from each other. "The most important man in your life once you decide to leave your husband," writes Carol Mindey, "is your attorney."[22] (Note her assumption that all lawyers are men!) It may or may not be true that women are less helpless when they hire female lawyers, but it is true that with our existing laws both sexes are excessively dependent on the vagaries of legal counsel.

For many divorcing couples, their biggest headaches begin after they retain their respective attorneys. Recently, we talked with the ex-wife of a famous and wealthy stage actor. It had taken her three years to obtain a divorce in California, which is one of the more progressive states! In her words, "Once the lawyers smelled money, they acted in cahoots to bleed us and draw out the proceedings." Although their separation had started out amicably, they grew to loathe each other; she believes that both his lawyers and her own successfully manipulated her and her husband into feeling victimized by each other. Together they paid a total of twenty thousand dollars for the divorce and consulted eight different lawyers. This woman was convinced that most of them strongly identified with her husband. Her hard feelings were intensified by the fact that three of them tried to date her, and all of them told her that she "shouldn't worry her pretty little head about anything." Finally she turned to a well-known female lawyer and had a much better experience.

In another case, which did not involve people of means, a divorced woman sought legal help because her ex-husband stopped paying her monthly alimony after she went to work (though he kept up child support) on the grounds that her income was nearly the same as his and that he had a larger family to support than she did. The divorce decree contained no specific provision for the cessation of those payments, however, and she wanted the law to force him to live up to the original agreement. She was represented by a lawyer whose specialty was tax law, not matrimonial law, and he advised her to take her grievance to Family Court, which she did. However, in New York, it is not the job of Family Court to enforce contracts but to determine the needs of families and settle questions on the equitable distribution of incomes. Her lawyer was apparently unaware that Civil Court, not Family Court, enforces contracts. When the Family Court judge announced that she would get little satisfaction from Family Court, she was humiliated and stunned, and helplessly asked, "What am I doing here then?" Very simply, she was led to the wrong court by an incompetent attorney, and by the time the matter was clarified by the judge (four all-day visits to court), her lawyer had washed his hands of her case and she had hired another attorney. Meanwhile, the first lawyer, who charged sixty dollars an hour for his questionable services, billed the ex-husband (who is usually required to pay *all* legal and court fees) nine hundred dollars for their inconclusive fiasco in court. (On good legal advice, he did not pay the bill.) Cases such as this could be reconciled without any lawyers if couples were routinely advised upon divorce where to turn for judicial help when they have an economic grievance. In this case, the judge had ready access to all the pertinent financial data and there was absolutely no reason for either party to hire counsel except that it is customary and expected.

As we have seen, some attorneys are content to support the status quo, exploit the ignorance of their clients, and become embroiled in warfare. Others are beginning to take a broader and more humane view of their own role and to resent the fact that the law conspires to make them into charlatans. We are sympathetic with the competent lawyers who are sensitive to the divorce lawyer's low prestige. Donald Cantor, who recognizes and justifiably resents this reality, calls for a radical reorganization of divorce law so that divorce will become a personal right. (See Chapter 17.) Some people argue that divorce lawyers have bad reputations because of the emotions they deal with. It is understandable why many lawyers try to avoid divorce cases.[23] As one attorney wryly remarked, "Divorce law is the corn liquor of jurisprudence." [24] Anthropologist Paul Bohannan accurately perceived that divorce lawyers rate low primarily because divorced people are treated like deviants and criminals.[25]

Among the articulate lawyers who are sensitive to the brutality of American divorce are those who wisely call for restraint on the part of lawyers and clients. Norman Sheresky, for example, tries to show that the law seduces both lawyers and clients into a tough-guy posture which frequently backfires and hurts everybody. In *Uncoupling*, he and Marya Mannes persuasively argue that husbands and wives should not try to use lawyers as instruments of their personal revenge. It may be true, as they assert, that "crazy clients" are largely to blame for getting lawyers hopelessly embroiled in endless warfare, but the buck really shouldn't stop there. In many cases, as we have shown, the law requires people to behave as if they were mad and sometimes the lawyer gets the brunt of it. Rational appeals for compromise and maturity are inconsistent with the philosophy of contemporary divorce law.

We believe that both the fear of widespread divorce and the contempt for all divorced people are the sociological and psychological bases on which divorce laws have been constructed, and that until there is a positive change of attitude, lawyers will be sullied by association in the process. Divorce law, at present, is a repressive instrument of government and is therefore the enemy of married couples who want their freedom. It is hard for even the most well-meaning lawyer to enhance and protect the rights of clients because everybody cheats in the divorce game. The rules themselves are so demoralizing that all the participants in divorce actions have reason to feel guilty. The matrimonial lawyer, according to one anthropologist, scarcely knows what his proper role should be; in our opinion, the fact that lawyers participate in the divorce process and are more aware than laymen are about what actually goes on gives them a moral obligation to protest the abuses of the system.

If some of the legal cleverness and human passion that now go into the divorce game could be rechanneled, lawyers could help devise ways for divorce to become less costly and painful. Perhaps the notable lack of leadership from within the legal profession is related to the fact that the struggle for a more humane and dignified divorce system will inevitably result in a smaller role for the lawyer. Nobody wants to work to put himself or herself out of business. One lawyer, sensitive to the proposal that divorce reform should entirely eliminate the role of the lawyer, speculates on whether there is a legitimate and necessary function for lawyers to perform that entitles them to a substantial fee. He concludes that lawyers are needed to determine the nature and extent of marital assets, to explore the question of reconciliation, and to act as the client's "guide and spokesman at trial." [26]

The proposed elimination of legal counsel, at least in uncontested divorce cases, recently came in concrete form from James Winder, an enterprising Rochester, New York, barber. Convinced that divorce laws and lawyers were too rotten and corrupt to be supported, he designed and marketed a "Divorce Yourself" kit for seventy-five dollars. The kit taught couples how to fill out certain forms and how to file for divorce without legal aid, which usually costs between five hundred dollars and seven hundred and fifty dollars, if there are no long-drawn-out complications. Winder's stated purpose was to give the law back to the people.[27] He successfully guided about eighty customers through divorce until he was legally stopped.

Predictably, the Monroe County Bar Association and the state attorney general's office joined forces in initiating action against Winder. In June 1972, the New York State Supreme Court imposed a permanent injunction against him on the grounds that he was "dispensing advice concerning the laws of divorce and separation" and thereby was practicing law illegally.[28] Winder plans to appeal to the Appellate Division. We are not competent to judge his technical guilt or innocence, but it is certainly more humane and dignified, and a lot less costly, to understand the law, draw up one's own petition, and appeal privately for the unbinding of a marriage contract than to go through the usual channels. Winder's case is an important reminder that in our country privileged professional groups jealously guard the prerogatives and mysteries of their lucrative crafts. Louis Nizer once remarked that divorce law was too intricate to "ever yield to a do-it-yourself kit." [29] It is not hard to relate this conviction to the vested interest many lawyers have in the existing system.

It seems to us that both the "Divorce Yourself" kit and the "no-fault" statute are feasible alternatives to more archaic practices, although they are not the final answer to the divorce problem. They are gaining support among people of good will who recognize that the counterpart of our cultural aversion to divorce has been a legal system based on guilt and punishment in which lawyers are duty-bound to take an adversary role.

# 17
# Toward Freedom and Equality in Divorce

> For the vast majority of women marriage is not only an emotional (and to many a sacred) relationship, it is also a way of life. It takes the place of an independent career. It is the woman's sole source of income and security.
> —Olive Stone,
> in *Family Law Quarterly*,
> December, 1969

> The question is not whether you have the right to render your people miserable, but whether it is not your interest to make them happy.
> —Edmund Burke

The modern proposals for divorce reform, although they move in the direction of freedom and dignity, have at least three serious shortcomings. First, they do not suggest any remedy for the blackmail and unhappiness that couples can inflict on each other when divorce is a contested issue. For example, both the "do-it-yourself kit" and the "no-fault" divorce depend for their success on the good will, cooperation and mutual consent of husband and wife. They are obvious improvements over the adversary system, but they are no guarantee of liberty from a marriage that is no longer satisfying to one spouse. Second, liberal reform proposals focus on the technical means of facilitating divorce. They lack the vision and insight necessary to remedy the inequities of post-divorce life. Not only the mechanical details but also the broader issues of child custody, financial support and traditional sex-linked roles will have to be re-examined. A radical critique of the mores of divorce is a prerequisite to meeting the real challenge of legal divorce reform. Third, judicial discretion, even in "no-fault" jurisdictions, impinges on the freedom of divorce.

Eliminating the concept of fault is an important step in encouraging tranquil divorce, but as these statutes now exist they are certainly not the final answer to the destructive and repressive laws of the past. The California no-fault provision was the model suggested in 1970 by the National Conference of Commissioners on Uniform State Laws. Max Rheinstein writes that if this "radical" proposal were followed, the liberal breakthrough in divorce law would be complete.[1]

In our opinion, California's new statute is not liberal enough nor is it a "breakthrough" in divorce reform. The reason it is not good enough is that it still gives courts the power to pass judgment on what is meant by the "irremediable breakdown" of a marriage. If one spouse demurs, arguing that the marriage is still viable, the judge is left with the task of evaluating whether the marriage can be saved or should be dissolved. California has tried to cope with this problem by authorizing and funding court-ordered conciliation services and by defining sufficient evidence of irreconcilable differences.[2] Evidence is defined as "those grounds which are determined by the court to be substantial reasons for not continuing the marriage and which make it appear that the marriage should be dissolved."[3] It is hard to see how such double-talk and vague terminology can be construed as a *definition* at all, or as a guide to the trial judge. In practice, one judge may believe that a single argument is substantial, while a second judge, believing in the sanctity of marriage, might refuse divorce on any grounds.[4]

In short, the no-fault concept helps those people who have already agreed to divorce to do so with greater dignity; it leaves essentially untouched the sticky problem of the contested case, in which one spouse holds out on the other. The old-fashioned

United Press International
Time Magazine, 1970

A crowd of 3000 demonstrates in favor of divorce in Rome's Piazza Navona, 1969.

Dr. and Mrs. Alexander Goodman
have the honour of announcing
the Divorce of their daughter
Barbara Jane
from
Ronald Melvin what's his name
in the year of our Lord
nineteen hundred and seventy
Superior Court
Los Angeles, California

A PUT-ON? Not at all. The Goodmans and their actress daughter, whose stage name is Wendy Wilson, were so happy about the untied knot that they sent embossed announcements to 110 friends and relatives. Explained Wendy: "It beats calling people and saying, 'Well, I'm free again.'" The result has been a number of dates and some divorce gifts. Her former husband, Ronald Melvin Charnak, she said, "laughed like mad."

*"It's Cynthia, she wants to know if we'd like to come round and see the slides of her divorce evidence against Rodney?"*

Punch, 1972

adversary system never deterred agreeable partners from getting divorced, although they had to adjust their situation to fit the statutory grounds of their state; therefore, unless legislators can propose a solution for the *contested* divorce case, the no-fault reform will be a fundamentally meaningless change which, ironically, gives the most relief to the people who need it least.

The California statute did in fact turn out to be a model for similar legislation in other jurisdictions, but their acts are no better. In October 1971, Oregon became the second state to pass no-fault legislation. Since the passage of the Oregon Marriage Annulment and Dissolution Act, the courts have been struggling with problems involving the *standards for dissolution and the adjudication of contested cases.*[5] Under the new act, the court must find both "irreconcilable differences" and "irremediable breakdown" to dissolve a marriage.[6] Evidence of specific acts of misconduct is eliminated from most proceedings, and when both parties stipulate that their marriage is destroyed, the dissolution decree is likely to be issued as a matter of course, particularly if there are no children.[7] But if the parties do not agree that the marriage is irremediably broken, the degree of conflict becomes a question for the courts to resolve, and fault evidence may be necessary to demonstrate marital breakdown.[8] Therefore the court is again back in the position where it has to dig up hard facts about the actual condition of the marriage. In summary, writes one lawyer, the drafters of the Oregon Act placed great reliance on judicial discretion in interpreting and resolving questions of the standard for dissolution, the scope of admissibility of evidence of misconduct, and the use of investigations and conciliation services.[9] The legislative history of the no-fault concept indicates a deliberate refusal to list specific grounds for dissolution because such specifications would merely resurrect in principle the adversary system. Therefore the vagueness of the no-fault provisions means that judges are left to decide on a case-by-case basis whether divorce is warranted.[10]

It is clear that neither partner has the "right" to divorce as long as the other partner has to agree to it.[11] In order for this to happen, judicial power must be considerably limited and the prerequisites of mutual consent and grounds for divorce must be completely eliminated.

Unlike the decision to marry, the decision to divorce is not considered a private and personal privilege and is not protected as such by state laws. An irate husband recently complained that a marriage contract is a bond between two consenting adults, not a club held over two children by church and state. It is none of the state's business, he argued, when and where a woman loves a man, or how, when and where a man cherishes a woman.[12] Some enlightened lawyers take hope that repressive laws will change in light of recent Supreme Court decisions which reflect the growing view that sexual behavior in private is not the proper concern of the state.[13] (It should be noted, however, that the courts have looked very harshly upon divorced lesbian mothers who fight for custody of their children. In a recent New Jersey ruling, a mother was ordered to give up her lover in exchange for the privilege of keeping her children.)

The "right to divorce" does not yet exist, but in the legal history of America, new rights have from time to time been incorporated into the constitutional system. The "right to privacy," for example, was grafted to the Constitution after Samuel Warren and Louis Brandeis had outlined the strategy in their famous *Harvard Law Review* article on "The Right of Privacy" in 1890. This precedent suggests how, in broad outline at least, a similar "right to divorce" may be introduced. The constitutional guarantees of individual liberty in the Bill of Rights and in the Fourteenth Amendment to the Constitution have been broadened in the past; we are calling for a new generation of optimistic lawyers who, like attorney Donald Cantor, can envision divorce as a constitutionally protected right that will not depend upon the discretionary power of individual state legislatures.[14]

Other possible legal arguments could support the case for a "right to divorce." The established constitutional guarantee of a "right of association" could imply the freedom *not* to associate with a spouse no longer loved or loving.[15] The presumed sanctity of the marriage contract is a formidable obstacle to overcome in the creation of a right to divorce. Legal marriage is buttressed by the constitutional prohibition on "impairing the obligation of contracts." But a still-valid Supreme Court decision, Maynard v. Hill, 125 U.S. 190 (1888), found that marriage was not such an inviolable contract under the Constitution. Ample opportunity exists for lawyers to forge creative legal arguments that can facilitate their clients' freedom to divorce.

After the task is accomplished of converting divorce into a "right," all other issues related to family reorganization can be dealt with in a more wholesome climate. Divorce itself could be a fairly inexpensive administrative procedure in which a trained lay person or paraprofessional could gather and itemize the basic pertinent data that judges would need in arriving at equitable settlements when money and property are contested issues. If there were persistent financial matters on which the couple could not agree, they could seek the help of a professional arbitrator [16] who would not be cornered into taking sides, as the average divorce lawyer now is. If one partner felt depressed, frightened, or enraged because the other partner decided upon divorce, he or she could seek psychological counseling. There are at least some reputable counselors and social agencies in most major cities and towns. The ability to pay and the mature cooperation of both partners should not, as they now do, play a crucial role in determining whether a person can easily get a divorce. Easy divorce does not imply that either parent is absolved of responsibility for the children, but it does imply that they will no longer be able to use children as instruments of hostility when they want to suppress each other's freedom.

Whether it has been easy or hard for them to jump the hurdle of legal divorce, couples with children have to confront another set of resistances and expectations that now contribute to the trauma associated with divorce. When the allied issues of custody, child support and alimony emerge, parents are up against centuries of sex-role indoctrination. In particular, their post-divorce lives will be organized around the premise that mothers should routinely and "naturally" get custody of the children. In 80 to 90 per cent of American divorce cases, judges assume that children are better off with their mothers than with their fathers.[17] Even Judge Nanette Dembitz, of New York, a woman with the reputation of being an enlightened jurist, argues that "all things being equal, I think a child should go to its mother." [18] As Max Lerner once observed, "American courts, by a curious quirk of gallantry and a tenacious belief in mother love, almost invariably award the child to the mother." [19]

The mere fact that we have a custody tradition in America does not mean that it is a rational or healthy tradition. Perhaps it is true that this prejudice against men is the result of the "corrective" to the old prejudice against women, in which they were treated as their husband's property.[20] Thus, the children have now become her property. Whatever the historical reason, the tradition of nearly automatic custody to women can be highly destructive for divorced families. It can needlessly exacerbate the hatred between the spouses by implying that the father is by definition the less competent parent. The custody tradition also reinforces the woman's economic dependency on her ex-husband and her psychic dependency on her children; it encourages her to lean on her role as mother as a primary element in her definition of her identity. Ultimately, she may grow to resent these children, especially if she has felt driven by custom and social pressure to sacrifice her own development to become "both mother and father" to them. As anthropologist Jules Henry once observed, "There is a limit to how much people can sacrifice their own comfort for someone else, without turning against him." [21] Or she may use her children as a rationale for her inability to find happiness. The common practice of sole female custody, based on the unproved assumption that mothers both want and deserve it, causes many divorced women to expect excessive satisfaction and gratitude from the children, making it difficult for them to separate from her and establish their independence.

When custody is a contested issue in divorce, both parents will again be at the mercy of legal counsel and judicial discretion. They will have no guarantee that the judge hearing their case knows any more than most people about the emotional needs of divorced families. "The more conscientious the judge," writes Dr. J. Louise Despert, "the more likely he is to see that in cases involving the custody of children he stands on the edge of a field of knowledge in which he is not at home." [22] However learned judges are, they are not free from the biases that affect most people, including the potent American mystique of motherhood. But judges are in a unique position to impose their prejudices because of the power that has been vested in them to settle personal issues pertaining to divorce. While the law grants domestic court judges very wide discretion, it also permits people to appeal judicial decisions to higher courts. However, in divorce matters, higher courts are reluctant to upset the decisions of a judge who presumably knew the case; furthermore, such appeals are very costly.[23]

The sanctity of motherhood in America, which is perpetuated by law, ironically operates to denigrate women. Since it is culturally determined that her primary role is child and home care, the divorced mother cannot choose to pursue a career or just be by herself and relinquish custody without feeling "unnatural" and therefore guilty. Though she may eternally resent her ex-husband who is "free as a bird" (while he may in fact be aching for custody), she cannot conceive of demanding similar freedom for herself. Society has reinforced the myth of motherhood with both laws and propaganda, "laws that made woman a chattel, denied her education and personal mobility, and madonna propaganda that she was beautiful and wonderful doing it and it was all beautiful and wonderful to do." [24] In our society, not to want to be a mother is to be a freak, and not to be a *blissful* mother is to be a witch.[25] As one psychiatrist aptly observed, "Women don't need to be mothers any more than they need spaghetti. But if you're in a world where everyone is eating spaghetti, thinking they need and want it, you will think so too. Romance has really contaminated science." [26] Thus the woman of today who is not granted custody of her children suffers a major loss of status, which of course impels her to fight for it whether she wants it or not.[27] Even if she is incompetent as well as unhappy, and the father could be a more wholesome and cheerful custodial parent, she will wind up with the children. Fathers can sue for custody, but they will have a herculean task trying to prove that mother is cruel or negligent, or flamboyantly and drastically ill, mentally or physically.[28] Even if one or more of these characteristics are present, the humane father will often forgo the process of gathering legal evidence because of his reluctance to subject the children to the sordid details of an ugly court struggle.

Although the presence of the father is deemed crucial to the child's healthy development, the law gives him a peculiar and ambiguous role after divorce. Divorce decrees usually specify visiting hours, during which time he has the "right" to see his children. Not only is the father rarely granted custody, but he can be prevented from visiting in excess of his allotted time. In spite of such institutionalized hostility, the law expects dad to feel important, assume the entire burden of child support if he can, and act emotionally loving. In actuality, divorced fathers are legally relegated to the role of "father by permission of the mother." [29]

One rationale for preferring mothers over fathers as custodial parents is that women are more likely and more willing to stay home all day and care for children. These assumptions should be examined more closely. Although there are as yet no national statistics, private detectives report a quantum leap in the number of runaway wives they are hired to retrieve by baffled husbands. One private investigator in New York reports that in 1969 only 2 per cent of his quarry was female; in 1973, the figure soared to 56 per cent.[30] More and more mothers are abandoning their supposedly sacred duties. Except in the most affluent circles, divorced mothers who would love to stay home are driven out to work in order to make ends meet. What then is the difference between a divorced mother working all day and making alternative child-care arrangements and a divorced father working all day and doing the same thing? As an observant judge recently commented, many competent and interested fathers would be happy to rear their children but the courts systematically prevent them from doing so. The result is that children are often reared by doting grandmothers who cannot really guide them or are reared in other more haphazard arrangements.[31]

It seems to us that a father with a good income could hire a competent housekeeper during the day. (The children could then have the male *and* female "identification models" the experts claim they need at home). On the other hand, a woman cannot readily "hire" a man to stay home with her children while she goes out to work. Fathers with custody would see their children often, but the children would not simultaneously be deprived of female attention, since they see women all the time in nurseries, schools and playgrounds. As long as isolated nuclear families are *the* mode of rearing children, it makes more sense to urge fathers to take custody. Of course if the government took a genuine interest in the economic and emotional vicissitudes of divorce, it would move rapidly toward designing and supporting warm and wholesome day-care centers, staffed by men and women of all ages. Recent White House decisions seem to be going in the other direction. Considering their reputation as "second-best" parents, and the courts' hostility to them, it is not surprising that so many fathers feel it is a hopeless battle to try to defy established customs.[32]

Although inertia, cultural tradition, psychological brainwashing, economic self-interest and other factors conspire to inhibit change, a major focus of efforts to restructure American society should be our archaic divorce customs. Instead of reinforcing narrow sex roles, divorce law should be transformed so that its concern and protection are equally available to all parties. If the law simply dedicates itself to upholding reactionary ideals, it will lose the respect of the public that it is supposed to guide and protect. If, for example, both mother and father seem to be equally capable, loving and interested parents, legal custody should not give one parent the power to regulate or restrict the other parent's involvement in the child's life. Visiting time should be as open-ended as possible, and the parent with "legal" custody should be told that the privilege of custody is predicated on his (her) agreement not to interfere with the desire of the children and the ex-spouse to see each other as frequently as they mutually wish to. In cases where the noncustodial parent abuses the right of visitation by inconvenient and frequently unannounced visits it may become necessary for the other parent to appeal to the courts for a more structured arrangement until this problem is resolved.

Some people would retort that an open-ended, unstructured settlement opens a Pandora's box of conflict for the children, especially if the parents compete for their loyalty and attention. It has been our clinical and personal experience, however, that regardless of how specific or structured the visiting routine is on paper, parents of good will adopt the above policy anyway, while parents at war systematically do battle over visitation. In our opinion, the most and the best the law can hope to do (assuming that both parents behave reasonably toward the children) is to encourage the children to feel that mother and father are equally caring and competent; if that is not the case, the child will learn soon enough which parent satisfies his needs and will make his or her preferences very explicit. The law should protect the child's right to spend a great deal of time with both parents. Custody is not a declaration of relative parental innocence, but a matter of convenience for the sake of giving the child a stable home base. Sometimes one parent gradually seems to lose interest in being with the children, or the children express a decided preference for the company of one parent; the visitation stipulations should not be so fixed or rigid as to compel people to be together when they prefer to be apart. Neither should children be so bound and influenced by a fixed visiting schedule that they do not *permit themselves* to desire or request changes.

The fact that so many divorced mothers seem to want custody of the children should not mislead us into assuming that this is an entirely natural or wholesome request. Not all of their motives are laudable and healthy. Some mothers bitterly resent the financial and emotional hardships imposed by husbands who "dumped" the kids on them. On the other hand, many women say they would "rather die than let that man get his clutches on my children." Women are becoming aware, at long last, of the perverse nature of their "overwhelming sense of responsibility to their children." Recently, there was a wholesome and daring panel discussion at Barnard College among a group of divorced mothers, all of whom wanted and got custody at the time of divorce. They believed that child care was their primary if not exclusive domain. Some even admitted feeling that the more personal sacrifices they made, the better mothers they were. When we asked them why they hadn't urged their ex-husbands to play a larger role in raising the children, some of the women replied that they just assumed the fathers "wouldn't want to." Others confessed that they really felt more comfortable about having *exclusive control* over their children's lives. One jocular, introspective woman recalled that on Sundays, when her daughter went out with Daddy, she prepared her child a "picnic lunch" so that Daddy wouldn't have to "be bothered figuring out what Cindy likes to eat!" Another mother, who had tried living in a commune with her two children, found that shared responsibility was a strain on her because she was forced to relinquish control over a number of minor day-to-day child-care decisions.

Even mothers in marriage sometimes have trouble letting fathers "take over," and tend, therefore, to treat their husbands like children. One of the panelists sheepishly remembered that even when she was married, if she left her son with his father for a whole day, she picked and laid out the child's clothes for the day and pre-prepared all the meals. If women are to be instrumental in altering traditional child-care patterns so that both parents can function competently, they will have to reconsider the question of how much their personal sense of worth and identity are linked to the exclusive control of, and power over, children.

Mothers who are willing to relinquish formal custody can devote more time and energy to education and job training and can move more rapidly toward economic self-sufficiency, a goal many divorced women cherish but never achieve. In doing so, in pursuing inherently satisfying personal goals, many women might find themselves more relaxed, secure, fulfilled, and better mothers.

# 18
# Limitations of the Law:
# The Money Question

> There is much to be said for the answer one
> woman recently gave to her best friend upon
> being asked whether she married for money.
> She smiled and said in a pleasant voice: "Why
> no, I divorced for it!"
>
> *Family Law Quarterly* (1969)

Happily, some lawyers, feminists and politicians are emerging out of the dark ages of divorce and are shedding light on new ways to alleviate suffering and to enhance the emotional well-being and the economic equality of post-divorce life. Future generations of women may not have to look forward to the humiliation of taking alms each month from men who do not love them and whom they do not love. They will not have to rely forever on the conscience and good will of their ex-spouses who may be unreliable about sending monthly checks. Men may be freed of what is often an onerous and unfair burden, and children, hopefully, will cease to be pawns in the parental struggle over money.

220

Divorce insurance is the most plausible innovation to date for the relief of inequities and financial deprivation after divorce. New York State Senator Donald Halperin (Democrat of Brooklyn) has presented a coherent plan to the legislature; it is actively supported by Diana DuBroff, a Fellow of the American Academy of Matrimonial Lawyers.[1] Divorce insurance is a form of financial protection intended to provide for a family, for a specified time after divorce, until the members have recovered economically from the sudden division of income.[2] Since mothers usually have custody and generally do not earn fabulous salaries of their own, the children, argue Halperin and DuBroff, become the financial casualties of divorce. Women with no skills, who receive little or inconsistent support, are sometimes forced to seek public assistance; this fact is not only demoralizing for the woman but may deter her from seeking a divorce that she earnestly wants. Divorce insurance, even for a limited period of time, would give the woman a chance to adjust to her new economic status, would give the couple one less issue to argue about as they separate, and might even enable parents and judges to make custody decisions free of glaring economic considerations.

Mrs. DuBroff envisions divorce insurance as something like a trust fund, or a nest egg, taken out immediately before or after marriage, like accident, fire, or life insurance. It would be used primarily to insure adequate child support in the event of divorce, but should the marriage prove a lasting one, the insurance could be converted to other uses, such as education, retirement, or life insurance.[3] It would also be valuable for a divorced couple without children because the payments would give the less skilled partner time to acquire vocational training. In our opinion, divorce insurance would help discourage people from remaining unhappily married, especially in cases where they are doing so for primarily economic reasons.

Divorce insurance advocates visualize a system based on a minimum standard of support; judges would retain the power to set higher support figures, which would be met by the wealthier parent. The levels of support provided by such insurance would have to be higher than those offered by local welfare departments in order to make the idea attractive and reasonable. According to Mrs. DuBroff, there is increased pressure on employers from individuals and trade unions to include divorce insurance in job contracts.

The difficulties with divorce insurance ought not to be minimized. A purely voluntary plan would, as Senator Halperin noted, probably not be effective. Such insurance would have to be government sponsored and mandatory to be effective. This form of state involvement in divorce, however, would enhance individual freedom and would have precisely the opposite effect than does the present situation, where the weight of government power is thrown against happiness and equality in divorce.

It is unlikely that newlyweds will acknowledge the impermanence of marriage or see the wisdom in such a precaution as divorce insurance. Even the most naïve romantics know that death is inevitable and that accidents happen, so there is much less resistance to overcome in deciding to purchase other forms of insurance. Although there are now 455 divorces for every 1,000 new marriages,[4] the American dream does not anticipate divorce at all; planning for it at wedding time would, of course, be out of the question. Initially, after a flood of actuarial studies, divorce insurance will probably be sold by private companies on a voluntary basis to a small number of enlightened realists. With the use of our now extensive divorce statistics, computation of premiums is feasible.[5] It is at least one way of trying to make divorce less awesome and of assuring minimum financial security to divorced families. It would be especially attractive to women who plan to be out of the labor market for many years and to women who do not have professional skills. Only after the gross economic burdens of divorce are lifted will people be able, *objectively*, to evaluate whether or not divorce inevitably has to be catastrophic and debilitating. Resistance to divorce insurance will no doubt come in the form of an argument that such insurance would foster divorce; the attitude that any nonpunitive reform is essentially "conducive to easy divorce" is by now a familiar one which ignores the fact that divorce is a part of contemporary social existence and is here to stay.[6]

The realm of alimony is the most dank and murky region in post-divorce life. It probably causes far more suffering than it alleviates. In most states it has been a lifetime right, since judges have bent over backward to protect the woman's income and keep her off the welfare rolls.[7] It is a concrete thing around which all the feelings concerning the divorce are likely to gather. Animosities that might otherwise have been burned out with the passage of time are rekindled each time the check is mailed. When alimony was originated, men were entitled to the entire wealth and earnings of the women they married. In the event that they became legally separated, the husband did not lose his marital rights on his wife's property, with the result that she was left with no independent means of support. To prevent the wife from becoming destitute, the ecclesiastical courts, upon granting separation, ordered the husband to provide money for his wife's maintenance. This payment, called alimony, derived from the Latin word *alimonia*, meaning "nourishment" or "sustenance." (The Married Woman's Property Act, passed in the United States in the nineteenth century, stripped husbands of control over their wives' property, but that law had no bearing on his obligation to support her.[8]) Alimony is based on the common-law obligation of the husband to support his wife, which is not removed by her asking for or obtaining a divorce or a separation. The *right of alimony*, both temporary and permanent, was recognized in ecclesiastical law and refers specifically to the wife's maintenance, as distinguished from *child support*.[9]

The controversy that now surrounds alimony is reflected in contradictory and sometimes arbitrary judicial practices. (See Chapter 14.) In *theory*, alimony and child support are based on the wife's need and the husband's ability to pay. Lawyers write that if the wife has an adequate income of her own, the courts will not unduly burden the husband.[10] In *practice*, there are often extreme and unexplained variations in the amounts of alimony and support ordered for ex-wives in almost identical financial situations in the same geographic area.[11] A recent survey by the American Bar Association of more than five hundred domestic relations judges revealed that many of them are overtly hostile to working mothers, while others believe that men should never stop supporting the women they marry. One judge's attitude is that "marriage is a woman's business. When the marriage is bankrupt, the woman is bankrupt." [12] Alimony reflects an archaic legal divorce tradition and is often used to punish the "guilty" and to reward the "innocent." Too often, the amount depends on whatever moral or immoral conduct the court knows about.[13] In countless cases the payment has no bearing at all on whether a woman is economically needy; traditionally, she is "entitled" to alimony until she remarries. Many shrewd women exploit this custom by living with men whom they do not marry. Common-law relationships protect the divorced woman from losing her ex-husband's payment. (A Chicago judge recently deprived a divorced woman of her eight-hundred-dollar-a-month alimony payment on the ground that she was using the money to support a paramour as well as herself.) [14] There are now twenty-seven states that permit alimony to be awarded to the husband.[15]

To our knowledge there is only one reliable nation-wide study of alimony and child support.[16] It indicates that alimony is awarded in only a very small percentage of cases, that nearly 90 per cent of the petitioners waive it, and that in only 2 per cent of all divorce cases is it a permanent award.[17] Nevertheless, alimony is a major source of debate and vindictiveness for thousands of divorcing couples.

People who believe that women should be self-supporting argue that women demand alimony primarily because they want to punish their ex-mates. Instead of helping women in the transition to self-sufficiency, argues one male author, alimony turns into a "pension for injuries sustained in marital combat." [18] According to another author, male, of course, alimony is the ultimate form of having your cake and eating it too. John Rodell writes that because the law sanctions alimony, "it encourages contempt for the law among otherwise law-abiding men," more than all the loopholes in the tax structure and the abuses of big business combined.[19] Some lawyers claim that judges try not to let divorced women become "alimony-drones," that is, self-indulgent or indolent women.[20] Leading members of the Committee for Fair Divorce and Alimony Laws are sensitive to this issue and have taken the position that because alimony is a dole for the wife and a punishment for the husband, it should be limited to one year, unless the wife is sick, aged, or has preschool children to care for. The Committee has filed a bill to this effect in the New York State Senate.[21] There seems to be a trend—albeit a slow one—to limit both the amount and the duration of alimony.[22]

Women's rights groups protest that alimony is not a pension, grant, or dole, but a salary legitimately earned by years of keeping house, performing domestic duties, and caring for children. According to the Citizen's Advisory Council on the Status of Women, ex-wives are rarely overcompensated in alimony, compared with how hard they have toiled.[23] Many women do deserve at least some financial compensation for years of unpaid labor which enabled their husbands to prosper. Feminist organizations like the National Organization for Women (NOW) or Women in Transition demand community property laws and enforcement of support orders.

We are convinced that the alimony issue is not amenable to abstract theoretical solution, and that the law, even if it could assume a perfectly "just" position, would be ignored, by and large. The man's obligation to support his wife and children may be fundamental in marriage, but after divorce this expectation is largely unenforceable and unenforced. However well parent and child are provided for in theory by the courts, statistics show that within one year after divorce only 38 per cent of the fathers are in full compliance with those orders. By the tenth year after divorce, 79 per cent of the fathers are making no payments at all.[24]

The historical principle of alimony and the abstract moral question of whether needy people deserve help have little bearing on present-day law and practice. In some cases, divorced women continue to receive alimony even when it can be demonstrated that they are independently wealthy or otherwise self-supporting. On the other hand, there are women in desperate need, unskilled, middle-aged, and poor, who never see a dime of alimony. There does not seem to be any effective means of insuring justice in this area; even if the courts put a recalcitrant man in jail, the woman does not benefit financially. Some people have suggested that men's salaries be garnisheed if they do not make their payments. In New York, however, the legal maximum that can be deducted is 10 per cent of a salary, and that is far below the average alimony allotment. Besides, for poor people who do not have secure jobs, or who are not well paid, the revenue available by this remedy could not support an adult. Court decrees in reference to alimony are circumvented and ignored so systematically and successfully that alimony laws, whether they protect or punish divorced families, do so in an entirely haphazard way. (In order to combat this particular problem in Israel, the Knesset, Israel's parliament, has instituted a system of government support for alimony recipients. The law has been altered so that the National Insurance Institute makes payments to divorced women whose ex-husbands perpetually default. The government is then responsible for taking men to court to enforce payments.) [25]

Since the law is largely impotent to protect men and women after divorce, it seems likely that spouses will have to take responsibility for their own economic well-being in the years to come. Women will have to fight valiantly for social and economic equality before and during marriage; they have little choice but to pursue jobs and careers that insure their economic independence, for nothing and no one else will.

Happily, divorced parents can expect a small measure of help to ease the economic burdens of post-divorce life. The Internal Revenue Service now permits parents to deduct as much as four hundred dollars a month for daytime child care.[26] The IRS has also made a ruling (retroactive to 1970) that the parent who contributes more than half the support of a child is entitled to claim the child as an exemption.[27]

As one colleague of ours recently suggested, it is consistent with the new revolutionary position of women that alimony be abolished entirely. Women effectively destroy themselves as emancipated adults when they curtail their educational and vocational growth in the service of marriage, homemaking and child rearing. Alimony, as it is currently awarded, is a dubious form of justice and is too often a monthly reminder that men control women's lives and livelihoods.

Once couples begin to accept the impermanence of marriage as a fact of life, they will stop subordinating their individual needs and ambitions to the exclusive concerns of their private nuclear family. Gradually, smaller and smaller families will become popular, and women who choose not to have children at all will no longer feel like outcasts. Women who resent being asked to sacrifice the "right" to raise children should be reminded that men make that sacrifice all the time while they are out struggling to earn a livelihood for the family. We would agree that this generation of families, based largely on the traditional sexist division of labor, needs the "protection" of law in an urgent way. The law should at least try to compensate women who are trapped in untenable financial straits. We are certainly not advocating that the divorced mothers of today should be punished because they were successfully indoctrinated with a faulty and self-destructive set of values. A committee of economists could be appointed by the government to publish a set of guidelines in the various income brackets so that couples could know in advance roughly what to expect of each other in the event of separation. These guidelines would also reduce the wide latitude judges now have in fixing support payments. At least the inequities caused by arbitrary judicial decisions can be eliminated.

However, in order really to insure equality in post-divorce life, future generations will have to reconsider the importance of sharing "outside and inside" work more equitably. In theory it may be true that the parent who sacrifices outside work for inside work *deserves* a lifetime of compensatory support after divorce, but that is a "pseudo issue" since the law never has and never will be able to enforce that principle systematically. There is no evidence that the law either wants to or can effectively uphold an abstract principle of sexual, marital, or economic equality.

Although American matrimonial and divorce laws seem to be hopelessly bogged down in the service of an antiquated and repressive ideology, and firmly committed to the perpetuation of marriage, the proposed Equal Rights Amendment to the Constitution gives us reason for at least cautious optimism. It aims to protect women in marriage and divorce from discriminatory legal and labor practices, and it commits the law, at least on paper, to the equal protection of both sexes. For example, passage of the Equal Rights Amendment would mean that labor laws, as well as other forms of legislation, would have to be written in "sex-neutral" language, which precludes employers from preferring men to women simply because certain categories of jobs are arbitrarily designated as inappropriate for women. In relation to divorce, the Amendment promises to require each spouse to contribute to the family "in a fashion that would not leave the spouse with the children in a worse financial situation than the other spouse." [28]

For many optimistic men and women, the Equal Rights Amendment represents a major step in mutual emancipation and equality, but their enthusiasm is considerably dampened by the extent of opposition to its passage. At the time of this writing, it is seriously threatened with failure of ratification. It has been passed in twenty-eight states but is not likely to win the necessary ten more. Not only is opposition widespread and well funded (the AFL-CIO, for example, is against the ERA), but most state legislators are men. Labor groups recognize and fear that this Amendment threatens exclusive male access to the best-paying jobs. Considerable organized opposition has also appeared recently among women, led by Phyllis Schlafly, a conservative Republican from Illinois.[29] They argue that the Equal Rights Amendment threatens their "privileged status" as women and mothers.

While the Equal Rights Amendment aims to bar sex discrimination based on law, it cannot protect women from everyday discriminatory practices. It cannot guarantee that couples who have grown apart will not find ways to hurt each other and to circumvent the intent of the law, whether support payments are being made by the man or the woman. But passage of this Amendment can at least give us the legal tools to appeal for justice.

Equality in divorce will be a natural outgrowth of equality in marriage. In our opinion the law is largely to blame for allowing and encouraging divorced couples to hurt each other, to waste their precious financial resources in legal battle, and to be at the mercy of lawyers and judges who may exercise their power in inappropriate ways. We recognize that hard feelings cannot be legislated away, but they can be legislated into existence, or at least intensified, by law. If husbands and wives want to separate with dignity, they have to prepare themselves for independence, inside and outside of marriage.

When couples decide to have children, *both* partners commit themselves to the responsibilities of parenthood. Therefore, they should take an active role, together, in reshaping traditional patterns of marriage and family life. All parents should participate in fighting and lobbying for decent government-supported day-care centers that would free both parents to work and become self-supporting. (A new variety of highly respected careers would then open up for adults who want to work at daytime child rearing.) There are many untapped human resources in our communities for freeing the parents of young children, so that they could work and study outside the home. For example, there are millions of retired Americans whose only responsibility is to keep themselves alive. They have no useful role to play, no work to do, and therefore very little dignity in their lives. Their idleness helps them to grow feeble.[30] Many of these adults have raised children of their own and could be employed, individually and in teams, to help care for preschool youngsters. Parents should have access to these resources whether they are married, divorced, or single.

If the government encouraged men and women to become self-sufficient in their youth, there would be no need to panic at the thought of divorced women and children becoming public charges. Domestic relations lawyers and judges can speak in schools and to community organizations in order to inform young people of the economic realities of divorce. Educating the public, in our opinion, is a humanitarian and crucial task, which would not only alleviate pain for divorced families of the future but would also relieve some of the frustration of judges who often agonize over support problems. "After divorce," wrote one sensitive judge, "my problem is that of trying to provide food and shelter for the wife and children while leaving the husband enough so that he can eat and have a roof over his head. Most of the time I am in the position of our Lord Jesus, without His powers: that of trying, with one loaf and one fish, to feed a multitude." [31]

It would be unfair to berate a well-meaning judge, who every day faces the dilemma of trying to relieve one person's distress without magnifying the other's. Judicial incompetence and frustration in this area are by-products of the inefficient nuclear family, which stretches the earning capacity of the average adult well beyond the breaking point. Since the economic burdens at least double after divorce, when two households have to be supported instead of one, families of the future will have to find more creative and equitable ways of sharing their earning power. In our opinion, the members of the legal profession, who have firsthand knowledge of the financial strains of divorce, are uniquely qualified to be in the forefront of the struggle to reorganize family life. Collectives, extended families, group marriages and three-generation communities are the most hopeful alternatives for the future since they hold out the promise of extending intimacy and relieving the stress of two people depending on each other for all of their needs.

# Conclusion

Far from being the basis of the good society, the family with its narrow privacy and tawdry secrets is the source of all our discontents.

—Edmund Leach

The moral problems of social study . . . will be recognized and discussion will be possible. Then there will be greater self-awareness all around—which is of course a precondition for objectivity in the enterprise of social science as a whole.

—C. Wright Mills

Ideas and attitudes change. Even during the composition of this book a discernible shift in media treatment of divorce has been perceptible. Scattered television shows and magazine features have brought objective and sympathetic accounts of divorced families to mass audiences. It is hard to conceive of such media presentations just a few years ago, when the standard stereotypes reigned supreme: divorce was unrelieved misery and persons who went through with it were pathological specimens.

But a few public airings of the real issues does not amount to a thoroughgoing change in attitudes. Even those who do achieve divorce are confused and distracted by lingering feelings of guilt

231

and shame. Two thousand years of anti-divorce indoctrination cannot instantly be eradicated. It is necessary to study and understand this heritage and its contemporary manifestations if they are ever to be overcome.

A surprising prop to these old attitudes and values on divorce has been social science, and particularly sociological studies of the family. Despite the façade of objectivity to which social science pays obeisance, popular and academic sociology has been geared primarily to the perpetuation and improvement of nuclear family life. The classic sociological works on divorce,[1] works whose influence is still dominant in America, comprise an important part of the anti-divorce tradition. Sociologists have demonstrated a fairly consistent commitment to the status quo, a tendency toward reckless and unsound psychological theorizing, and a fundamental confusion between the concepts of "deviance" and "difference."

It is on precisely this last point that researchers have revealed their bias against divorce. Often their negativism is a by-product of the categories that social scientists use. "In measuring the breakdown of society," writes Margaret Mead, "it is customary for researchers to group together statistics on crime, juvenile delinquency, alcoholism, drug addiction, mental illness and divorce."[2] Covert value judgments are woven into the vocabulary of social science and thus gain the authority of scientific objectivity.

Research into the sociology of divorce has been dominated by William Goode, a respected scholar whose books are an important part of contemporary courses in family sociology. As recently as 1964 Goode wrote that divorce is a *catastrophe* which *inevitably* creates serious adjustment problems, and that it may be seen as a *personal misfortune* for one or both spouses in any society.[3] In *The Family* he implies that parents cease to discharge their proper role obligations to their children when they decide to divorce.[4] Indoctrinating people to associate divorce with breakdown, loss and hardship, social scientists have reinforced the traditional view that divorce must be a disaster.

For the past forty years, even prior to Goode's research, the standard sociological works on divorce were even more gloomy and moralistic. The writings of Willard Waller, Ernest Groves, Meyer Nimkoff and others were marred by a pious conventionality which indoctrinated people to revere marriage, dread divorce, suspect the unmarried, and disparage youthful experimentation. Divorce, the antithesis of marriage, was portrayed as a singularly horrendous experience leading to pervasive feelings of failure, thoughts of suicide, moods of desperate loneliness, illicit sexual relationships, insecure children, diminished income, unwise rebound marriages, and so on. But Goode, the contemporary dean of family sociology, expresses essentially the same outlook. The bias in all of their work is so pervasive that it accepts without question the normality and desirability of the nuclear American family.

The cumulative content of most books on marriage and family life may indeed be "rubbish," as one critic asserts,[5] but the idealization of bourgeois nuclear family life persists. Despite the fact that thousands of people and dozens of serious writers have argued that in its traditional patriarchal form marriage is a nearly defunct institution,[6] specialists still believe that the "rising tide of divorce" calls for reform by prevention, in the name of the sanctity of the family. With the still negligible exception of a few radical writers, mainly feminists, liberal reformers are mainly preoccupied with the early prevention of divorce through counseling and family life education.

In our opinion, the real objects of reform ought to be the institution of marriage and the myth of domesticity itself, of which the laws and customs surrounding divorce are the most curious expressions.[7] At the very least, divorce must be understood as part of "the passing of patriarchism and familism in America, and of the revolt of women." [8] Studies of divorced couples indicate that at least two main factors are associated with marital difficulty: the desire to escape home and the need to legitimize pregnancy.[9] Therefore the most sensible and feasible approach to the problem of hasty, ill-advised marriages would be to break down the traditional norm which teaches that marriage is the only genuine measure of adulthood and the only healthy foundation for family life.

It is the inability to translate personal problems into public issues that engenders much of the contemporary panic over the soaring divorce rates. Thus the distortion persists that divorce represents a total and negative breakdown of relationships between parents and children rather than a gradual but significant change in kinship patterns and cultural values. What divorce really does is *restructure* family relationships; parents who do not get "custody" need not kiss their children good-by and disappear. They can and should play an active role in the lives of their children. Contrary to legend, stepfamilies can be happy families, and parents who remarry need not feel that they are merely compounding their children's problems. Freed of the covert biases of traditional family sociology we may view the whole range of divorce relationships with a fresh viewpoint.

Lacking any clear sense of their capability to achieve a successful post-divorce life, or any sense of community with other divorced families, many couples never find the courage to split up, and remain locked in sad and unfulfilling marriages. Parents are still skeptical about the possibility of satisfactory post-divorce relationships with their children and are uninformed about the ways in which common problems can be handled. Existing literature, focusing almost exclusively on the dramatic events of separation, reinforces this unhealthy ignorance. For those who do manage to divorce there is often an unnecessary sacrifice of relationships with children and extended family, which in many cases probably could have been maintained in different, even better, forms than they existed in marriage.

In championing the courage to divorce we have not been advocating hasty or casual decisions to sever marital bonds. Our clinical and personal experience has convinced us that quite the opposite actually occurs most of the time; because of a variety of cultural and psychological pressures, unhappily married people are more likely to endure than to end bad marriages. In this book we have not been primarily concerned with the causes of divorce, but rather with the pressures that keep so many unfulfilling marriages formally "intact." We believe that these life-denying forces may be understood, countered and overcome.

# Notes

### INTRODUCTION
1. Robert Merton, "The Self-Fulfilling Prophecy," in *Social Theory and Social Structure* (Glencoe, Ill.: The Free Press, 1949), pp. 183–184.
2. Sidney Ditzion, *Marriage, Morals and Sex in America: A History of Ideas* (New York: Bookman Associates, 1953), p. 393.
3. Paul H. Jacobson, *American Marriage and Divorce* (New York: Rinehart & Co., 1959), p. 88.

### CHAPTER 1
1. William O'Neill, *Divorce in the Progressive Era* (New Haven: Yale University Press, 1967), p. 57; and James Barnett, "Divorce and the American Divorce Novel, 1858–1937," unpublished dissertation, University of Pennsylvania, 1939.
2. Simone de Beauvoir, *The Second Sex* (New York: Bantam Books, 1961), pp. 408–409.
3. Hugh Carter and Paul Glick, *Marriage and Divorce: A Social and Economic Study* (Cambridge: Harvard University Press, 1970), pp. 269–270.
4. Margaret Mead, "Anomalies in American Post-Divorce Relationships," in Paul Bohannan, ed., *Divorce and After* (Garden City, N.Y.: Doubleday & Co., 1970), p. 104; and Margaret Mead, "Double Talk About Divorce," *Redbook*, May, 1968, p. 47.
5. William Graham Sumner, *Folkways* (1906, reprinted New York: Dover Publications, Inc., 1959), p. 372.
6. C. Wright Mills, *The Sociological Imagination* (New York: Grove Press, 1961), p. 10.
7. Friedrich Engels, *The Origin of the Family, Private Property and the State* (New York: International Publishers, 1942), p. 65.
8. Bronislaw Malinowski, "Personal Problems," in Bronislaw Malinowski and Robert Briffault, *Marriage: Past and Present* (Boston: Porter Sargent Publishers, 1956), p. 80.

235

9. *Ibid.*, p. 83.

10. Alvin Toffler, *Future Shock* (New York: Random House, 1970), p. 221.

11. See Marjorie Smith, "Where Credit Is Due," *Ms*, Vol. 1, No. 4, October, 1972, pp. 36–37.

12. Dean Knudsen, "The Declining Status of Women: Popular Myths and the Failure of Functionalist Thought," *Social Forces* 48 (1969), pp. 183–193.

13. Marilyn Goldstein, "When the Marriage Ends, the Money Squeeze Begins," *Newsday*, April 13, 1972, p. 4A.

14. See John Rodell, *How to Avoid Alimony* (New York: Stein and Day, 1969) and Norman Sheresky and Marya Mannes, *Uncoupling: The Art of Coming Apart* (New York: The Viking Press, 1972).

15. We were pleasantly surprised to read of the 1970 decision of the Washington *Post* to repudiate the use of the word "divorcee" in that newspaper on the ground that it is a stereotyped and denigrating image that undermines the dignity of women.

16. Paul Bohannan, "Some Thoughts on Divorce Reform," in Paul Bohannan, ed., *Divorce and After*, p. 249. Note the tendency of many divorced women, for example, to retain the surname of their former husbands. This habit may reveal their continued emotional attachment to their ex-spouses, their desire to "protect" their children from potentially awkward questions, their need to "prove" that they are the parents of "legitimate" children, their shame at being divorced, or some combination of the above.

17. Mary Salpukas, "The Man Who Gets Ahead: Being Married Really Helps," *The New York Times*, July 24, 1972.

18. *Ibid.*

19. William O'Neill, *Coming Apart: An Informal History of America in the 1960's* (Chicago: Quadrangle Books, 1971), p. 107. This evidence contradicts Max Rheinstein's conclusion that Rockefeller was able to go through a migratory divorce without either losing prestige or having his political ambitions thwarted. Rheinstein is unduly optimistic in his assessment of the cultural climate. See Max Rheinstein, *Marriage Stability, Divorce and the Law* (Chicago: University of Chicago Press, 1972), p. 357.

20. Judson Landis and Mary Landis, *The Marriage Handbook* (New York: Prentice-Hall, 1948), p. 4.

21. Donald Michael, *The Next Generation: The Prospects Ahead for the Youth of Today and Tomorrow* (New York: Random House, 1965), p. 75.

22. John Sirjamaki, *The American Family in the Twentieth Century* (Cambridge: Harvard University Press, 1953), p. 56.

23. Hendrik Ruitenbeek, *The Male Myth* (New York: Dell Publishing Co., 1967), p. 51.

24. Judson Landis and Mary Landis, *Building a Successful Marriage* (Englewood Cliffs, N.J.: Prentice-Hall, 1968), p. 88.

25. Doris Jonas Freed and Henry Foster, Jr., "Divorce American Style," *Annals of the American Academy of Political and Social Science*, Vol. 383, May, 1969, p. 83.

26. Max Rheinstein, *Marriage Stability, Divorce and the Law*, Chapter 16, especially p. 430.

27. Theodore Lidz, M.D., *The Family and Human Adaptation* (New York: International University Press, 1963), p. 62.

28. Shulamith Firestone, *The Dialectic of Sex: The Case for Feminist Revolution* (New York: William Morrow & Co., 1970), p. 251.

29. Dr. Benjamin Spock, "Can a Mother Play a Father's Role?", *Redbook*, May, 1969, p. 43.

30. Max Rheinstein, *Marriage Stability, Divorce and the Law*, p. 435.

31. Betty Rollin, "Motherhood: Who Needs It?", in Arlene Skolnick and Jerome Skolnick, eds., *Family in Transition* (Boston: Little, Brown & Co., 1971), p. 352.

32. Morton Hunt, *The World of the Formerly Married* (New York: McGraw-Hill, 1966), p. 259.

33. Ralph Ober, "Parents Without Partners—With Children of Divorce," in Earl A. Grollman, ed., *Explaining Divorce to Children* (Boston: Beacon Press, 1969), p. 154.

34. *Ibid.*, p. 155.

35. John Thomas, "A Priest's View on Children of Divorce," in Earl A. Grollman, ed., *Explaining Divorce to Children*, p. 193.

36. William Goode, *The Family* (Englewood Cliffs, N.J.: Prentice-Hall, 1964), p. 100. Only 3 to 4 per cent of the adult population that is divorced is not remarried, *The Nation*, April 23, 1973, p. 527.

37. Paul Glick, *American Families* (New York: John Wiley & Sons, 1956), pp. 138–139.

38. William Goode, *Women in Divorce* (Glencoe, Ill.: The Free Press, 1957), Chapter XX.

39. Thomas Monahan, "The Changing Nature and Instability of Remarriages," *Eugenics Quarterly* 5 (June, 1958), pp. 73–85, quoted in Landis and Landis, *Building a Successful Marriage*, p. 152.

40. See, for example, the opinion of anthropologist Margaret Mead, in *Redbook*, May, 1968, p. 47.

41. Robert Merton, "The Self-Fulfilling Prophecy," in *Social Theory and Social Structure* (Glencoe, Ill.: The Free Press, 1949), pp. 421–436.

42. William and Ellen Hartley, "Stop Divorces Before They Start," *Good Housekeeping*, April, 1966, p. 89.

43. *Ibid.*, p. 230.

44. Norman Lobsenz, "How Young Divorced Mothers Learn to Stand Alone," *Redbook*, November, 1971, p. 83.

45. William J. Lederer and Don D. Jackson, *The Mirages of Marriage* (New York: W. W. Norton & Co., 1968), pp. 15–16.

46. Susan Pollack, "Child of Divorce," *Mademoiselle*, May, 1968, p. 172.

47. *Newsweek*, May 12, 1973, p. 47.

48. Norman Lobsenz, "How Young Divorced Mothers Learn to Stand Alone," p. 83.

49. *Ibid.*

50. Herb Gore, "This Marriage Couldn't Be Saved," *New York*, September 18, 1972.

51. See, for example, Norman Sheresky and Marya Mannes, *Uncoupling: The Art of Coming Apart*.

52. Bertrand Russell, *Marriage and Morals* (New York: Liveright Publishing Co., 1929), p. 57.

53. Elizabeth Janeway, "The Question Is, What Is a Family Anyway?", *The New York Times*, April 1, 1972.

54. While the "manifest functions" of Parents Without Partners are unique and admirable, the organization's "latent function," in our opinion, is to facilitate remarriage, since the professionals who are consultants to PWP are by and large in agreement that divorce is an unfortunate necessity which is not good for children. A California-based organization, called MOMMA, is beginning to fill this gap; it has branches in many cities and also publishes a magazine for single mothers.

55. Elizabeth Mulligan, "Divorce Court: Scene of Decay," *Marriage*, Vol. 52, No. 4, April, 1970, pp. 41–43.

56. John Deedy, *The New York Times*, September 3, 1972. However, the Catholic divorce rate is not substantially different from that of the national average—455 divorces for every 1,000 new marriages. Some estimate that as many as five million American Catholics are divorced and living in so-called invalid marriages.

57. Robert O. Blood, Jr., and Donald M. Wolfe, *Husbands and Wives* (Glencoe, Ill.: The Free Press, 1960), p. 80.

58. Judge R. A. Pfaff, of Los Angeles, quoted in William and Ellen Hartley, "Stop Divorces Before They Start," p. 89.

59. According to a United Press International poll, Dr. Brothers, who is a psychologist, is one of the ten most influential women in America. She is a nationally syndicated journalist and is advertised as "the

world's most widely read, seen and heard psychologist." See Joyce Brothers, *The Brothers System for Liberated Love and Marriage.* (New York: Peter Wyden: 1972).
60. George O'Neill and Nena O'Neill, *Open Marriage* (New York: M. Evans & Co., 1972), p. 20.
61. William J. Lederer and Don D. Jackson, *The Mirages of Marriage.*
62. Fred Bruning, "44 Hours That Will Change Your Life," *New York,* October 2, 1972, p. 44.

## CHAPTER 2

1. For an insightful evaluation and discussion of unsatisfying marriage "systems," see William J. Lederer and Don D. Jackson, *The Mirages of Marriage* (New York: W. W. Norton & Co., 1968), especially Part II.
2. *Newsweek,* March 12, 1973, p. 49.
3. William J. Lederer and Don D. Jackson, *The Mirages of Marriage,* p. 453.
4. For a vivid reminder of how potent the romantic appeal of the formal wedding still is in America, see Marcia Seligson's book, *The Eternal Bliss Machine* (New York: William Morrow & Co., 1973).
5. For an informative and lively discussion of the historical roots of new life-styles, and their relevance to the modern era, see Alvin Toffler's *Future Shock* (New York: Random House, 1970), especially Chapter 11.

## CHAPTER 3

1. See Jetse Sprey, "Children in Divorce: An Overview," in Earl A. Grollman, ed., *Explaining Divorce to Children* (Boston: Beacon Press, 1969), p. 57. See also William Goode, *Women in Divorce* (Glencoe, Ill.: The Free Press, 1956), p. vi.
2. William O'Neill, *Divorce in the Progressive Era* (New Haven: Yale University Press, 1967), pp. 221–222.
3. Jetse Sprey, "Children in Divorce: An Overview," pp. 57–58.
4. Oliver Spurgeon English and C. J. Foster, *Fathers Are Parents Too* (New York: G. P. Putnam's Sons, 1951), p. 239.
5. Irene Fast and Albert Cain, "The Stepparent Role: Potential for Disturbance in Family Functioning," *American Journal of Orthopsychiatry,* Vol. 36, 1966, p. 490.
6. Dr. Benjamin Spock, "Can a Mother Play a Father's Role?", *Redbook,* May, 1969, p. 46.
7. Dr. Lee Salk, *What Every Child Would Like His Parents to Know* (New York: McKay, 1972), pp. 187–188.
8. Esther Oshiver Fisher, "A Guide to Divorce Counseling," *The Family Coordinator,* Vol. 22, No. 1, January, 1973, p. 55. Esther

Fisher, LL.B., Ed.D., is Chairman of Training in Marriage and Divorce Counseling at the American Association of Religion and Psychiatry in New York City.

9. See, for examples, Nathan Ackerman, "Divorce and Alienation in Modern Society," in Jacob Fried, ed., *Jews and Divorce* (New York: KTAV Publishing House, 1968), p. 94; Catherine M. Bitterman, "The Multimarriage Family," *Social Casework*. Vol. XLIX, No. 4, April, 1968, p. 3; William Goode, *The Family* (Englewood Cliffs, N.J.: Prentice-Hall, 1964), p. 98; Meyer Nimkoff, *Marriage and the Family* (New York: Houghton Mifflin Co., 1947), p. 350; Dr. Benjamin Spock, "Can a Mother Play a Father's Role?", pp. 46–50; Isabella Taves, *Women Alone* (New York: Funk & Wagnalls, 1968), p. 271; and Willard Waller, *The Old Love and the New: Divorce and Readjustment* (Carbondale and Edwardsville: Southern Illinois University Press, 1958), pp. 22–23.

10. Paul Bohannan, *Social Anthropology* (New York: Holt, Rinehart and Winston, 1963), p. 121.

11. William Goode, *The Family*, p. 98.

12. *Ibid.*, p. 101.

13. Wayne E. Oates, "A Minister's Views on Children of Divorce," in Earl A. Grollman, ed., *Explaining Divorce to Children*, p. 172. Dr. Oates is professor of psychology, religion and pastoral care at the Southern Baptist Theological Seminary in Louisville, Kentucky.

14. Bernard Steinzor, *When Parents Divorce: A New Approach to New Relationships* (New York: Pantheon Books, Random House, 1969), p. 195. A practicing therapist in New York City, Steinzor is also a lecturer in the program of psychiatry and religion at the Union Theological Seminary.

15. Paul Bohannan, "The Six Stations of Divorce," in Paul Bohannan, ed., *Divorce and After* (Garden City, N.Y.: Doubleday & Co., 1970), p. 37.

16. William Goode, *The Family*, p. 98.

17. Bert N. Adams, *The American Family: A Sociological Interpretation* (Chicago: Markham Publishing Co., 1971), p. 341.

18. Paul Bohannan, "The Six Stations of Divorce," p. 53.

19. George O'Neill and Nena O'Neill, *Open Marriage* (New York: M. Evans and Co., 1972), p. 25.

20. Willard Waller, *The Old Love and the New: Divorce and Readjustment*, p. 26.

## CHAPTER 4

1. C. Wright Mills, *The Sociological Imagination* (New York: Grove Press, 1961), p. 21.

2. William O'Neill, *Divorce in the Progressive Era* (New Haven: Yale University Press, 1967), p. 273.

3. Herbert Holt and Charles Winick, "Some Psychodynamics in Divorce and Separation," *Mental Hygiene*, Vol. XLIX, July, 1965, p. 443.

4. Ernest R. Groves, *Conserving Marriage and the Family: A Realistic Discussion of the Divorce Problem* (New York: The Macmillan Co., 1944), p. 19. Groves was a sociologist and domestic counselor. He allegedly taught the first college course in preparation for marriage, at the University of North Carolina in 1927.

5. Willard Waller, *The Old Love and the New: Divorce and Readjustment* (Carbondale and Edwardsville: Southern Illinois University Press, 1958), p. 151.

6. Ronald Liefer, *In the Name of Mental Health* (New York: Science House, 1969), p. 25.

7. Seymour Halleck, M.D., *The Politics of Therapy* (New York: Harper & Row, 1971), p. 15.

8. Ronald Liefer, *In the Name of Mental Health*, p. 25.

9. Philip Lehrman, M.D., "Psychopathological Aspects of Emotional Divorce," *The Psychoanalytic Review*, Vol. 26, No. 1, January, 1939, p. 10.

10. Edmund Bergler, *Divorce Won't Help* (New York: Harper and Bros., 1948). Dr. Bergler was a practicing psychoanalytical psychiatrist from 1927 until his death in 1962. He published 22 books and 273 studies on the theory and treatment of neurosis.

11. *Ibid.*, pp. ix–x, 23.

12. *Ibid.*, p. 233.

13. J. Louise Despert, M.D., *Children of Divorce* (Garden City, Dolphin Books, 1962), p. 199.

14. Aaron Rutledge, "Should a Marriage Counselor Ever Recommend Divorce?", *Journal of Marriage and Family Living*, Vol. XXV, No. 3, August, 1963, pp. 320–321.

15. Rabbi Solomon Faber, in Jacob Fried, ed., *Jews and Divorce* (New York: KTAV Publishing House, 1968), p. 81.

16. Simone de Beauvoir, *The Second Sex* (New York: Bantam Books, 1961), p. 443.

17. Bernard Steinzor, *When Parents Divorce: A New Approach to New Relationships* (New York: Pantheon Books, Random House, 1969), p. 43.

18. Esther Oshiver Fisher, LL.B., Ed.D., quoted in the New York *Post*, July 28, 1973.

19. Esther Oshiver Fisher, "A Guide to Divorce Counseling," *The Family Coordinator*, Vol. 22, No. 1, January, 1973, pp. 55–56, 58.

20. Haim Ginott, *Between Parent and Child* (New York: The Macmillan Co., 1965), p. 204. The author was professor of psychology at New York University and served as United Nations expert in child psychotherapy and parent guidance.

21. Lawrence Kubie, M.D., in Earl A. Grollman, ed., *Explaining Divorce to Children* (Boston: Beacon Press, 1969), p. 8. Dr. Kubie is professor of psychiatry at the University of Maryland.

22. J. Louise Despert, M.D., *Children of Divorce*, p. 199.

23. Norman Reider, in Victor Eisenstein, M.D., ed., *Neurotic Interaction in Marriage* (New York: Basic Books, 1956), p. 311.

24. Herbert Holt and Charles Winick, "Some Psychodynamics in Divorce and Separation," p. 450.

25. Seymour Halleck, M.D., *The Politics of Therapy*, p. 43.

26. *Ibid.*, p. 56.

27. Among the significant authors whose work seriously challenges these conventional beliefs are Bruno Bettelheim, *The Children of the Dream* (London: The Macmillan Co., 1969); Shulamith Firestone, *The Dialectic of Sex: The Case for Feminist Revolution* (New York: William Morrow & Co., 1970); Jules Henry, *Pathways to Madness* (New York: Random House, 1971); and Ronald Laing, *The Politics of the Family and Other Essays* (New York: Vintage Books, Random House, 1969).

28. Paul Bohannan, *Social Anthropology* (New York: Holt, Rinehart and Winston, 1963), p. 114.

29. George Mohr, M.D., "The Threat of Divorce," *Child Study*, Vol. XXV, No. 1, Winter, 1947, pp. 7–9. The author was associate professor of psychiatry at the University of Illinois and a staff member of the Chicago Institute of Psychoanalysis.

30. Bernard Steinzor, *When Parents Divorce: A New Approach to New Relationships*, p. 175.

31. John Millet, "Marriage Terminable and Interminable," in Salo Rosenblum and Ian Alger, eds., *The Marriage Relationship* (New York: Basic Books, 1968), p. 320.

32. Theodore Lidz, M.D., *The Family and Human Adaptation* (New York: International University Press, 1963), p. 39.

33. *Ibid.*, pp. 34, 45.

34. Nathaniel Lehrman, M.D., in Jacob Fried, ed., *Jews and Divorce*, pp. 42–43.

35. Emily Mudd, in Emily Mudd, Maurice Karpf, Abraham Stone, and Janet Fowler, eds., *Marriage Counseling: A Casebook* (New York: Association Press, 1958), p. 475.

36. Thomas French, M.D., "Contributions to a Therapeutic Solution to the Divorce Problem: Psychiatry," University of Chicago Law

School, Conference on Divorce, Conference Series No. 9, February 29, 1952, p. 63.

37. Ronald Laing, the *Politics of the Family and Other Essays*, p. 23.

38. Norman Reider, in Victor Eisenstein, M.D., ed., *Neurotic Interaction in Marriage*, p. 323.

39. The widespread use of drugs, such as Ritalin, for example, to suppress "hyperactivity" in school children, and the use of Valium and Thorazine in prisons, suggests that the use of drugs as a form of social control is gaining, not losing, popularity.

40. Ray L. Birdwhistell, "The Idealized Model of the American Family," *Social Casework*, Vol. LI, No. 4, April, 1970, p. 197. Ray Birdwhistell is professor of communications at the University of Pennsylvania Annenberg School.

41. John R. Cavanagh, M.D., *Fundamental Marriage Counseling: A Catholic Viewpoint* (Milwaukee: The Bruce Publishing Co., 1963), p. 363.

42. See the Reverend Walker Gwynne, D.D., *Divorce in America Under State and Church* (New York: The Macmillan Co., 1925), p. 11, and the Reverend Ralph Ferris, quoted in Alfred Cahen, *A Statistical Analysis of American Divorce* (New York: Columbia University Press, 1932), p. 47. The Reverend Ferris was a professor at the Chicago Theological Seminary.

43. David Hubbard, *Is the Family Here to Stay?* (Waco, Texas: Word Books, 1971), *passim*.

44. Jacob Fried, ed., *Jews and Divorce*, introduction, p. IX.

45. Alvin Chenkin, in *ibid.*, pp. 83–84.

46. Rhoda Simon, in *ibid.*, p. XII.

47. Earl A. Grollman, ed., *Explaining Divorce to Children*, p. 229.

48. Nathan Ackerman, in Jacob Fried, ed., *Jews and Divorce*, p. 93.

49. Nathan Ackerman, *The Psychodynamics of Family Life* (New York: Basic Books, 1958), p. 8.

50. Nathan Ackerman, in Jacob Fried, ed., *Jews and Divorce*, p. 91.

51. Martin Duberman, "Homosexual Literature," *The New York Times Book Review*, December 10, 1972.

52. Seymour Halleck, M.D., *The Politics of Therapy*, p. 302.

53. William Graham Sumner, *Folkways* (1906, Reprinted, New York: Dover Publications, Inc., 1959), p. 377.

54. Gunnar Myrdal, *Objectivity in Social Research* (New York: Pantheon Books, Random House, 1969), p. 5.

### CHAPTER 5

1. William Goode, *Women in Divorce* (Glencoe, Ill.: The Free Press, 1956), p. 307.

2. Max Lerner, *America As a Civilization* (New York: Simon and Schuster, 1957), p. 597.

3. Nathan Ackerman, *The Psychodynamics of Family Life* (New York: Basic Books, 1958), p. 149.

4. Edmund Bergler, *Divorce Won't Help* (New York: Harper and Bros., 1948), p. 162.

5. Robert A. Harper, "Marriage Counseling and the Mores: A Critique," *Journal of Marriage and Family Living*, Vol. XXI, February, 1959, pp. 14–15.

6. Ruth Dickson, *Marriage Is a Bad Habit* (New York: Award Books, 1969), p. 150.

7. *Ibid.*, p. 153.

8. Earl A. Grollman, ed., *Explaining Divorce to Children* (Boston: Beacon Press, 1969), p. 4.; and Morton Hunt, *The World of the Formerly Married* (New York: McGraw-Hill, 1966), p. 258.

9. Mary McCarthy, *Birds of America* (New York: New American Library, 1965), p. 101. For a lengthy and thorough exploration of the treatment of divorce in American fiction, see James Barnett, "Divorce and the American Divorce Novel, 1858–1937," unpublished dissertation, University of Pennsylvania, 1939.

10. J. Louise Despert, M.D., *Children of Divorce* (Garden City: N.Y.: Dolphin Books, 1962, p. 55.

11. E. E. LeMasters, "Parents Without Partners," in Arlene Skolnick and Jerome Skolnick, eds., *Family in Transition* (Boston: Little, Brown & Co., 1971), p. 409.

12. *Ibid.*

13. *Ibid.*, p. 410.

14. John F. McDermott, Jr., M.D., "Parental Divorce in Early Childhood," *American Journal of Psychiatry*, Vol. 124, No. 10, April, 1968, p. 1,424.

15. Alexander Plateris, "Children of Divorced Couples: United States, Selected Years," U.S. Department of Health, Education and Welfare, Vital and Health Statistics, Series 21, No. 18, February, 1970, p. 2.

16. *Ibid.*

### CHAPTER 6

1. J. Louise Despert, M.D., *Children of Divorce* (Garden City: N.Y.: Dolphin Books, 1962), p. 59.

2. See Dr. Lee Salk, *What Every Child Would Like His Parents to Know* (New York: McKay, 1972), pp. 187–188.

3. Evelyn Goodenough Pitcher, "Explaining Divorce to Young Children," in Earl A. Grollman, ed., *Explaining Divorce to Children*, p. 70.

4. Bernard Steinzor, *When Parents Divorce: A New Approach to New Relationships* (New York: Pantheon Books, Random House, 1969), p. 78.

5. Catherine M. Bitterman, "The Multimarriage Family," *Social Casework*, Vol. XLIX, No. 4, April, 1968, pp. 219–220.

6. Jetse Sprey, "The Study of Single Parenthood: Some Methodological Considerations," *Family Life Coordinator*, Vol. XVI, January–April, 1967, pp. 29–34.

7. See Morris Rosenberg, "The Broken Family and Self-Esteem," in Ira Riess, ed., *Readings on the Family System* (New York: Holt, Rinehart and Winston, 1972).

8. *The New York Times*, March 3, 1973.

9. Michael J. Arlen, "Saturday Father," *McCall's*, February, 1973, p. 38.

10. William Goode, *Women in Divorce* (Glencoe, Ill.: The Free Press, 1956), p. 309.

11. Eva Figes, *Patriarchal Attitudes* (New York: Stein and Day, 1970), pp. 172–173.

12. Ruth E. Hartley, "Sex Role Pressures and the Socialization of the Male Child," *Psychological Reports*, Vol. 5, 1959, p. 459.

13. Hendrik Ruitenbeek, *The Male Myth* (New York: Dell Publishing Co., 1967), p. 72.

14. Donald E. Payne and Paul H. Mussen, "Parent-Child Relations and Father Identification Among Adolescent Boys," *Journal of Abnormal and Social Psychology*, Vol. 52, 1956, p. 358.

15. J. C. Flügel, *The Psychoanalytic Study of the Family* (London: Hogarth Press and the Institute of Psychoanalysis, 1931), pp. 223–224.

16. *Ibid.*

17. Robert R. Bell, *Marriage and Family Interaction* (Homewood, Ill.: Dorsey Press, 1967), p. 490.

18. Lee Burchinal, "Characteristics of Adolescents from Unbroken, Broken, and Reconstituted Families," *Journal of Marriage and the Family*, Vol. XXVI, No. 1, February, 1964, p. 50.

19. *Ibid.*

20. Ivan Nye, "Child Adjustment in Broken and Unhappy, Unbroken Homes," *Marriage and Family Living*, Vol. 19, No. 4, November, 1957, p. 361.

21. Ralph Ober, "Parents Without Partners—With Children of Divorce," in Earl A. Grollman, ed., *Explaining Divorce to Children*, p. 149.

22. Bernard Steinzor, *When Parents Divorce: A New Approach to New Relationships*, p. 45.

23. *Ibid.*

24. Seymour Halleck, M.D., *The Politics of Therapy* (New York: Harper & Row, 1971), p. 256.
25. "The Broken Family: Divorce U.S. Style," *Newsweek*, March 12, 1973, p. 50.
26. Bernard Steinzor, *When Parents Divorce: A New Approach to New Relationships*, p. 56.
27. Donald Cantor, *Escape from Marriage* (New York: William Morrow & Co., 1971), p. 158.
28. Theodore Lidz, A. Cornelison, S. Fleck, D. Terry, "The Intrafamilial Environment of Schizophrenic Patients: Marital Schism and Mental Skew," *American Journal of Psychiatry*, Vol. 114, 1959, p. 246.
29. Margaret Mahler and Ruth Rabinovitch, "The Effects of Marital Conflict on Child Development," in Victor Eisenstein, M.D., ed., *Neurotic Interaction in Marriage* (New York: Basic Books, 1956), p. 53.

## CHAPTER 7

1. J. Louise Despert, M.D., *Children of Divorce* (Garden City: Dolphin Books, 1962), p. 54.
2. Earl A. Grollman, "Prologue," in Earl A. Grollman, ed., *Explaining Divorce to Children* (Boston: Beacon Press, 1969), p. 21.
3. Bernard Steinzor, *When Parents Divorce: A New Approach to New Relationships* (New York: Pantheon Books, Random House, 1969), p. 122.
4. This kind of parental behavior may help explain one sociologist's tentative finding that the self-esteem of children of divorce is lower than that of children from intact homes. See Morris Rosenberg, "The Broken Family and Self-Esteem," in Ira Riess, ed., *Readings on the Family System* (New York: Holt, Rinehart and Winston, 1972).
5. Robert A. Harper, "Marriage Counseling and the Mores: A Critique," *Journal of Marriage and Family Living*, Vol. XXI, February, 1959, p. 15.
6. Judson T. Landis, "The Trauma of Children When Parents Divorce," *Journal of Marriage and Family Living*, Vol. XXII, No. 1, February, 1960, p. 9.
7. Jules Henry, *Pathways to Madness* (New York: Random House, 1971), p. 60.
8. Norman Lobsenz, "How Young Divorced Mothers Learn to Stand Alone," *Redbook*, November, 1971, p. 139.
9. Dr. Benjamin Spock, "Can a Mother Play a Father's Role?", *Redbook*, May, 1969, p. 50.
10. Bernard Steinzor, *When Parents Divorce: A New Approach to New Relationships*, p. 55.

11. Richard A. Gardner, M.D., *The Boys and Girls Book About Divorce*, (New York: Bantam Books, 1971), pp. 22–23.
12. We are in no way comparing divorce to wartime bombing raids, but we are trying to show that whatever the external situation may be, parents profoundly affect their children's attitudes.
13. Margaret Mahler and Ruth Rabinovitch, "The Effects of Marital Conflict on Child Development," in Victor Eisenstein, M.D., ed., *Neurotic Interaction in Marriage* (New York: Basic Books, 1956), pp. 51–52.
14. Robert A. Harper, "Marriage Counseling and the Mores: A Critique," p. 15.
15. William Goode, *Women in Divorce* (Glencoe, Ill.: The Free Press, 1956), p. 307.
16. Jules Henry, *Pathways to Madness*, p. 252.
17. Ralph Ober, "Parents Without Partners—With Children of Divorce," in Earl A. Grollman, ed., *Explaining Divorce to Children*, p. 145.

### CHAPTER 8
1. Bernard Steinzor, *When Parents Divorce: A New Approach to New Relationships* (New York: Pantheon Books, Random House, 1969), p. 52.
2. *Ibid.*, p. 57.
3. *Ibid.*, p. 169.

### CHAPTER 9
1. Paul Bohannan, "Divorce Chains, Households of Remarriage, and Multiple Divorces," in Paul Bohannan, ed., *Divorce and After* (Garden City, N.Y.: Doubleday & Co., 1970), p. 121.
2. Jetse Sprey, "Children in Divorce: An Overview," in Earl A. Grollman, ed., *Explaining Divorce to Children* (Boston: Beacon Press, 1969), p. 57.
3. William Goode, *Women in Divorce* (Glencoe, Ill.: The Free Press, 1956), p. 339.
4. Else P. Heilpern, "Psychological Problems of Stepchildren," *Psychoanalytic Review*, Vol. 30, April, 1943, p. 171.
5. Edward Podolsky, "The Emotional Problems of Stepchildren," *Mental Hygiene*, Vol. 39, January, 1955, p. 52.
6. Catherine M. Bitterman, "The Multimarriage Family," *Social Casework*, Vol. XLIX, No. 4, April, 1968, pp. 220–221.
7. Jessie Bernard, *Remarriage: A Study of Marriage* (New York: The Dryden Press, 1956), pp. 318–319.

8. Morris Rosenberg, "The Broken Family and Self-Esteem," in Ira Riess, ed., *Readings on the Family System* (New York: Holt, Rinehart and Winston, 1972), p. 527.

9. *Ibid.*, p. 528.

10. *Ibid.*

11. Margaret Mahler and Ruth Rabinovitch, "The Effects of Marital Conflict on Child Development," in Victor Eisenstein, M.D., ed., *Neurotic Interaction in Marriage* (New York: Basic Books, 1956), p. 53.

12. Francis L. Beatman, "When a Child Gets a New Parent," *The New York Times Magazine*, January 29, 1961.

13. Bernard Steinzor, *When Parents Divorce: A New Approach to New Relationships* (New York: Pantheon Books, Random House 1969), p. 189.

14. Paul Bohannan, *Social Anthropology* (New York: Holt, Rinehart and Winston, 1963), p. 122.

15. Janet Pfleger, "The Wicked Stepmother in the Child Guidance Clinic," *Smith College Studies in Social Work*, Vol. XVII, No. 3, March, 1947, pp. 161–162.

16. Paul Bohannan, "Divorce Chains, Households of Remarriage, and Multiple Divorces," p. 119.

17. Saul Bellow, *Herzog* (New York: The Viking Press, 1964).

18. For an example of professional bias against stepfamilyhood, see Irene Fast and Albert Cain, "The Stepparent Role: Potential for Disturbance in Family Functioning," *American Journal of Orthopsychiatry*, Vol. 36, 1966, pp. 485–490.

19. Ernest S. Burch, Jr., "Marriage and Divorce Among the North Alaskan Eskimos," in Paul Bohannan, ed., *Divorce and After* (Garden City, N.Y.: Doubleday & Co., 1970), pp. 163–164.

20. *Ibid.*

21. John Sirjamaki, *The American Family in the Twentieth Century* (Cambridge: Harvard University Press, 1953), p. 116.

22. Irene Fast and Albert Cain, "The Stepparent Role: Potential for Disturbance in Family Functioning," p. 489.

23. Else P. Heilpern, "Psychological Problems of Stepchildren," p. 174.

### CHAPTER 10

1. Nathan Ackerman, *The Psychodynamics of Family Life* (New York: Basic Books, 1958), p. 53.

2. Robert Seidenberg, quoted in *The Wall Street Journal*, February 7, 1972, p. 13. Dr. Seidenberg is clinical professor of psychiatry at Upstate Medical Center in Syracuse, New York.

3. Anne C. Schwartz, "Reflections on Divorce and Remarriage," *Social Casework*, Vol. XLIX, No. 4, April, 1968, p. 215.

4. Esther Oshiver Fisher, "A Guide to Divorce Counseling," *The Family Coordinator*, Vol. 22, No. 1, January, 1973, p. 57.

5. William Nichols, "Marriage Counseling, A Brief Overview," *The Family Coordinator*, Vol. 22, No. 1, January, 1973, p. 11.

6. This course was introduced into the marital counseling curriculum in the fall of 1972 by Esther Fisher. It was offered again in 1973 as a series of seminars by Fellows of the Matrimonial Law Association.

7. When Anne Schwartz made this observation in 1968, she was referring specifically to the Jewish Family Service, of Cleveland, Ohio. (See "Reflections on Divorce and Remarriage".) But this fact is also borne out by the experience of practitioners who, like ourselves, have worked for a number of years in family agencies and community clinics.

8. George Rothman, in Jacob Fried, ed., *Jews and Divorce* (New York: KTAV Publishing House, 1968), p. 114.

## CHAPTER 11

1. Stuart Queen and John Adams, *The Family in Various Cultures* (New York: J. Lippincott & Co., 1952), p. 111.

2. *Ibid.*, p. 118.

3. Abram Leon Sachar, *A History of the Jews* (New York: Alfred A. Knopf, 1965), pp. 94–95.

4. *Ibid.*

5. *Ibid.*, p. 144.

6. *Ibid.*, p. 145.

7. *Ibid.*, p. 154.

8. Menachem M. Brayer, "The Role of Jewish Law Pertaining to the Jewish Family, Jewish Marriage and Divorce," in Jacob Fried, ed., *Jews and Divorce* (New York: KTAV Publishing House, 1968), p. 8.

9. Edward Westermarck, *The History of Human Marriage*, Vol. III (New York: The Allerton Book Co., 1922), p. 309.

10. Julius Kravetz, "Divorce in the Jewish Tradition," in Jacob Fried, ed., *Jews and Divorce*, p. 156.

11. Boaz Cohen, "Concerning Divorce in Jewish and Roman Law," reprinted from the Proceedings of the American Academy for Jewish Research (New York, 1952), Vol. XXI, p. 21.

12. Contemporary practice in Israel is guided by the principle that a divorce cannot take place unless the husband agrees to it. In Orthodox communities around the world, the same practice is followed. Recently, in New York, a fifty-year-old man who refused to apply for an Orthodox divorce, thus leaving his religious wife unable to remarry, was

kidnapped and beaten by a group of Hasidic Jewish men who detained him until he "changed his mind." *The New York Times*, May 16, 1973.

13. Edward Westermarck, *The History of Human Marriage*, p. 307.

14. For an extended, scholarly discussion of Hebrew divorce, see Ze'ev Falk, *Jewish Matrimonial Law in the Middle Ages* (London: Oxford University Press, 1966).

15. Stuart Queen and John Adams, *The Family in Various Cultures*, pp. 130–131.

16. Morton Hunt, *The Natural History of Love* (London: Hutchinson & Co., 1960), p. 57.

17. Michael J. Whaling, "The No-Fault Concept: Is This the Final Stage in the Evolution of Divorce?", *Notre Dame Lawyer*, Vol. 47, April, 1972, p. 959.

18. S. B. Kitchin, *A History of Divorce* (London: Chapman & Hall, 1912), p. 1.

19. Edward Westermarck, *The History of Human Marriage*, p. 320.

20. Stuart Queen and John Adams, *The Family in Various Cultures*, p. 137.

21. *Ibid.*, p. 141.

22. Morton Hunt, *The Natural History of Love*, p. 58.

23. Stuart Queen and John Adams, *The Family in Various Cultures*, p. 141.

24. Morton Hunt, *The Natural History of Love*, p. 61.

25. Stuart Queen and John Adams, *The Family in Various Cultures*, p. 142.

26. Morton Hunt, *The Natural History of Love*, p. 61.

27. Stuart Queen and John Adams, *The Family in Various Cultures*, p. 146.

28. For further discussion of Roman divorce practices see S. B. Kitchin, *A History of Divorce*.

### CHAPTER 12

1. Stuart Queen and John Adams, *The Family in Various Cultures* (New York: J. Lippincott & Co., 1952), p. 151.

2. Morton Hunt, *The Natural History of Love* (London: Hutchinson & Co., 1960), p. 100.

3. Stuart Queen and John Adams, *The Family in Various Cultures*, p. 152.

4. S. B. Kitchin, *A History of Divorce* (London: Chapman & Hall, 1912), p. 81.

5. *Ibid.*, p. 21.

6. Titus 2:4–5.
7. Stuart Queen and John Adams, *The Family in Various Cultures*, p. 156.
8. *Ibid.*, p. 143.
9. *Ibid.*, p. 152.
10. Morton Hunt, *The Natural History of Love*, p. 100.
11. Stuart Queen and John Adams, *The Family in Various Cultures*, p. 163.
12. Morton Hunt, *The Natural History of Love*, p. 109.
13. *Ibid.*
14. *Ibid.*, p. 113.
15. Stuart Queen and John Adams, *The Family in Various Cultures*, p. 101.
16. Morton Hunt, *The Natural History of Love*, p. 111.
17. *Ibid.*, p. 112.
18. S. B. Kitchin, *A History of Divorce*, p. 65.
19. George Elliott Howard, *A History of Matrimonial Institutions*, Vol. 1 (New York: Humanities Press, 1964), p. 336.
20. S. B. Kitchin, *A History of Divorce*, p. 74.
21. George Elliott Howard, *A History of Matrimonial Institutions*, Vol. II, pp. 56–57.
22. S. B. Kitchin, *A History of Divorce*, p. 77.
23. For a greater understanding of the Roman Church's involvement in divorce, see S. B. Kitchin, *A History of Divorce* and George Elliott Howard, *A History of Matrimonial Institutions*, Vol. II.
24. Morton Hunt, *The Natural History of Love*, p. 188.
25. *Ibid.*, p. 189.
26. George Elliott Howard, *A History of Matrimonial Institutions*, Vol. II, p. 61.
27. Morton Hunt, *The Natural History of Love*, p. 190.
28. George Elliott Howard, *A History of Matrimonial Institutions*, Vol. I, p. 389.
29. Morton Hunt, *The Natural History of Love*, p. 193.
30. Edward Westermarck, *The History of Human Marriage*, Vol. III (New York: The Allerton Book Co., 1922), p. 334.
31. S. B. Kitchin, *A History of Divorce*, p. 116.
32. Morton Hunt, *The Natural History of Love*, p. 203.
33. *Ibid.*
34. S. B. Kitchin, *A History of Divorce*, pp. 120–121.
35. George Elliott Howard, *A History of Matrimonial Institutions*, Vol. II, p. 69.
36. *Ibid.*

37. S. B. Kitchin, A *History of Divorce*, p. 110.
38. George Elliott Howard, A *History of Matrimonial Institutions*, Vol. II, p. 71.
39. Morton Hunt, *The Natural History of Love*, p. 212.
40. *Ibid.*, p. 213.
41. *Ibid.*
42. For further discussion of Protestant divorce developments, see S. B. Kitchin, A *History of Divorce*, and George Elliott Howard, A *History of Matrimonial Institutions*, Vol. II.

### CHAPTER 13

1. Carl Bridenbaugh, *Vexed and Troubled Englishmen, 1590–1642* (New York: Oxford University Press, 1968); Marcus Hansen, *The Atlantic Migration, 1607–1860* (New York: Harper Torchbooks, 1961), Chap. 1 and pp. 77–78.
2. Nelson Manfred Blake, *The Road to Reno: A History of Divorce in the United States* (New York: The Macmillan Co., 1962), pp. 34–35.
3. *Ibid.*
4. John Demos, A *Little Commonwealth: Family Life in Plymouth Colony* (New York: Oxford University Press, 1970), pp. 93–94.
5. L. Kinvin Wroth and Hiller B. Zobel, eds., *The Legal Papers of John Adams* (Cambridge: Harvard University Press, 1965), pp. 281–283.
6. William O'Neill, *Divorce in the Progressive Era* (New Haven: Yale University Press, 1967), p. 11.
7. Doris Jonas Freed and Henry Foster, Jr., "Divorce American Style," *Annals of the American Academy of Political and Social Science*, Vol. 383, May, 1969, p. 75.
8. For these early feminist struggles, see Eleanor Flexner, *Century of Struggle: The Women's Rights Movement in the United States* (New York: Atheneum, 1968), Part I.
9. Nelson Manfred Blake, *The Road to Reno: A History of Divorce in the United States*, Chapters 5–9, *passim.*
10. *Ibid.*, Chapter 6.
11. Henry S. Cohn, "Connecticut's Divorce Mechanism, 1636–1969," *American Journal of Legal History*, Vol. 14, January, 1970, pp. 35–54; Nelson Manfred Blake, *The Road to Reno: A History of Divorce in the United States*, pp. 59–61.
12. Benjamin Trumbull, quoted in Morris Ploscowe, *The Truth About Divorce* (New York: Hawthorne Books, 1955), pp. 2–3.
13. Timothy Dwight, quoted in Nelson Manfred Blake, *The Road to Reno: A History of Divorce in the United States*, p. 58.

14. William O'Neill, *Divorce in the Progressive Era*, pp. 6–7, building upon the insights in Christopher Lasch, "Divorce American Style," *New York Review of Books*, February 17, 1966.

15. Henry James, Sr., quoted in Nelson Manfred Blake, *The Road to Reno: A History of Divorce in the United States*, p. 83.

16. Elizabeth Stanton, quoted in *ibid.*, p. 99.

17. Nelson Manfred Blake, *The Road to Reno: A History of Divorce in the United States*, Chapter 8.

18. *Ibid.*, pp. 132–134.

19. Theodore Dwight Woolsey, quoted in *ibid.*, p. 131.

20. President Theodore Roosevelt, Message to Congress, January 30, 1905, quoted in J. P. Lichtenberger, *Divorce—A Social Interpretation* (New York: Whittlesley House, 1931), p. 189; Roosevelt, Sixth Annual State of the Union Message, December 3, 1906, in Fred Israel, ed., *The State of the Union Messages of the Presidents, 1790–1966* (New York: Chelsea House, 1966), p. 2,219.

21. Justice Felix Frankfurter in Vanderbilt v. Vanderbilt (1957), quoted in Nelson Manfred Blake, *The Road to Reno: A History of Divorce in the United States*, p. 186.

22. See Max Rheinstein, *Marriage Stability, Divorce and the Law* (Chicago: University of Chicago Press, 1972) which conclusively demonstrates this point.

23. Hugh Carter and Paul Glick, *Marriage and Divorce: A Social and Economic Study* (Cambridge: Harvard University Press, 1970), p. v.

### CHAPTER 14

1. Judge Paul Alexander, "Follies of Divorce, a Therapeutic Approach to the Problem," *University of Illinois Law Forum*, Winter, 1949, p. 704.

2. Roger J. Leo, "Oregon's No-Fault Marriage Dissolution Act," *Oregon Law Review*, Vol. 51, 1972, p. 716.

3. *The Nation*, April 23, 1973, p. 527.

4. Lee Allen Hawke, "Divorce Procedure: A Fraud on Children, Spouses and Society," *Family Law Quarterly*, Vol. 3, September, 1969, p. 243.

5. Max Rheinstein, *Marriage Stability, Divorce and the Law* (Chicago: University of Chicago Press, 1972), pp. 104–105. In other countries, such as China, the law says that when two people agree to a divorce, it is to be granted, provided adequate provision is made for the children. Felix Greene, "A Divorce Trial in China," *China* (New York: Grove Press, 1965).

6. Robert S. Taft, "Tax Implications of Divorce and Separation," *Family Law Quarterly*, Vol. 3, June, 1969, p. 146.

7. Donald Cantor, *Escape from Marriage* (New York: William Morrow & Co., 1971), p. 21.

8. Diana DuBroff, "Not for Women and Children Only" (New York: National Organization to Improve Support Enforcement, 1972), pp. 6–7.

9. Judge Paul Alexander, "Follies of Divorce, a Therapeutic Approach to the Problem," p. 698.

10. Donald Cantor, *Escape from Marriage*, pp. 34, 38.

11. Judge Paul Alexander, quoted in University of Chicago Conference on Divorce, 1952, p. 51.

12. Judge Paul Alexander, "Divorce Without Guilt or Sin," *The New York Times Magazine*, July 1, 1951. His court had the financial backing it needed for a staff of 93 professionals. Only about 30 per cent of the divorce actions have been dismissed through reconciliation. Lee Hawke, "Divorce Procedure," p. 247.

13. Judge Paul Alexander, University of Chicago Conference on Divorce, p. 54.

14. There are methods by which affluent, intelligent people can circumvent the rigidities of state law and accomplish what are essentially bigamous marriages without being punished by the law. See Louis Nizer, *My Life in Court* (New York: Doubleday & Co., 1961), pp. 184–188.

15. Doris Jonas Freed and Henry Foster, Jr., "Divorce American Style," *Annals of the American Academy of Political and Social Science*, Vol. 383, May, 1969, p. 80. For a detailed analysis of comparative conciliation proceedings in nations throughout the world, see Max Rheinstein, *Marriage Stability, Divorce and the Law*, Chapter 16, especially pp. 436–443.

16. Prior to Haitian and Dominican divorces, Mexican decrees were popular and legal.

17. Donald Cantor, *Escape from Marriage*, p. 108.

18. See Louis Nizer, *My Life in Court*, pp. 184–188.

19. Norman Sheresky and Marya Mannes, *Uncoupling: The Art of Coming Apart* (New York: The Viking Press, 1972), p. 183.

20. Isabel Drummond, *Getting a Divorce* (New York: Alfred A. Knopf, 1931), p. 22.

## CHAPTER 15

1. Fortunately the New York State Court of Appeals ruled on March 23, 1973, that local governments have to pay certain expenses of divorce proceedings for indigent people receiving welfare payments. *The New York Times*, March 23, 1973.

2. Max Rheinstein, *Marriage Stability. Divorce and the Law* (Chicago: University of Chicago Press, 1972), pp. 406, 432, 435.

3. Lee Allen Hawke, "Divorce Procedure: A Fraud on Children, Spouses and Society," *Family Law Quarterly*, Vol. 3, September, 1969, pp. 242, 248.

4. Diana DuBroff, "Not for Women and Children Only" (New York: National Organization to Improve Support Enforcement, 1972), p. 9.

5. *Equal Rights Amendment and Alimony and Child Support Laws* (Washington, D.C.: Citizen's Advisory Council on the Status of Women, 1972), p. 7.

6. Karen Sacks, "Social Bases for Sexual Equality: A Comparative View," in Robin Morgan, ed., *Sisterhood Is Powerful* (New York: Vintage Books, Random House, 1970), pp. 460–462.

7. Una Rita Quendstedt and Colonel Carl Winkler, "What Are Our Domestic Relations Judges Thinking?" *American Bar Association Journal*, Monograph No. 1, July, 1965, p. 6.

8. Lawrence Kahn and Robert Kahn, "The Case for No-Fault Divorce," *Signature*, March, 1973, p. 6.

9. Julia Perles, quoted in the New York *Post*, July 28, 1972.

10. Havelock Ellis, *Sex and Marriage: Eros in Contemporary Life* (New York: Random House, 1952), p. 114.

11. Meyer Elkin, "Conciliation Courts: The Reintegration of Disintegrating Families," *The Family Coordinator*, Vol. 22, No. 1, January, 1973, p. 70.

12. *Newsweek*, March 12, 1973, p. 50.

13. David Merder, "The Need for an Expanded Role for the Attorney in Divorce Counseling," *Family Law Quarterly*, Vol. 4, September, 1970, p. 280.

14. Doris Jonas Freed and Henry Foster, Jr., "Divorce American Style," *Annals of the American Academy of Political and Social Science*, Vol. 383, May, 1969, p. 79.

15. Nelson Manfred Blake, *The Road to Reno: A History of Divorce in the United States* (New York: The Macmillan Co., 1962), p. 219.

16. Meyer Elkin, "Conciliation Courts: The Reintegration of Disintegrating Families," p. 66.

17. *Ibid.*, p. 67.

18. *Ibid.*, p. 64.

19. Emily Mudd, "Contributions to a Therapeutic Solution to the Divorce Problem: Social Work and Marriage Counseling," University of Chicago Conference on Divorce, 1952, pp. 67–68.

20. Lawrence Kahn and Robert Kahn, "The Case for No-Fault Divorce," p. 6.

21. Thomas French, M.D., "Contributions to a Therapeutic Solution

to the Divorce Problem: Psychiatry," University of Chicago Law School, Conference on Divorce, Conference Series No. 9, February 29, 1952, p. 62.

22. See Nicholas Kittrie's discussion of the emergence of the "therapeutic state" in America in his book *The Right to Be Different: Deviance and Enforced Therapy* (Baltimore: Johns Hopkins University Press, 1972), *passim*.

23. David Merder, "The Need for an Expanded Role for the Attorney in Divorce Counseling," pp. 282–283.

24. Max Rheinstein, *Marriage Stability, Divorce and the Law*, p. 442.

25. Michael J. Whaling, "The No-Fault Concept: Is This the Final Stage in the Evolution of Divorce?", *Notre Dame Lawyer*, Vol. 47, April, 1972, p. 969.

26. David Merder, "The Need for an Expanded Role for the Attorney in Divorce Counseling," p. 283.

27. Peter Platten, a Pennsylvania divorce lawyer, quoted in *The Nation*, April 23, 1973, p. 529.

28. David Merder, "The Need for an Expanded Role for the Attorney in Divorce Counseling," p. 283.

29. Meyer Elkin, "Conciliation Courts: The Reintegration of Disintegrating Families," p. 63.

30. Alice Murray, "Conciliation: Is It Worth a Try?", *The New York Times*, September 3, 1972.

31. *Ibid.*

32. Max Rheinstein, *Marriage Stability, Divorce and the Law*, pp. 440–441.

33. *Ibid.*, p. 360. In Sweden, conciliation proceedings were recently declared to be empty formalities. In Denmark, conciliation is under attack as a "relic of the pre-individualistic age." *Ibid.*, p. 152.

34. William Goode, *Women in Divorce* (Glencoe, Ill.: The Free Press, 1956), p. 342.

## CHAPTER 16

1. John Mariano, *The Use of Psychotherapy in Divorce and Separation Cases* (New York: American Press, 1958).

2. *Ibid.*, pp. 7, 35.

3. *Ibid.*, p. 8.

4. *Ibid.*, p. 70.

5. Nester C. Kohut, "Therapeutic Separation Agreements," *Journal of the American Bar Association*, Vol. 51, No. 8, August, 1965, p. 757.

6. *Ibid.*, p. 756.

*7.* Max Rheinstein, *Marriage Stability, Divorce and the Law* (Chicago: University of Chicago Press, 1972), p. 443.

8. Haskell C. Freedman, "The Child and the Legal Procedures of Divorce," in Earl A. Grollman, ed., *Explaining Divorce to Children* (Boston: Beacon Press, 1969), p. 134.

9. Lawrence Kahn and Robert Kahn, "The Case for No-Fault Divorce," *Signature*, March, 1973, p. 6.

10. Henry Foster, quoted in *The Nation*, April 23, 1973, p. 528. Mr. Foster is professor of law at New York University.

11. David Merder, "The Need for an Expanded Role for the Attorney in Divorce Counseling," *Family Law Quarterly*, Vol. 4, September, 1970, pp. 288–289.

12. Peter Platten, a Pennsylvania divorce attorney, quoted in *The Nation*, April 23, 1973, p. 529.

13. Isabel Drummond, *Getting a Divorce* (New York: Alfred A. Knopf, 1931), p. 23.

14. Donald Cantor, *Escape from Marriage* (New York: William Morrow & Co., 1971), p. 164.

15. David Merder, "The Need for an Expanded Role for the Attorney in Divorce Counseling," pp. 285–286.

16. *Ibid.*, p. 293.

17. Louis Nizer, *My Life in Court* (New York: Doubleday & Co., 1961), pp. 213–214.

18. *Ibid.*, Chapter 2.

19. Norman Sheresky and Marya Mannes, *Uncoupling: The Art of Coming Apart* (New York: The Viking Press, 1972), p. 54.

20. See John Rodell, *How to Avoid Alimony* (New York: Stein and Day, 1969), p. 120.

21. Norman Sheresky and Marya Mannes, *Uncoupling: The Art of Coming Apart*, p. 7.

22. Carol Mindey, *The Divorced Mother: A Guide to Readjustment* (New York: McGraw-Hill, 1969), p. 53.

23. Hugh Carter and Paul Glick, *Marriage and Divorce: A Social and Economic Study* (Cambridge: Harvard University Press, 1970), pp. 376–378. One lawyer friend of ours claims that divorce law is relatively low-paying because lawyers have to "live with" their clients for years afterward.

24. William Boyden, "Property Aspects of the Law," University of Chicago Conference on Divorce, 1952, p. 16.

25. Paul Bohannan, "The Six Stations of Divorce," in Paul Bohannan, ed., *Divorce and After* (Garden City, N.Y.: Doubleday & Co., 1970), p. 39.

26. Stuart Walzer, "The Role of the Lawyer in Divorce," *Family Law Quarterly*, Vol. 3, September, 1969, pp. 212–214.

27. James Winder, quoted in the Plainfield, New Jersey, *Courier News*, May 12, 1972, p. B–1.

28. State Supreme Court Justice James Boomer, quoted in *The New York Times*, June 28, 1972.

29. Louis Nizer, *My Life in Court*, p. 197.

### CHAPTER 17

1. Max Rheinstein, *Marriage Stability, Divorce and the Law* (Chicago: University of Chicago Press, 1972), p. 316.

2. Roger J. Leo, "Oregon's No-Fault Marriage Dissolution Act," *Oregon Law Review*, Vol. 51, 1972, p. 720.

3. California Civil Code 4507.

4. Michael J. Whaling, "The No-Fault Concept: Is This the Final Stage in the Evolution of Divorce?", *Notre Dame Lawyer*, Vol. 47, April, 1972, p. 968.

5. Roger J. Leo, "Oregon's No-Fault Marriage Dissolution Act," p. 715.

6. *Ibid.*, p. 717.

7. *Ibid.*, p. 720.

8. *Ibid.*, pp. 718, 721.

9. *Ibid.*, p. 722. In Oregon, the role of evidence of specific acts of misconduct in child-custody cases is still unclear. In most cases such evidence is still relevant and admissible. *Ibid.*, pp. 718, 723.

10. *Ibid.*, pp. 719–720.

11. Donald Cantor, *Escape from Marriage* (New York: William Morrow & Co., 1971), p. 89. In the Scandinavian countries, especially Sweden, the courts conclude the existence of deep and permanent discord by the mere fact of one party's petitioning for separation. Max Rheinstein, *Marriage Stability, Divorce and the Law*, p. 146.

12. The New York *Post*, July 28, 1972.

13. Donald Cantor, *Escape from Marriage*, p. 111.

14. *Ibid.*, p. 109.

15. See Glenn Abernathy, *The Right of Assembly and Association* (Columbia: University of South Carolina Press, 1961).

16. The American Arbitration Association, based in New York City at 140 West 51 Street, has branch offices in twenty-three states.

17. Parents Without Partners, Statistical Compilation, as of 1967, in Benjamin Schlesinger, *The One-Parent Family, Perspectives and Annotated Bibliography* (Toronto: University of Toronto Press, 1969), p. 113.

18. Judge Nanette Dembitz, quoted in the New York *Post*, June 17, 1972.

19. Max Lerner, *America As a Civilization* (New York: Simon and Schuster, 1957), p. 597.

20. Bernard Steinzor, *When Parents Divorce: A New Approach to New Relationships* (New York: Pantheon Books, Random House, 1969), p. 70.

21. Jules Henry, *Pathways to Madness* (New York: Random House, 1971), p. 257.

22. J. Louise Despert, M.D., *Children of Divorce* (Garden City, N.Y.: Dolphin Books, 1962), p. 198. For a series of interesting custody decisions made during the past century, see Robert Bremner, *Children and Youth in America: A Documentary History* (Cambridge: Harvard University Press, 1971), Vol. II, pp. 127–137.

23. *Ibid.*, pp. 196–197.

24. Betty Rollin, "Motherhood: Who Needs It?", in Arlene Skolnick and Jerome Skolnick, eds., *Family in Transition* (Boston: Little, Brown and Co., 1971), p. 348.

25. *Ibid.*, p. 350.

26. Dr. R. Rabkin, quoted in Rollin, "Motherhood: Who Needs It?", p. 346.

27. Helen Thomson, *The Successful Stepparent* (New York: Harper & Row, 1966), p. 83.

28. Exceptions arise, especially when a case of proved adultery is brought before a judge who happens to have a profound personal conviction that women who have lovers cannot be good mothers to their children or provide wholesome atmospheres for them to grow up in.

29. Jim Egleson and Janet Frank Egleson, *Parents Without Partners* (New York: E. P. Dutton, 1961), p. 75.

30. *Newsweek*, March 12, 1973, p. 50.

31. Una Rita Quendstedt and Colonel Carl Winkler, "What Are Our Domestic Relations Judges Thinking?", *American Bar Association Journal*, Monograph No. 1, July, 1965, p. 2.

32. Bernard Steinzor, *When Parents Divorce: A New Approach to New Relationships*, pp. 70–71.

### CHAPTER 18

1. Mrs. DuBroff is also founder of the National Organization to Improve Support Enforcement. Her pamphlet "Not for Women and Children Only" is published periodically and can be obtained from NOISE, 12 West 72 Street, New York City, New York 10023. The organization currently has a mailing list of more than 7,000 men and women.

2. Diana DuBroff, "Not for Women and Children Only" (New York: National Organization to Improve Support Enforcement, 1972), p. 9.
3. As of January, 1973, Senator Halperin was planning to resubmit his bill, establishing a study commission on offering such insurance for sale in New York State, to the legislature. Last year it never got out of committee. See *The New York Times*, January 15, 1973.
4. *The New York Times*, January 5, 1973.
5. Michael J. Whaling, "The No-Fault Concept: Is This the Final Stage in the Evolution of Divorce?", *Notre Dame Lawyer*, Vol. 47, April, 1972, p. 972.
6. *Ibid.*
7. *The Nation*, April 23, 1973, p. 528.
8. Morris Ploscowe, "Alimony," *Annals of the American Academy of Political and Social Science*, Vol. 282, May, 1969, p. 16.
9. Robert S. Taft, "Tax Implications of Divorce and Separation," *Family Law Quarterly*, Vol. 3, June, 1969, pp. 147–148. Since "absolute divorces" were not decreed in ecclesiastical courts, alimony was granted only as an incident to "bed and board" divorce.
10. *Ibid.*, p. 148.
11. Una Rita Quendstedt and Colonel Carl Winkler, former chairmen of the Support Committee of the Family Law Section of the American Bar Association, made a survey of the attitudes and practices of 575 court personnel. See findings in Monograph No. 1, *American Bar Association Journal*, July, 1965, especially p. 1.
12. Stuart Walzer, "Divorce and the Professional Man," *Family Law Quarterly*, Vol. 4, December, 1970, p. 364.
13. Paul Bohannan, "The Six Stations of Divorce," in Paul Bohannan, ed., *Divorce and After* (Garden City, N.Y.: Doubleday & Co., 1970), p. 44.
14. The New York *Post*, February 19, 1973.
15. *The Nation*, April 23, 1973, p. 528.
16. Una Rita Quendstedt and Colonel Carl Winkler, Monograph No. 1.
17. *Ibid.*
18. Bernard Steinzor, *When Parents Divorce: A New Approach to New Relationships* (New York: Pantheon Books, Random House, 1969), p. 97.
19. John Rodell, *How to Avoid Alimony*, (New York: Stein and Day, 1969), p. 114.
20. Norman Sheresky and Marya Mannes, *Uncoupling: The Art of Coming Apart* (New York: The Viking Press, 1972), p. 16.
21. Marilyn Goldstein, "When the Marriage Ends, the Money Squeeze Begins," *Newsday*, April 13, 1972, p. 5A.

22. *The Nation,* April 23, 1973, p. 528.

23. Marilyn Goldstein, "When the Marriage Ends, the Money Squeeze Begins," p. 5A.

24. *The New York Times,* January 15, 1973. Also see *Equal Rights Amendment,* pp. 6–7.

25. The New York *Post,* March 23, 1972.

26. *Newsweek,* March 12, 1973, p. 48.

27. The New York *Post,* April 27, 1973.

28. *Equal Rights Amendment and Alimony and Child Support Laws,* published by the Citizen's Advisory Council on the Status of Women, p. 10.

29. *The New York Times,* February 21, 1973.

30. Seymour Halleck, M.D., *The Politics of Therapy* (New York: Harper & Row, 1971), pp. 130–131.

31. A Wisconsin judge, quoted in Una Rita Quendstedt and Colonel Carl Winkler, Monograph No. 1, p. 3.

## CONCLUSION

1. See listings in the Selected Bibliography under the following authors: Ernest Groves, Meyer Nimkoff and Willard Waller.

2. Margaret Mead, "Double Talk About Divorce," *Redbook,* May, 1968, p. 47.

3. William Goode, *The Family* (Englewood Cliffs, N.J.: Prentice-Hall, 1964), pp. 92–93.

4. *Ibid.,* especially Chapter 9.

5. Mervyn Cadwallader, "Marriage As a Wretched Institution," *Atlantic,* Vol. 218, No. 5, November, 1966, p. 63.

6. See, for examples, Hugo Beigel, "Romantic Love," *American Sociological Review,* Vol. 16, No. 3, June, 1951, p. 333; Theodore Dreiser, "Modern Marriage Is a Farce," in Bertrand Russell, ed., *Divorce* (New York: The John Day Co., 1930), pp. 43–53; Shulamith Firestone, *The Dialectic of Sex: The Case for Feminist Revolution* (New York: William Morrow & Co., 1970), p. 254; Margaret Mead and Francis Kaplan, eds., *American Women, the Report of the Presidential Commission on the Status of Women* (New York: Charles Scribner's Sons, 1965), pp. 163–172; Carl Rogers, *Becoming Partners: Marriage and Its Alternatives* (New York: Delacorte Press, 1972), *passim;* Alvin Toffler, *Future Shock* (New York: Random House, 1970), pp. 221–223.

7. See the essay by Christopher Lasch, "Divorce American Style," *New York Review of Books,* February 17, 1966, p. 4.

8. A. Calhoun, quoted in Christopher Lasch, *ibid.,* p. 3.

9. Ruth Shonle Cavan, *American Marriage: A Way of Life* (New York: Thomas Crowell Co., 1959), p. 127.

# Selected Bibliography

### BOOKS

Marvin Albert, *The Divorce* (New York: Simon and Schuster, 1965).
An interesting historical account of the divorce of Henry VIII from
Catherine of Aragon. Rather detailed and probably of special interest
to students of the period.

Stephen Pearl Andrews, ed., *Love, Marriage and Divorce* (New York:
Stringer & Townsend, 1853).
A lively debate on the merits and morality of divorce between Henry
James, Sr., Horace Greeley and Stephen P. Andrews. Fascinating
reading.

Philippe Ariès, *Centuries of Childhood: A Social History of Family Life*
(New York: Vintage Books, Random House, 1962).
A beautifully written history of the evolution of the modern concep-
tion of family life, oriented around the child and his education.

Edmund Bergler, *Divorce Won't Help* (New York: Harper and Bros.,
1948).
Long considered a "classic" in divorce literature, this book, written
by a psychiatrist, is an attempt to show that people who divorce are
emotionally sick and can only be cured with intensive psychotherapy.
Takes no account of other causative factors in marital conflict and
is both outdated and biased.

Jessie Bernard, *Remarriage: A Study of Marriage* (New York: The Dryden Press, 1956).
A complete and unbiased treatment of remarriage, based on careful
study.

Nelson Manfred Blake, *The Road to Reno: A History of Divorce in
the United States* (New York: The Macmillan Co., 1962).
A highly readable and well-documented account of divorce in
America, written by a historian. Emphasis is on the philosophical
and moral positions of influential Americans. An excellent source
book on divorce history.

Paul Bohannan, ed., *Divorce and After* (Garden City, N.Y.: Doubleday & Co., 1970).

An interesting book on various sociological, anthropological and legal aspects of divorce and post-divorce life.

Ernest W. Burgess and Harvey J. Locke, eds., *The Family: From Institution to Companionship* (New York: The American Book Co., 1953).
A book of sociological readings on different types of families and their modes of accommodation to crises. Thorough summaries of family research but nothing original on divorce.

Alfred Cahen, *A Statistical Analysis of American Divorce* (New York: Columbia University Press, 1932).
A dated yet classic evaluation of divorce based on careful study. The author reveals some fascinating attitudes held by professionals at the time this book was written.

Donald Cantor, *Escape from Marriage* (New York: William Morrow & Co., 1971).
An unusually outspoken appeal, by a divorce lawyer, for radical reforms in divorce law. Cantor calls for the transformation of divorce so that it becomes a personal right for every individual. A well-argued and moving plea for change.

Hugh Carter and Paul Glick, *Marriage and Divorce: A Social and Economic Study* (Cambridge: Harvard University Press, 1970).
This book is of interest mainly for its comprehensive and fascinating statistics on divorce in America.

John R. Cavanagh, M.D., *Fundamental Marriage Counseling: A Catholic Viewpoint* (Milwaukee: The Bruce Publishing Co., 1963).
A conservative discussion of the aims of Catholic counseling, with special emphasis on the advisability of condemning divorce.

J. Louise Despert, M.D., *Children of Divorce* (Garden City, N.Y.: Dolphin Books, 1962).
An attempt at a "balanced" account of the effects of divorce on children, this book nevertheless supports the traditional views that parents in divorce are neurotic and that children cannot escape the experience entirely unscathed.

Isabel Drummond, *Getting a Divorce* (New York: Alfred A. Knopf, 1931).
An old but perceptive account of the historical injustices surrounding divorce law in ancient and modern history. The author is particularly lucid in condemnation of the excessive power of judges in America.

Jim Egleson and Janet Frank Egleson, *Parents Without Partners* (New York: E. P. Dutton, 1961).
This open-minded book attempts to describe divorced persons in a humane and unprejudiced light. Unfortunately its presentation of

remarriage after divorce is riddled with biased and unsupported notions.

Victor Eisenstein, M.D., ed., *Neurotic Interaction in Marriage* (New York: Basic Books, 1956).
An excellent anthology of essays by clinicians who work with married couples. Some attempt is made to clarify the proper role of the therapist in marital and divorce intervention and to clarify the objective stresses inherent in marriage.

Friedrich Engels, *The Origin of the Family, Private Property and the State* (New York: International Publishers, 1942).
The classic Marxist account of the genesis of domestic institutions.

Ze'ev Falk, *Jewish Matrimonial Law in the Middle Ages* (London: Oxford University Press, 1966).
A scholarly and useful resource book which addresses itself primarily to the philosophical and rabbinical debates that surrounded the practice of divorce in the Middle Ages. Difficult reading for lay people.

Jacob Fried, ed., *Jews and Divorce* (New York: KTAV Publishing House, 1968).
Proceedings of the Commission on Synagogue Relations of the Federation of Jewish Philanthropies of New York. Concerned primarily with the quality and perpetuation of Jewish family life, the contributors are alarmed by divorce rates.

Richard A. Gardner, M.D., *The Boys and Girls Book About Divorce* (New York: Bantam Books, 1971).
This unusually forthright book offers the children of divorce a great deal of support for their feelings and advice in handling their relationships with adults. A must for parents and children of divorce.

Haim Ginott, *Between Parent and Child* (New York: The Macmillan Co., 1965).
Intended as a popular and readable guidebook for parents, this author's treatment of divorce is pessimistic, poorly thought out, and probably detrimental to parents and children. A highly conservative and unoriginal assessment.

William Goode, *The Family* (Englewood Cliffs, N.J.: Prentice-Hall, 1964).
The application of social theory to family structure. An attempt to achieve a greater understanding of familial changes during the past decades.

————, *Women in Divorce* (Glencoe, Ill.: The Free Press, 1956).
An important research study on the post-divorce adjustment of women; the data refute many negative assumptions about divorce but their positive conclusions have not sufficiently influenced public

opinion. However, Goode shares with other writers the bias that *remarriage* is the saving grace of divorce, which otherwise represents a catastrophic loss for children.

Germaine Greer, *The Female Eunuch* (New York: Bantam Books, 1970).
A fascinating book by a leading feminist. She discusses the position of women in contemporary society and brilliantly explores the problems that modern women face in their marriages.

Earl A. Grollman, ed., *Explaining Divorce to Children* (Boston: Beacon Press, 1969).
This edited volume presents a number of expert but negative views about divorced adults and their children. Most of the authors present the child of divorce as victimized and inevitably scarred.

Ernest R. Groves, *Conserving Marriage and the Family: A Realistic Discussion of the Divorce Problem* (New York: The Macmillan Co., 1944).
A completely unrealistic discussion of the divorce question by a marriage counselor who was committed to the belief that divorced people could not live happily ever after. A maudlin collection of stories about people who lived to regret their decision to divorce. The title alone belies any possibility of an objective analysis of marriage and divorce.

Seymour Halleck, M.D., *The Politics of Therapy* (New York: Harper & Row, 1971).
An excellent and successful attempt to demonstrate that psychiatric work is neither politically nor socially "neutral" but has traditionally been used to support the status quo in America. A moving and personal appeal for all therapists to re-examine their biases and intentions. A long-overdue critique on the abuses of modern psychiatry.

Jules Henry, *Culture Against Man* (New York: Random House, 1963).
A fascinating exploration of the interrelationship between the individual psyche and the powerful forces of cultural indoctrination in America.

————, *Pathways to Madness* (New York: Random House, 1971).
A brilliantly written account of an anthropologist's extended home visits with five American families, all of whom had at least one member diagnosed as emotionally ill. A penetrating and fascinating analysis of the relationship of traditional nuclear family life to the potential for mental disturbance and emotional breakdown. A crucial book for laymen and professionals.

Morton Hunt, *The Natural History of Love* (London: Hutchinson & Co., 1960).

Written for a popular audience, this is an excellently researched survey of the "institutionalization" of love in various cultures. Contains a brief but lucid discussion of how marriage and divorce patterns reflect the changing status of women.

————, *The World of the Formerly Married* (New York: McGraw-Hill, 1966).
A lively, readable, still relevant antidote to the usual assumptions about the misery and loneliness of post-divorce life in America. Gives a good feeling of the life-style of divorced adults, their pleasures as well as their struggles.

S. B. Kitchin, *A History of Divorce* (London: Chapman & Hall, 1912). One of the most complete historical treatments of divorce; highly readable.

Aileen Kraditor, *The Ideas of the Woman Suffrage Movement, 1890–1920* (Garden City, N.Y.: Doubleday & Co., 1971).
An interpretive commentary on the history of feminism and the social problems of the progressive era. In relation to marriage and divorce, the author shows the distinction between the thought and activity of women who demanded marital reforms and those who called for the freedom of divorce.

Ronald Laing, *The Politics of the Family and Other Essays* (New York: Vintage Books, Random House, 1969).
An excellent and important anthology of the author's most searching work on the future of the traditional nuclear family. A critical and successful attempt to show the kind of psychic harm created by unhappy families.

William J. Lederer and Don D. Jackson, *The Mirages of Marriage* (New York: W. W. Norton & Co., 1968).
A thorough psychological analysis of why so many American marriages fail, and how people can make their marriages work if they recognize that a marriage is more than just the sum of two people legally bound to each other. Probably the most sane and responsible of all the books written in the "how to save your marriage" tradition.

Bronislaw Malinowski and Robert Briffault, *Marriage: Past and Present* (Boston: Porter Sargent Publishers, 1956).
A collection of essays by two anthropologists based on a radio debate held in England. Malinowski, the more conservative of the two, argues for marriage as the foundation of society. Briffault calls for group marriage and opposes the oppression of women in marriage.

John Mariano, *The Use of Psychotherapy in Divorce and Separation Cases* (New York: American Press, 1958).
This lawyer-counselor outlines his vision of "psychotherapeutic juris-

prudence," a euphemism for pressuring couples into remaining married. The best example we found of an inappropriate and authoritarian approach to divorce law.

C. Wright Mills, *The Sociological Imagination* (New York: Grove Press, 1961).
A radical examination of the complacency of official American sociology. A crucial work for the student of contemporary social issues.

Carol Mindey, *The Divorced Mother: A Guide to Readjustment* (New York: McGraw-Hill, 1969).
An unliberated and unsophisticated account of how women are helpless after divorce without the aid of their "men," including psychiatrist and lawyer.

Meyer Nimkoff, *Marriage and the Family* (New York: Houghton Mifflin Co., 1947).
A conservative, widely read sociologist looks at divorce in America. He sees deviance, crisis and tragedy, and likens the experience to death. A best-selling text, this book went into a second printing. The author speculates on the biological, social and constitutional inferiority of divorced people to married ones. A near-classic example of the failure of social scientists to acknowledge and examine their own biases.

George O'Neill and Nena O'Neill, *Open Marriage* (New York: M. Evans and Co., 1972).
An attempt by two married anthropologists to show how modern, sophisticated couples can shore up their marriages by agreeing to live as independent but equal partners. Contains a typical diatribe against the alternative of divorce. Unoriginal on every score.

William O'Neill, *Divorce in the Progressive Era* (New Haven: Yale University Press, 1967).
An informative study of changing attitudes toward divorce in the period 1890–1920. Demonstrates the gradual accommodation of progressive attitudes on divorce to the dominant values in support of marriage and the family as institutions. Emphasizes divorce as the safety valve to preserve the conjugal system.

Stuart Queen and John Adams, *The Family in Various Cultures* (New York: J. Lippincott & Co., 1952).
A good source for historical information on marriage and divorce, particularly during the Roman and Early Christian periods.

Max Rheinstein, *Marriage Stability, Divorce and the Law* (Chicago: University of Chicago Press, 1972).
A comparative study of the legal and social aspects of divorce in major areas of the world. Despite the author's personal anti-divorce

bias, this book is a rich source of information on the relation between marriage breakdown and the harshness of divorce law. Too heavy and dry for casual reading.

John Rodell, *How to Avoid Alimony* (New York: Stein and Day, 1969).
A crass and sexist account of how men have to play rough with their conniving ex-wives and their weakling lawyers. The author's cynicism is a reflection of the impact of the divorce tradition on the average person, and is therefore worth examining.

Norman Sheresky and Marya Mannes, *Uncoupling: The Art of Coming Apart* (New York: The Viking Press, 1972).
Allegedly a guide to "sane divorce," lawyer Sheresky and journalist Mannes describe the horrors commonly associated with the disintegration of marriage. On one level, an argument for sanity, caution and compromise between partners; but it reads like a laundry list of all the ugly scenarios they have witnessed.

Arlene Skolnick and Jerome Skolnick, eds., *Family in Transition* (Boston: Little, Brown & Co., 1971).
An excellent anthology of essays on the family, with some particularly radical accounts of new life-styles; the contributors raise some searching questions about the inherent "rightness" of the traditional American life-styles.

Bernard Steinzor, *When Parents Divorce: A New Approach to New Relationships* (New York: Pantheon Books, Random House, 1969).
A clearly written and fairly balanced account of how post-divorce conflict can be minimized, with special emphasis on the need of each parent to allow the other an autonomous relationship with the child. The author's pro-marriage bias does not detract from the value of this book.

University of Chicago Forum: Conference Series No. 9, February 29, 1952.
An important collection of essays on the theme of a "therapeutic approach" to divorce from the disciplines of law, psychiatry, social work and sociology. The over-all theme is that methods should be found to preserve marriage and deter divorce, outside the framework of the adversary proceeding.

Willard Waller, *The Old Love and the New: Divorce and Readjustment* (Carbondale and Edwardsville: Southern Illinois University Press, 1958).
A guided tour into the inferno of divorce by a sociologist who was convinced that it should be a last resort, when all avenues of recourse have failed. In the negative tradition of Bergler, Groves and others.

Edward Westermarck, *The History of Human Marriage*, Vol. III (New York: The Allerton Book Co., 1922).
A well-written three-volume history of marriage with a wealth of fascinating information on non-Western marriage customs.

### ARTICLES

Paul Alexander, "Divorce Without Guilt or Sin," *The New York Times Magazine*, July 1, 1951.
A lucid appeal for "no-fault" divorce which would focus on the recognition of marital breakdown as sufficient ground for divorce. Now outdated by more sophisticated work, this article typifies the thinking of liberals within the legal profession.

Joseph Baer and Muller Davis, "Merit in No-Fault Divorce," *Illinois Bar Journal*, Vol. 60, June, 1972, pp. 766–775.
The authors argue that dead marriages should be buried without consideration of "fault" but that "merit" or "relative fault" should be recognized as an important factor in determining alimony and property allowances.

James Barnett, "Divorce and the American Divorce Novel, 1858–1937," unpublished dissertation, University of Pennsylvania, 1939.
A thorough and interesting review of American fiction, demonstrating how writers were influenced by conservative thought on divorce and showing how little insight they had into the psychological complexity of divorce.

Ray L. Birdwhistell, "The Idealized Model of the American Family," *Social Casework*, Vol. LI, No. 4, April, 1970, pp. 195–198.
In this lucid article Birdwhistell argues that our traditional model of family life is ill-adapted to deal with the stresses of present-day life.

Catherine M. Bitterman, "The Multimarriage Family," *Social Casework*, Vol. XLIX, No. 4, April, 1968, pp. 218–221.
A negative, pessimistic and one-sided view of the problems facing post-divorce families.

Lee Burchinal, "Characteristics of Adolescents from Unbroken, Broken, and Reconstituted Families," *Journal of Marriage and the Family*, Vol. XXVI, No. 1, February, 1964, pp. 44–51.
A classic study of the effects of divorce on children. The author found an absence of inimical effects usually associated with separation and divorce.

Meyer Elkin, "Conciliation Courts: The Reintegration of Disintegrating Families," *The Family Coordinator*, Vol. 22, No. 1, January, 1973.
A vivid description of the conservative anti-divorce thrust of modern

law under the guise of a liberal approach to enhance the welfare of American families.

Esther Oshiver Fisher, "A Guide to Divorce Counseling," *The Family Coordinator*, Vol. 22, No. 1, January, 1973, pp. 55–63.
An essay by a marriage and divorce counselor full of pejorative inuendoes, though the author calls for compassion, objectivity and the explicit statement of clinical values. She has nothing positive to say about divorced people except that sometimes they are not sick.

Robert A. Harper, "Marriage Counseling and the Mores: A Critique," *Journal of Marriage and Family Living*, Vol. XXI, February, 1959, pp. 13–16.
This is a sound and well-written appeal for objectivity on the part of marriage counselors. The author makes a number of interesting statements about the origin of some of society's traditional beliefs on divorce.

Nester C. Kohut, "Therapeutic Separation Agreements," *Journal of the American Bar Association*, Vol. 51, No. 8, August, 1965, pp. 756–761.
A Catholic lawyer's approach to divorce, which emphasizes the use of the lawyer's authority and skill as a means of deterring people from their fateful decision.

Judson T. Landis, "The Trauma of Children When Parents Divorce," *Journal of Marriage and Family Living*, Vol. 22, No. 1, February, 1960, pp. 7–13.
This famous research study found an interesting relationship between children's predivorce environment, their perceptions of that environment, and the actual effect of divorce on these youngsters.

Christopher Lasch, "Divorce and the Family in America," *Atlantic*, Vol. 218, No. 5, November, 1966, pp. 57–61.
This article offers historical insights into marriage and family life and gives the reader greater perspectives on contemporary issues in divorce.

Gerald Leslie, "Personal Values, Professional Ideologies and Family Specialists," *Marriage and Family Living*, Vol. 21, February, 1959, pp. 3–12.
A critical and well-thought-out evaluation of current family life education as it is taught in the schools.

George Levinger, "Marital Cohesiveness and Dissolution: An Integrative Review," *Journal of Marriage and the Family*, Vol. XXVII, February, 1965, pp. 19–28.
A good solid review of research data on those forces (religious, social and economic) that act as restraining elements in keeping couples in marriage.

Elizabeth Mulligan, "Divorce Court: Scene of Decay," *Marriage*, Vol. 52, No. 4, April, 1970, pp. 38–43.

A Catholic view of divorce, with heavy emphasis on how traumatized and hysterical people become in divorce court; a silly attempt, based on biased ideas, to deter couples from contemplation of divorce.

*Seventeen*, "Would a Broken Home Break You?" March, 1968, p. 144.

A group of teen-agers has a panel discussion on reactions to growing up in divorced families. The panelists' insights and optimism are refreshing and valuable antidotes to the common myths about the detrimental effect of divorce on children.

Jack Westman and David Cline, "Divorce Is a Family Affair," *Family Law Quarterly*, Vol. 5, March, 1971, pp. 1–10.

This is a brief but clearly written and thoughtful survey of some of the typical patterns of post-divorce adjustment which intensify the stresses imposed upon children. Both authors are psychiatrists.

Michael J. Whaling, "The No-Fault Concept: Is This the Final Stage in the Evolution of Divorce?", *Notre Dame Lawyer*, Vol. 47, April, 1972, pp. 959–975.

A broad and thorough survey of the evolution of the no-fault concept, with some exploration of its advantages and shortcomings. The author favors mandatory conciliation and psychiatric efforts to preserve marriage.

# Index

hostility of ex-spouse and, 118, 120ff.
household tasks and, 119
"illegitimate," 51
legal reform and, 229
liberation of, by divorce, 90ff.
"loss" of parent and, 90–92
loyalty conflicts of, 98–99, 118, 141
"making up" to, 118–19
misplaced commitment to, 79ff., 94, 99–101
models for, 56, 94–95, 113, 130
myth of damaged, 79ff., 129
narcissism of, 129
neurosis in, 88–89, 98
outside adult relationships for, 113, 130
parental post-divorce relationships and, 91ff., 217–18
parenthood image and, 29–31
protection of, 49, 81, 108, 124
psychosexual development of, 94–96
reinterpreting divorce to, 82, 86, 101ff., 110
remarriage and, 54ff., 111, 128ff. See also Stepfamilies.
research on, 48–49, 87–89, 97
society and, 81, 82
statistics on, 84, 88
as status symbols, 30, 128
therapy and, 47–48, 80
traumatizing ingredients of divorce and, 31, 110ff.
two homes, advantage of, 125
as "victims," 31, 34, 39, 55, 79ff., 81–82, 91, 103, 104
visitation of, 91, 93, 94, 119,

217–18. See also Visitation.
Child support, 56, 111, 182, 213, 223, 225
and sex-role indoctrination, 213
deductibility of, 226
Christian divorce, 157ff. See also Protestantism; Roman Catholic Church.
Church of England, 166
Citizen's Advisory Council on the Status of Women, 225
Clinicians, see Mental health professions; Therapy.
Collusive divorce, see Law.
Colorado, 189
Commission on Synagogue Relations, 72
Committee for Fair Divorce and Alimony Laws, 225
Common-law relations, 224
Community property states, 188–89
Conciliation, 181, 194ff., 199–200
Connecticut, 170, 173
Constantine, 160, 161
Constitution, U.S., 173, 179, 189, 212, 213, 228
Contested divorce, 179–80, 209–11
Contract, marriage, 212–13
Corinthians, 159
Counseling, 63, 118
adaptation increase and, 71
anti-divorce ideology in, 65–66, 71ff.
bias in, 66, 145
children and, 80
coercive vs. voluntary, 194

# About the Authors

Susan Gettleman is a practicing clinical social worker, a supervisor at the Metropolitan Center for Mental Health, in New York City, and a lecturer on divorce at the New School for Social Research. She has specialized in the treatment of severely disturbed children and their families, at Bronx State Hospital, Jewish Family Service, and Linden Hill School, a residential treatment center affiliated with the Jewish Board of Guardians.

Mrs. Gettleman married at the age of twenty, divorced at twenty-two, and subsequently married a man who has two sons by his former marriage. She lives in Manhattan with her husband, their two daughters, and her two "step-sons" who spend considerable time in their second home.

Janet Markowitz, a clinical social worker, is affiliated with a Manhattan mental health clinic; as a senior therapist she treats children and adults in individual and family therapy. She has worked for a number of years treating very troubled families at the Jewish Child Care Association Foster Home Division, Elmhurst Hospital Psychiatric In-Patient Service and at the Linden Hill School of Jewish Board of Guardians. She has also served children and parents through her work at Project Head Start.

Mrs. Markowitz married at the age of twenty-two and now resides with her husband and son in Englewood, New Jersey.